UNITED WE WIN

UNITED WE WIN

The Rise and Fall of La Raza Unida Party

Ignacio M. García

MASRC
The University of Arizona • Tucson

About the Author

Ignacio García conducted research for four years on La Raza Unida Party. As a journalist he wrote extensively about the party and the Chicano Movement. He served as coordinator of publications for the Mexican American Studies & Research Center at the University of Arizona for five years. He also served as historian for the Alianza Hispano-Americana Project at the Center.

MASRC

Library of Congress Cataloging-in-Publication Data

García, Ignacio M.
   United We Win:
   The Rise and Fall of La Raza Unida Party

Bibliography: p.
   Includes index
   1. Mexican Americans—Politics and suffrage.   2. Mexican Americans—Nationalism.   3. Southwest—Race relations.
   I. Title.
ISBN 0939363-01-1   89-61349

CONTENTS

FOREWORD: A LEGACY UNTOLD

For a brief time in the recent history of Chicanos, a powerful and intense social movement focused attention on the Mexican American communities of the Southwest. The Chicano Movement, as this social phenomenon is now called, brought with it the proliferation of community organizations which sought to better the socioeconomic conditions of La Raza. One of these organizations, La Raza Unida, rapidly became one of the dominant currents of the Chicano Movement.

La Raza Unida advocated empowerment and self-determination for the Chicano communities of the Southwest. Its main thrust sought to implement social change in the barrios and to improve social conditions for La Raza by mobilizing its massive political potential and making its influence felt at the ballot box. But instead of choosing to work within either the Republican or Democratic parties, the leaders opted to organize their own independent Chicano party—La Raza Unida. In scarcely half a decade, La Raza Unida Party won an impressive number of elections in several South Texas counties, capturing political control in at least two, Zavala and La Salle. In Crystal City (Zavala), the party won control of all government units—the county commisioners court, the city council, and the school board.

The story of La Raza Unida's meteoric rise to power, and its short-lived existence on the political landscape, is well documented in *United We Win*. The author, Ignacio García, has done an admirable job in researching previously published and unpublished works, as well as integrating primary information provided by *partido* members, who made available their personal files and consented to be interviewed. *United We Win* is the most complete work to date on La Raza Unida. The book takes the reader from the formative stages of the Mexican American Youth Organization (MAYO) years to the party's last race for governor in 1978 and José Angel Gutiérrez's departure from Crystal City in 1982. The text is filled with rich details that offer insights into the thinking of the leaders and the partido organizers. Through it all, García maintains an objective detachment that is sure to irk at least a few of the die-hard loyalists, since he judiciously avoids favoritism in his treatment of the various personalities that made up the partido leadership.

It is precisely García's objectivity that makes *United We Win* a valuable and timely contribution. Chicanos and non-Chicanos alike have previously received only journalistic interpretations of La Raza Unida's accomplishments and historical significance. The mass media has seldom treated objectively organizations or individuals that challenge the hegemony of white America and its institutions over non-whites. One would be hard-pressed to find evidence to support the statement that the mass media gave objective coverage to La Raza Unida. García's book corrects this bias by offering an objective account of the partido and its leaders, whom the media sought to discredit.

The book is important for another reason. It is a most comprehensive work on La Raza Unida that is long overdue. It can be used in Chicano studies courses at colleges and universities, as well as in high school Chicano history classes. This is not a small point to make; history that is not accessible because of academic jargon or style normally serves only to gather dust on library shelves at university campuses. The average reader, however, will have no problem reading or understanding García's account of La Raza Unida. Similarly, Chicanas and Chicanos who are just entering college and who were not yet born or were too young to remember the party's heyday will be able to get in *United We Win* a complete view of one very important phase of contemporary Chicano political history. True, other scholarly works have been written previously; but none are as complete and comprehensive as García's book. Most of these works, moreover, are written in academic styles suited mainly for researchers. It is this "street history" quality that makes *United We Win* unique, although García did not sacrifice thorough, rigorous research to achieve it.

To be sure, some critical comments can be made in evaluating *United We Win*. For example, the book does not include any extensive discussion about the role and contributions of *las Chicanas del partido*, a fact the author acknowledges. Also, more information about the party's rank and file members would have enriched the wealth of material that is included. These difficiencies will surely offend those who sacrificed their families and careers for the advancement of the party.

Other criticisms can be leveled at García's treatment of well-known controversies. One is the issue of whether La Raza Unida should have followed José Angel Gutiérrez's preference for a regional rather than a state party. As history has now recorded, the decision was made to organize the partido at the state level. García's discussion of the issue doesn't shed any new light on this dispute. Thus, the question of which was the better strategy will have to await new research and further interpretation. Similarly, García's discussion of the "schism" that existed between rural and urban chapters will probably generate controversy because little research on this question has previously been available. He suggests that a more profound conflict existed between rural and urban Raza Unida chapters than was visible publicly during the Muñiz campaigns in 1972 and 1974. Some readers may find this refreshingly new information, while others may disagree with his analysis. This may hold true particulary of his suggestion that some urban chapters were socialist, while others seemingly lacked attachment to a clearly defined ideology.

In the final analysis, these weaknesses do not diminish the importance of *United We Win*. The legacy of La Raza Unida is the key role it played in accelerating the "liberation" of Chicanos and overthrowing the deeply entrenched perception that La Raza was forever doomed to be subordinate and inferior to whites. In the words of César Chávez, when the odds makers and political experts continually prophesied doom, La Raza Unida (and MAYO before it) kept saying and demonstrating *que si se puede*. With its tenacious adherence to cultural nationalism and ethnic pride, La Raza Unida struck a responsive chord and mobilized thousands of Chicanos to take control of their destiny and the political and social institutions in places where they were the majority. What resulted is an *apertura* in race relations and the political process that changed permanently the way Anglos treat Chicanos.

United We Win documents how La Raza Unida, it members, organizers, and leaders, went about accomplishing this feat of no small proportions, given the crushing weight of oppression that permeated the daily lives of Chicanos. It is the story of how Chicanas and Chicanos asserted their right to full and equal participation in American society by forcing their way into a political system that had ignored or deliberately kept them out for so long. It is the story of how powerful an idea and a handful of organizers can be in the face of seemingly insurmountable odds. It is the story that explains why Chicanas and Chicanos can now walk tall and proud in a previously rigidly racist environment. *United We Win* will allow our future generations to learn how their ancestors in La Raza Unida worked, fought and sacrificed in order that they be free from the exploitation and opression that pervaded and over-whelmed the daily existance of their ancestors—*sus madres y padres, abuelas y abuelitos, primas y primos, lo igual que sus tías y sus tíos.*

Madison, Wisconsin   Mario Compean
Cinco de Mayo 1989

PREFACE

The mid-1960s and most of the 1970s were years of social unrest in many of the Mexican American neighborhoods of the Southwest. This turmoil came to be known as the Chicano Movement, a political, social, and cultural catharsis that produced numerous self-help and militant organizations seeking to better the conditions of the Mexican American population. During this intense, sometimes divisive, often rhetorically violent period, a third political party was founded by young Chicanos and Chicanas who saw the Republican and Democratic parties as the "the same monster with two heads eating from the same trough."

The party was known as El Partido de la Raza Unida.* In a way it became the most threatening political organization of the Chicano Movement because it sought to displace Anglos from power and to restructure the American political system. It was separatist in orientation, if not in practice, and for a time it seemed capable of attracting thousands to an open electoral and social rebellion on a scale never before seen among the so-called passive Mexicans of the Southwest.

La Raza Unida's militant ideology attracted some of the best and the brightest in the barrios as it spread throughout the Southwest, Midwest, and even to the East and West coasts. For those of us who watched it develop or who participated in its growth, La Raza Unida seemed a fulfillment of some unknown prophecy that

---

*"The Party of the United People." *Raza* in this context does not mean "race".

Chicanos would rise from the ashes of discrimination, political powerlessness, and economic hardships to take their rightful place in the sun. That it would be led by young people was even more inspiring. The dream did not last a decade, but it did more to change the way we saw ourselves than any other experience. Even those who later repudiated the party's confrontational politics became more sensitive of their people's plight.

Many other things changed through the activities of La Raza Unida and the Chicano Movement as a whole. Mexican Americans participated in the electoral process in larger numbers and more of them ran for political office. People gained the courage to protest injustices, and a profound cultural renaissance produced plays, poems, novels, music, and *obras de teatro*. A sense of *carnalismo*, brotherhood, seemed for a time to prevail in the Mexican American community.

After the decline of the party, I waited to see if anyone would chronicle this period and interpret it for those of us who had been deeply involved or for those who had never been exposed to it. In 1984 I was encouraged by a friend to pursue the project myself. When I did, I found that many friends and colleagues were skeptical that it could be done. Not enough time had elapsed and feelings were still too tender, they said. Nevertheless, for the most part they were encouraging, and some of them proved to be extremely helpful.

When I began my research, I found that there were two dissertations, one monograph, one book, and several journal articles dealing with the party. Numerous other references to it appeared in book chapters on the Mexican American experience. But most of the works were either studies of particular periods and regions, or theoretical analyses, and they did not attempt to provide a wide overview of the party's activities.

United We Win, then, is the first comprehensive work on La Raza Unida Party (RUP) from beginning to end. It takes the reader from the founding of the Mexican American Youth Organization (MAYO) and the convening of the first Chicano Youth Liberation Conference, which preceded the party, to the departure of the last Raza Unida member from political office. It looks at the issues of the times, the personalities, the conflicts, the ideologies, the strategies, the electoral victories and defeats, and the Anglo reaction to this new militancy. There is no attempt to develop a theoretical framework for La Raza Unida, because this is an interpretive

work, not a case study or a social history. In reviewing the literature, I did not identify any variations in theoretical models that I
could have confidently applied in evaluating the multiplicity of
themes presented here. Questions on organizational development,
accessibility to political power, ideologies, cultural nationalism,
class consciousness, and so on are likely to come out of this study,
but these will have to be answered by scholars with interest and
expertise in them.

My purpose is to furnish the necessary spadework, identify
the sources, and provide an interpretive context in which to understand the significance of a Chicano third political party. I chose to
integrate the interpretation within the text of each chapter and to
summarize in the concluding chapter. This decision resulted from
the desire to see *United We Win* serve as a resource for the study of
the period of the Chicano Movement regardless of the readers'
theoretical inclinations. The most important aspect of this book
may not be, to my chagrin, its interpretations, but rather its
panoramic view and its details of "history"—dates, figures, personalities, events, and so forth.

No doubt there are events and issues that are not covered in
this work. Some I chose to leave out because I lacked information,
others because they demanded more time and expertise than was
at my disposal. I do not dwell much on Crystal City, the mecca of
Chicanismo, and I shortchange the RUP chapters in Arizona, Colorado and northern California. The role of women in the party is
not developed as a separate theme from the general history and this
in part reduces the Chicana presence in the book. Nevertheless, I
believe (and hope) that this work will stimulate more research on
the party and on the Chicano Movement as a whole. Overall, I am
convinced that what was included was the most essential.

The interpretations herein are based on three factors I identified as existing in the 1960s and which gave rise to the Raza Unida
Party. When these factors ceased to exist, the party declined. The
first was a heightened activism among Mexican Americans, much
of it caused by César Chávez's farm-worker movement, landownership conflicts in New Mexico, the rise of a militant nationalism in
Colorado, and short-lived electoral victories by Mexican Americans in Texas. This activism occurred within a larger context of
social rebellion in this country brought about by the war in Vietnam, the War on Poverty, and the Black Power Movement. The
second factor, partly a result of the first, was that the American

political system was no longer viewed as legitimate, nor were the "leaders" of the period. Among Mexican Americans there was a vacuum of leadership, not so much because there were not any individuals who wanted to lead, but because their politics seemed irrelevant to the times and the issues.

Third, a new core group of activists appeared in the 1960s anxious to challenge those in power in a confrontational manner and with prescribed ideals that were, if not revolutionary, at least militant reformist. What they found was a community aroused, unable to reach solutions in a system no longer considered legitimate. The activists took advantage of the fertile political soil to establish a party of their own and to conduct voter-registration drives, political orientation sessions, grassroots campaigns, and statewide electoral efforts.

In time, and in part because of the party's successes, conditions changed. The electoral system opened, Mexican Americans became prime targets for recruitment by the mainstream parties, and a number of them were elected to office. Political and educational institutions in this country made a comeback and regained their legitimacy in the eyes of many. Finally, the activists at the core of the movement suffered the consequences of their rebellion: lost jobs, judicial harassment, and surveillance and provocation by federal, state, and local agencies. By the late 1970s, many of these leaders had ceased to be functional.

To these external pressures we may add the mistakes of youth, as many activists were in their twenties when the party was founded. They were not well versed on organizational theory, electoral campaigns, and they were often rash in their decision-making. Ideology quickly became a major point of debate and division. Revolutionary nationalism, progressive nationalism, liberalism, Marxism, and other *isms* became points of contention among the leadership and the rank and file as the party sought to develop a direction. Power struggles also split La Raza Unida as national, state, and local leaders battled for political "turf" and control of the party structure.

These conflicts, viewed outside the context of the party's short duration and the external pressures it suffered, have led some scholars to declare that the party had no ideology and was simply a militant reformist movement. Such was the conclusion of two well-respected colleagues, Mario Barrera and Carlos Muñoz, in their otherwise excellent article, "La Raza Unida Party and the Chicano Student Movement in California." While they might be right factually, conceptually Barrera and Muñoz place too stringent a theoretical framework for discussion of the party's philosophical tendencies.

Ideology is the end product of an extensive process of intellectual discussion and debate as well as a series of action and reaction strategies. In their embryonic stage ideologies are basically principles by which unity is achieved on behalf of a cause or movement. In which case five to ten years—the life span of most of the party chapters—is simply not enough time by which to judge whether La Raza Unida Party had or, better put, *would have had* an ideology. I chose a less dialectical approach in examining the organic ideologies that arose within La Raza Unida. Otherwise, I might have delegitimized what was truly a "people's" social revolution in the 1960s and 1970s. It is an approach others might consider using while conducting further research on the Chicano Movement.

I experienced this period both as a spectator and as a county chairman for the party in Kingsville, Texas. I was one of two people who sat in a hotel in San Antonio with the RUP gubernatorial candidate on election day 1978 and watched the party fade into history.

I was fortunate to know a number of the party leaders and to have their trust. As I interviewed them, I found them frank and open about their experiences. They shared information and expressed feelings that they had previously kept tightly within. Some reviewed early drafts of the manuscript and pointed out factual errors, but none of them attempted to change my view or interpretation even when the text was critical of them.

I traveled extensively to interview numerous participants and to locate memos, letters, *movimiento* newspapers, position papers and other documents. Collections at the libraries of Stanford University, the University of California, Berkeley, and the University of Texas at Austin were particularly useful, as were the files of the *Corpus Christi Caller-Times* and the *San Antonio Express-News*. Also helpful were the bound collections of the socialist newspaper *The Militant*, as well as the Chicano periodicals *El Grito del Norte*, *El Gallo*, *La Raza Magazine*, and others found at the University of Arizona library. Juan José Peña shared his large personal collection of Raza Unida Party documents and letters of the New Mexico chapter and the national party. José Angel Gutiérrez allowed me access to his thousands of pages of papers obtained under the Freedom of Information Act. He also provided critical comments that forced me to reanalyze several parts of the manuscript. Another helpful critic was Mario Compean, one of the originators of the idea for the book. He opened many doors and remained a constant supporter throughout the project. No one was more critical or helpful than this good friend. Mario T. García, who also reviewed the manuscript, inspired me early in the writing when he praised an early version of the first chapter.

Many other kind individuals went out of their way to facilitate this work. Stephen Casanova conducted several of the taped interviews in Texas and provided two unpublished manuscripts on the Raza Unida Party press and the MAYO boycotts. His assistance helped accelerate the work. Richard Santillán, the first person to write at length about La Raza Unida, helped me to understand the role the party played in California. His dissertation also provided valuable background and enlightening information on the concept of cultural nationalism.

I am also indebted to Juan García, Oscar Martínez and Roberto De Anda, all of the University of Arizona, who read the manuscript and offered advice. At the university's Mexican American Studies & Research Center, Tom Gelsinon and Natalia Ochotorena proved to be crucial to the finishing of this long project. Tom read, reread, and edited the manuscript and provided an "outsider's" view. Ms. Ochotorena prepared the manuscript in record time and was indispensable in putting the bibliography together. Kimberly Vivier was the final manuscript editor and did a superb job.

Macario Saldate IV, director of the center, was the first person to suggest that I pursue this project. His gentle encouragement was backed by travel and research funds that enabled me to gather the data. He also allowed me ample time to finish the manuscript. Even as the project stretched on, his enthusiasm remained constant. Without his support, the work would never have reached completion.

Finally, this book is dedicated to Alejandra, my wife and friend. As companions we marched, picketted, and worked together for *La Causa*. Without her loving encouragement, this book would never have been written. Gracias mi amor.

Tucson, Arizona   Ignacio M. García
June 1989

PRELUDE

Southwestern society in the mid-1960s was marked by an obvious disparity between the dominant Anglo population and the mostly lower-class Mexican Americans. Two different worlds coexisted, and their inhabitants intermingled only when the job required it or circumstances briefly brought them together. In many small towns the railroad tracks separated the two; in others prejudice and discrimination, both de facto and de jure, indicated the dividing line and made sure everyone knew his or her place. Cultural, linguistic, and economic barriers separated Anglos from Mexican Americans, and in most places there also existed a distrust of motives. The Southwest was an Anglo world, and even in small rural communities like Pearsall, Texas; Greeley, Colorado; Las Vegas, New Mexico; Morenci, Arizona, and others where Mexican Americans were a significant part of the population, Anglo economic and political power stood firm and was used to its full extent to keep the races segregated. Occasionally challenged by Mexican Americans wanting change, Anglo dominance rarely gave way.

So entrenched was the culture of segregation that laws or court decisions outlawing it were ferociously opposed by many Anglo citizens.[1] When the Supreme Court ruled against the concept of "separate but equal," a furious Texas citizenry presented the governor with 165,000 signatures opposing federal intrusion into this segregated environment. In 1956, referenda promoting segregated schools, prohibiting interracial marriages, and supporting local

1

control over federal intervention were placed on the Texas ballot and passed overwhelmingly.[2]

Understanding their subordinate status, Mexican Americans avoided conflict with the *patrón*, *sherife*, *la corte*, and other symbols of Anglo power by keeping their contacts with them on a formal basis. They worked hard, stayed away from the affluent sections of town, and avoided the police at all costs. When they failed to do this, or when they were perceived to have failed, conflicts erupted, and it was usually the Mexican Americans who lost. They lost their jobs, were brutalized by law enforcement agents, and were made to feel like victims without recourse. And they had no recourse from local and state courts. In its report to President Richard Nixon, the United States Commission on Civil Rights declared:

> Our investigations reveal that Mexican American citizens are subject to unduly harsh treatment by law enforcement officers, that they are often arrested on insufficient grounds, receive physical and verbal abuse, and penalties which are disproportionally severe. We have found them to be deprived of proper use of bail and of adequate representation by counsel. They were substantially underrepresented on grand and petit juries and excluded from full participation in law enforcement agencies, especially in supervisory positions.[3]

Discrimination was not limited to those in rural areas or to workers on the lowest rung of society, but was a pervasive characteristic of southwestern society which suffocated the aspirations of many of those who sought to improve their bleak social standing.

Nowhere did discrimination seem more pronounced than in the region's public schools, which were segregated at a time when they should not have been. The 1950s had been a decade of litigation over desegregation, when Mexican Americans led by such organizations as the League of United Latin American Citizens (LULAC) and the American G.I. Forum had continually challenged the school systems in the courts. Between 1950 and 1957, fifteen suits charging discrimination were filed in Texas courts alone. In an effort predating the black civil rights movement, Mexican American lawyers had won important victories.[4] Unfortunately, the school systems' biases proved resilient, and board members and administrators found loopholes in the decisions or simply took advantage of a lack of enforcement of the law.

Where it was not possible to segregate the brown children,

they were often treated as second-class students by teachers, administrators, and school committees that decided on everything from homecoming queen to class valedictorian. In integrated schools a minuscule number of Anglo students occupied most of the positions of power and prestige. The method of electing class officers, cheerleaders, homecoming queens, most-likely-to-succeed, and so on changed as the population majorities in the schools went from Anglo to Mexican American. Anglo students had been allowed to choose their peer group leaders, but Mexican American students lost that right to school committees.

The educational system responded to Mexican American students in two ways. The more "sensitive" approach called for Americanizing the culturally different children with the foreign tongue. Executed with a missionary zeal, this approach had the purpose of making children different from parents, and instilling in them middle-class values and a patriotic fervor for the United States. Teachers were quick with the paddles and the tongue-lashings in the hope that with firmness they could discourage the children from being what they were.[5]

The well-entrenched culture and language the students brought from home, educators still believed in the 1960s, kept them from trying harder. It was widely accepted as fact that passive, "mañana-oriented" attitudes were the reason for Mexican Americans' slow learning and that their inability to defer gratification caused them to drop out of school. As far as the teachers and administrators were concerned, Mexican American parents were not interested in their children's education. One clear indication, they pointed out, was the parents' unwillingness to teach their children English. Anyone speaking Spanish during school hours received a swift retribution. Spanking, a trip to the principal's office, and suspension were all remedies for those who used Spanish. Administrators in some schools even assigned Spanish "monitors," students who mingled discreetly among their peers during recess to find out who was speaking Spanish in order to report them to the school authorities.[6]

The second approach to the Mexican American educational problem bordered on benign and, at times, deliberate neglect. Some school districts had large numbers of uncertified instructors, unmotivated teachers, and educators waiting to retire. The quality of their teaching was poor, and their popularity among the students was nonexistent. Unwilling to take the time to teach students with so many disadvantages, they simply herded them into remedial courses or vocational education shops where they could "use their hands" and stay away from trouble. A small number of Mexican American students were selected every year to be encouraged to go on to college, but few could afford the tuition and even fewer had received the proper counseling. By 1960 only 13 percent of Mexican Americans had four years of high school and less than 6 percent had some years of college education.[7]

Stephen Castro, a graduate of Sidney Lanier High School in San Antonio in 1969, complained that "counselors only bring ex-convicts to our school to scare us away from jail. Those are not role models."[8] Other students protested that there were few pre-paratory courses for college, and that more time was spent advising them against smoking, premarital sex, and violence than encour-aging them to seek a profession. The school policy seemed one of containment and avoidance of problems rather than one of educating. Urban schools, in particular, had problems with youth group violence, though rarely was it directed at the teachers or administrators.

Although some educators cared, many became discouraged in a few years because of the school systems' attitude toward their students and the seeming lack of support from the parents. A few of them understood that the schools were programmed to fail be-cause they did little to overcome the disadvantages the students brought with them. The majority of teachers, though, simply blamed the circumstances on the children and rarely tried to change their approach to teaching or the schools' policies toward educating.[9]

The tragedy of years of poor schooling showed in the economic state of the Mexican American population of the 1960s. Only 19 percent of Mexican Americans were employed in white-collar occupations, and 57 percent worked in low-skill manual jobs in which they earned, per capita, only forty-seven cents for every dollar of Anglo income. This rate of pay fell below that of other nonwhites and kept nearly 35 percent of all Mexican Americans in the Southwest below the poverty line of three-thousand dollars in annual income.[10] The unemployment rate for Mexican Americans was twice as high as that for Anglo workers and only slightly less than that for other nonwhites. In 1964 Gunter Myrdal said of America's poor:

Something like a caste line is drawn between the people in the urban and rural slums and the majority of Americans who live in a virtual full employment economy. ... There is an underclass of people in the poverty pockets who live an ever more precarious life and are increasingly excluded from any job worth having, or who do not find any jobs at all.[11]

Sixteen percent of the Mexican American population worked in the fields, following the migrant streams north to Idaho, Nebraska, Wisconsin, and Michigan, west to California, and Washington, and south to Florida to pick the crops. Theirs was a life of constant travel, harsh living conditions, and back-breaking work for six to eight months, and stringent budget-watching for the last four to six. The migrant workers' difficult existence seem destined to be perpetuated through their children, who rarely completed school and thus were unable to gain the skills necessary to leave the fields. They represented a living tragedy for which there existed no formal policy of assistance. James Sundquist explained the mood of government about this issue: "When it comes to the solution of the poverty problem, a good many of the urban poverty thinkers have written off the rural areas and have concluded that the only way to deal with rural poverty is to let the people move and then handle them in the cities."[12] Migrant workers who moved to the cities often found that they still had to follow the crops because their lack of skills kept them underemployed.

Many Mexican Americans had left the fields for the cities in the preceding decades, but their poverty had followed them. Lewis Nordyke, in his book *The Truth About Texas*, described the condition of the urban Mexican American: "Many Latin families live in *jacales* or huts and shanties that have no plumbing; some of them have no water, and the people carry in buckets from wherever they can get it; they burn candles or kerosene lamps because there is no electricity."[13]

Every southwestern town and some major cities, such as San Antonio, Albuquerque, Los Angeles, Denver, and Phoenix, had Mexican sides: the *barrios*, poor neighborhoods where people lived in substandard housing and where there were few street lights, many unkempt streets, and often no drainage for rainwater. Although in the 1960s poverty had been rediscovered and federal monies were available for poor communities to start revamping themselves, many Anglo-run town governments did not seek these funds and chose instead to remain "independent" of the federal government and to keep taxes low. In the cities, where federal funds were requested, the planning for such programs as Model Cities and Urban Renewal was sometimes so carelessly done that the resulting development created inconvenience and forced people to leave their communities, causing a financial burden and social displacement.

The powerlessness of the Mexican American population made it easier for government to be insensitive. In town after town in the Southwest, predominantly Mexican American communities were governed by Anglo officeholders who had been elected and reelected by a small minority of voters. In Tucson the Mexican American population lost its majority in the early 1900s and with it went its political power. Only a few elite families participated in coalitions with Anglos, mostly at a subservient level.[14] In California a wholesale gerrymandering of legislative and county districts diluted Mexican Americans' voting strength.[15] Another problem resulted from the fact that a large portion of the Spanish surname population did not have citizenship status. Colorado had an active community, but its numbers were too small to have much impact. As for New Mexico, Mexican Americans were an important minority—almost 40 percent—and they did have political power, but the governing policy was a blend of Anglo conservatism and Mexican elitism. The state's limited tax base and lack of significant industry coupled with the political orientation left many Mexican Americans without a voice.[16]

Texas undoubtedly was the most repressive of the states.[17] Two kinds of Anglo politicians governed the Lone Star State, and both kept the power away from the barrios. The old guard of the Texas Democratic Party had built its power in the late 1800s through the accumulation of land, usually at the expense of its former Mexican owners. These Anglos had taken over the land but did not completely discard the ways of the rich Mexican landowner. Evan Andres, in his book *Boss Rule in South Texas*, described the patrón relationship between the landowner and most of his laborers. As patrón, the rancher exercised almost complete social and economic control over his *peones*. The submissive workers could not quit their jobs or own property, and they needed their master's permission to marry, to leave the ranch, or to summon a doctor or some other outsider. The patrón also served as the local judge, who settled disputes among his peones, maintained order and discipline, and even assessed punishment.[18] On election day he herded them to the voting booth, citizens or noncitizens, and had them vote for him or for those in association with him. Since Mexican Americans were the overwhelming majority in areas such as South Texas, these politicians were guaranteed their stay in office. Occasionally, the political bosses would include a Mexican American or two on their slates, particularly if the rest of the Anglo ranchers were not happy over the power sharing. The trade-off was a number of votes for a benevolent feudalism.

As repulsive as this corrupt system seemed to reformers and present-day activists, it was no worse than the system that replaced it in many parts of rural and urban Texas in the late 1800s and early 1900s. The new politics were couched under the guise of Progressivism. The Progressive Era reformers were interested in transferring the power of the old bosses to new capitalist elites who claimed an interest in cleaning up the political spoils system and reducing government costs and waste. More often than not, though, they sought to curb the voting power of the lower, immigrant-ethnic classes who had formed the base of the political machines they were seeking to replace. In the decade-long struggle between the "Progressives" and the "bosses," Mexican Americans lost almost all the controlled but valuable electoral strength that had given them some limited benefits.[19]

The new reformers, having eliminated many of the bosses—not all of them, in the case of South Texas—did little to change the social or economic status of the Mexican American workers and families in their communities. They developed voter eligibility requirements, disallowed the use of Spanish in the voting place, and intimidated the few individuals who overcame the first two obstacles. These new power brokers and their constituencies were the ones responsible for the enactment of segregating laws and the ones to perceive that there was a "Mexican" problem. These men believed in less, not more, government and consequently did not see any role for government in helping the poor Mexican American. Remnants of both of these types of politics remained at the beginning of the 1960s in South and West Texas.

The few Mexican American officeholders at the beginning of the 1960s owed their positions to their allegiance to one or another Anglo coalition. These officeholders proved to be unwilling or unable to improve the economic, educational, or social status of their fellow ethnics. There were, however, several Mexican American officeholders left over from the time of boss rule, such as those of the Guerra family in Starr County. They controlled local politics through an extended family network of politicians, businessmen, and party officials. Unfortunately, these leaders did not see anything wrong with the way they governed or the way most Mexican Americans lived.[20]

The only hope for what seemed a hopeless situation came from a small number of Mexican American politicians and intellectuals scattered across the United States. They were a more militant progeny of what historian Mario T. García described as the Mexican American Generation.[21] They were products of the Second World War and participants or at least witnesses of the litigation battles waged by members of organizations such as LULAC, the G.I. Forum, and La Liga Pro-Defensa Escolar against segregated school systems nationally. Their parents had been influenced by the assimilationist tendencies of the 1930s, when Mexican American intellectuals stopped looking at Mexico as the mother country or as the center of intellectual thought. Learning English and attaining citizenship was important, and so was demanding the civil rights conferred by that citizenship.

In "The Mexican American Mind: A Product of the 1930s," Richard García writes:

> The Mexican American mind emerged in the 1930s as a product of social differentiation, the crisis of the Depression, the Americanization role of such institutions as the family, the Catholic Church and the educational system, the Mexican and American ethos of the city, the idea and ideology of the exiled Mexican "rico" and the rise of the LULAC as well as the relative absence of constant immigration.[22]

J. Montiel Olvera, writing in 1939 in his *Latin American Yearbook*, admonished his readers: "The minds of the younger generation . . . must be trained to be subservient to no one; to feel and act 'equal' with others; to grow into manhood upright, with no complexes . . . *with loyalty to the [American] flag . . . and an abundance of patriotism in their hearts.*"[23] This generation felt that improvements had been made and could be enhanced if Mexican Americans tried harder to integrate into American society and to be less like the immigrant generation that had preceded them. Their perception of the role of the Mexican American in U.S. society prevailed until after the 1940s and then began changing in the 1950s.

Rodolfo Alvarez describes this juncture in the development of the Mexican American as a "period when the first relatively effective community protective organizations began to be formed. The organizing documents are so painfully patriotic as to demonstrate the conceptualized ambitions of the membership rather than their actual living experience." Alvarez also places a perspective on the advances this generation made by pointing out that the improvements in education, income, social acceptance, and so on were accomplishments only when compared to the lot of the migrant generation, which began with nothing. And in fact the Mexican American experienced only an "upward coasting with the general economy and was not directly influencing his own economic betterment."[24]

The activists of the 1950s promoted the concept of integration rather than assimilation. They began to note that there were differences between them and the majority population, but they were nonetheless Americans with full rights. Rarely successful in local politics, they were attracted to national elections and the major liberal politicians of the time. They also moved toward direct involvement in electoral politics, unlike LULAC and the G.I. Forum.[25] These Mexican American activists were optimistic, and they quickly joined John F. Kennedy's presidential campaign of hope. Viva Kennedy Clubs sprang up throughout the Southwest amid promises of Mexican American inclusion in the Kennedy administration.

This activism found a base in two new organizations. The Mexican American Political Association (MAPA) in California and the Political Association of Spanish-Speaking Organizations (PASSO) in Texas, though they did not field candidates, did endorse them and provided money and volunteers to those they felt would work for the benefit of the community.[26] This was the first time an organization had used the term "Mexican American" in its title or made politics a prominent feature of its agenda. Both groups were headed by feisty militants. Bert Corona, Jr., long-time unionist, was the president of MAPA, and Albert Peña, Jr., civil rights lawyer, occupied the presidency of PASSO. Both men represented the link to a yet-to-come activism of the Chicano Movement, while their constituency remained a composition of moderate New Dealers at best. These organizations had ties to labor and attempted to include the skilled working class and the war veterans. At the halfway point of the 1960s the leadership felt that there prevailed a "friendly atmosphere for change." President Lyndon B. Johnson had followed Kennedy's progressive rhetoric with a full agenda of social programs to combat poverty and illiteracy, and these programs created a small but aggressive and adequately financed group of educators, social workers, and community organizers.

Ironically, when the social activism of the 1960s began accelerating, both MAPA and PASSO lost momentum and were not able to capture the leadership of a movement they had helped initiate. There were several reasons for their decline. The first was that the membership was composed predominantly of professionals who were either established in their careers or at least were sampling the benefits of a growing economy. They were, in terms of economic stability and educational achievement, unrepresentative of the population at large, and though supportive of liberal remedies for the poor, they were nevertheless class conscious and moved away from the barrio and into integrated neighborhoods as soon as they could.[27] Their children were the first generation of Mexican Americans to have trouble speaking Spanish and relating to Mexican culture. A second reason was that, as MAPA and PASSO members worked in coalitions with Anglo liberals, they were forced to suppress their own nationalistic tendencies. Although they were supportive of their culture at the personal level, they did not consider it appropriate to flaunt it or to perpetuate its "public" existence. Third, they were extremely sensitive to the intense red baiting directed at the black civil rights movement. It was not uncommon for these activists to point out that they had refrained from rioting and protest marches and had chosen to suffer discrimination with dignity.[28]

The preoccupation with dignity and legitimacy often led to bitter infighting that weakened the organizations. The fatal blow for PASSO came after an impressive electoral victory in the small South Texas town of Crystal City. There PASSO united with the International Brotherhood of Teamsters to sponsor an all-Mexican American slate that swept the city council elections in 1963. The victory sent shock waves throughout the state, as it was the first time Mexican Americans had successfully challenged their subordinate status through the ballot box. Peña and Albert Fuentes, PASSO's executive secretary, took credit for the strategy and for a time vowed to repeat the process throughout Texas.[29]

Liberals statewide praised the Crystal City "miracle," but other PASSO members, led by Hector García, founder of the American G.I. Forum, were troubled by the association with the Teamsters and the negative publicity in the conservative Texas press. William Bonilla, a García lieutenant, expressed the feeling of a significant minority when he said, "Many of our professional and business people feel that PASSO has received unfavorable publicity because of the Crystal City elections, and they do not know if it's worthwhile for them to give of their time to work for the organization."[30]

At the PASSO convention of 1964 some delegates also felt that the all-Mexican slate was open to charges of "discrimination in reverse." Crystal City mayor Juan Cornejo had to explain to the delegates that the teamsters-PASSO coalition had tried to balance the slate with Anglos but had been unsuccessful in attracting any of them. Just as reluctant had been the "educated Latins." "Instead, we poor Latin Americans with fifth grade education had to run," said Cornejo. For many middle-class Mexican Americans, the Crystal City officials, who were defeated in 1965 after a disastrous and divisive two years, were an embarrassment. The teamsters-PASSO association became a major issue at the convention and led to the walkout of García when Peña was reelected. The organization never recovered from that schism.[31]

By the late 1960s the PASSO-MAPA style of activism had come in for strong criticism from new activists involved in what came to be known as the Chicano Movement.[32] This movement brought a new world view of the barrio and its relationship to Anglo society. The new activists had no interest in legitimacy in the eyes of the Anglos, they were avowed nationalists, they spoke as much Spanish as English even though they were young and educated, and they believed in the confrontation politics of the civil rights movement. They were deeply influenced by the rhetoric of black militants such as H. Rap Brown, Stokely Carmichael, and Malcolm X and were discovering a new cultural identity in the symbolism of the United Farm Workers' movement. Their heroes were César Chávez of the UFW; Reies López Tijerina, leader of a movement to win back land grants in New Mexico; and Rodolfo Gonzales, a charismatic, urban politico from Denver, Colorado, who sought to organize *Cholos* and street-gang members into a revolutionary vanguard.

By the latter part of the 1960s the movement had spread nationally, and initially it gave rise to a consensus of the needs of the Mexican American community, something that the regionalism of the prior organizations had made impossible. This movement not only awoke the political sensibilities of the southwestern barrios, but it also encouraged a renaissance of Chicano art, literature, and culture. It became a breeding ground for young intellectuals who had their own ideas on how to change the condition of the Mexican American. They were impatient with the slow-moving changes. Many had been sheltered from the many struggles that had taken place in earlier generations, and for a time they believed that their own parents and grandparents had been passive and accommodating to discrimination and exploitation. These militants were the first generation to see its economic and social status within the context of a bountiful America. An educated group, it believed many benefits were unattainable because of Anglo society's preoccupation with color, accent, and national origins. To them, America's moral legitimacy had been lost, and what began as an opposition to specific issues became a repudiation of the whole American system and its moral foundations.[33]

Armando B. Rendón, in his *Chicano Manifesto*, expressed the feeling of many activists when he said:

> The North American culture is not worth copying: it is destructive of personal dignity; it is callous, vindictive, arrogant, militaristic, self-deceiving, and greedy; it is a gold-plated ballpoint pen; it is James Eastland and Richard Nixon; it is Strom Thurmond and Lyndon Johnson; it is a Mustang and old-folk's homes; it is medicine and OEA; it is an $80 billion defense budget and $75 a month welfare; it is a cultural cesspool and a social and spiritual vacuum for the Chicano.[34]

By 1967 the mood was calling for a new kind of approach to organizing mass resistance to Anglo society. Militant Chicanos no longer just wanted to eliminate the disparities between the two worlds, they wanted to destroy the structures that had made those differences possible. "Chicano Power!" became the new slogan and "Viva La Raza!" the call to arms.

Para los Gringos
todos los Mexicanos
son frijoles de la
misma hoya.

To the Gringo,
all Mexicans are
beans from the same
pot.

—*El Chile*, October 1975

LOS CINCO DE MAYO

The barrios in the city of San Antonio were seething during the summer of 1967. The three hundred fifty thousand or so citizens of Mexican ancestry there had watched half a decade of civil rights conflict and legislation after legislation of New Frontier and Great Society programs unfold before them. Yet they remained powerless, unable to elect any significant numbers of Mexican Americans to office or to break down the barriers to economic upward mobility even as their sons went to war in large numbers. Although political and social activism had been prevalent in San Antonio, most outsiders would have categorized Mexican Americans there as a flock without a shepherd, lost within the confines of their own barrios.

Against this backdrop five young men came together at the Fountain Room, a local bar several blocks from St. Mary's University, a small, Catholic, liberal-arts college. They came to discuss politics, the Chicano student movement in California, and the conditions of Mexican Americans in general, and they came to drink beer.[1] Serving as the catalyst for the group was a political science graduate student named José Angel Gutiérrez, who had recently dropped out of the University of Houston's law school. Gutiérrez came to the meeting already a veteran of numerous political battles, including the 1963 Crystal City election, in which as a junior-college student he had registered voters and written propaganda flyers. Also, as an undergraduate at Texas A&I University he had forced PASSO to lower its age requirement from twenty-one to eighteen.[2]

15

At St. Mary's, Gutiérrez renewed his acquaintance with Charles Cotrell, a political science professor he had met at Texas A&I. Cotrell introduced Gutiérrez to other young men on campus who were involved in social activism.[3] In the early spring of 1967 he met two young men and became reacquainted with another who shared his ideas about the conditions of the Mexican American population. The three were Juan Patlán, a friend from high school and junior college; Willie Velásquez, a student and community activist who worked for the Catholic Bishop's Committee on the Spanish-Speaking; and Ignacio "Nacho" Pérez, a nonstudent who was active in raising money for the Texas chapter of the United Farm Workers Organizing Committee.[4] The four talked for hours one spring evening. Their topics ranged from the Black Movement to the current crop of Mexican American political leaders. Nothing, except a decision to meet again, came of the meeting.

Several weeks later Gutiérrez met Mario Compean, a former migrant farm worker in his late twenties who had grown up in the tough barrios of San Antonio's west side and was then a freshman political science student. They met at a picnic sponsored by the department. After teaming up to win several games of horseshoes—a game neither had played before, but did so to beat a few "gringos"—they discussed Gutiérrez's political views. Compean recalled the meeting years later:

> We talked a lot about what was going on with the Black Movement ... the farm workers' movement ... César Chávez in California, and other events. We discussed leaders like [Stokeley] Carmichael, Martin Luther King, and others. We also discussed some of the recognized political leaders in the Chicano community in Texas and particularly San Antonio ... and organizations such as LULAC and the American G.I. Forum.[5]

In Compean, Gutiérrez found a disciple. Compean had attended school at Edgewood High School in San Antonio, which had a predominantly Mexican American student population. By his own admission, there he had learned to distrust Anglos and to develop nationalistic ideas.[6]

After talking to Gutiérrez, Compean agreed to meet with the other young men. Three weeks later Gutiérrez, Compean, and the other three met at the Fountain Bar and then began to meet regularly afterward. This time the meetings were not merely rap sessions, but study sessions.

The five began to read books on political theory and works by black nationalists such as Carmichael, Eldridge Cleaver, and Malcolm X.[7] The group also followed the newspaper accounts of what was happening with the Alianza de Pueblos Libres of Reies López Tijerina in New Mexico and the Crusade for Justice of Rodolfo "Corky" Gonzales in Colorado. Tijerina led a movement to reclaim thousands of acres of federal land for the descendants of the original owners, who had received land grants from the Spanish Crown. The Alianza had had by then several violent confrontations with state and federal authorities. Tijerina had also been the target of the largest federal manhunt in the country. Gonzales had a regional reputation for his fiery nationalistic speeches that smacked of separatism and for the Chicano liberation gatherings he sponsored.[8] The five also looked up old organizers like Eluterio Escobar and María Hernández, who began their activism in the 1930s and 1940s.

In their discussion sessions the five reaffirmed their dislike for the *políticos* of the barrio. They felt that these political leaders' approach to the problems of the Mexican American community did not yield meaningful results. They viewed these leaders as accommodationists who were only too willing to work within the system and who agitated in favor of their community only as long as it did not adversely affect their economic or political standing or as long as it gave them credibility without consequences.[9] The five also concluded that they were not interested in forming another mass membership organization, of which there were many in the Mexican American barrios, but rather were attracted to organizations such as the Students for a Democratic Society, a white anti-war group, and the Students Nonviolent Coordinating Committee, a black activist movement, as possible models for Mexican Americans.

They traveled—sometimes together, sometimes alone—into the South to talk with Carmichael and Martin Luther King's people, and they headed west to Albuquerque to interview Tijerina. They listened attentively, took notes, and came back and reported to those left behind.[10]

Through these travels and study sessions, they concluded that they should establish an entity of organizers, young activists who would subsist on a minimum of resources. They were to get involved in issues of discrimination, police brutality, labor organizing, and especially education and the treatment of Mexican American students in the schools. Beyond that, they were to foster a new pride in being Chicano. The new organization, they decided, would consist of natural leaders who could be developed without too much training. By the late summer of 1967 the five had recruited a second layer of young men, mostly high-school dropouts. These new recruits came from the ranks of Compean's acquaintances, although Gutiérrez did most of the recruiting.[11] These teenagers had little regard for the society around them and were in fact considered its failures. In the second year a third layer of youth joined the growing group of activists-to-be. They were teenagers in school, mostly from the poorest districts deep in the west side of San Antonio. At the same time, the five began to contact other young men around the state. Most of these recruits were involved in the farm workers' unionizing efforts or in self-help programs in the poor barrios. These men, too, came in for extensive study sessions.

Guadalupe Youngblood, a prominent young activist from Robstown, Texas, recalled "long study and discussion sessions in which we talked about what we wanted and how we were going to do it. It was a philosophy based on cultural nationalism."[12] This philosophy embodied cultural components such as family, Mexican history, music, and the use of the Spanish language as part of the group's political views. It was also based on a new political rhetoric whose confrontational nature sought to arouse the attention of the Anglos, who would be shocked by it, and to capture the imagination of young Mexican Americans, who would applaud its audacity and valor. "We set out to come up with a lexicon of . . . terms," said Compean, "terms like 'La Raza,' 'Chicano liberation,' . . . and the word 'Chicano.' We began personifying the system through the use of the word 'gringo.'"[13]

These young leaders were bent on discarding what they referred to as the "lone wolf approach" of the old Mexican American political guard: "writing letters, [calling] press conferences, [using] the style of diplomacy . . . very proper, very formal, raising substantive issues, but in a nice voice."[14] These were the methods of once feisty organizations like LULAC and the G.I. Forum, which by the 1960s relied on litigation and support from sympathetic Anglos to achieve their goals. Compean recalled:

> What we needed was an approach similar to what the Black Movement was using . . . demonstrating, marching in the streets. To that we incorporated a Saul Alinsky component of confrontation politics. And we said that was going to be the

strategy ... MAYO [Mexican American Youth Organization] was going to be using. Use confrontational politics based on information ... well researched, but also foregoing the use of nice language.[15]

Gutiérrez, Pérez, and Compean tried out this approach in the summer of 1967 when they set up an informational picket line outside the Alamo, where a July 4th commemoration was being held.[16] While the band played and patriotic speeches were still ringing in the air, the three chanted and carried signs taunting the crowd. Expressions such as "What about La Raza?" "What about independence for La Raza?" and "When is that coming?" were painted on large signs where the celebrants could see them. There were always substantial numbers of Mexican Americans at these functions, and the three wanted to inaugurate their new rhetoric. For the most part they were ignored, except for a Mexican American veteran who became angry and tried to get them arrested. Nevertheless, for the three the protest was a success. They had introduced their style of activism to other Chicanos and to the media.[17]

The five also followed Pérez's lead in getting involved in a farm workers' strike in the Rio Grande Valley where Chávez's people were trying to organize. They went down to the fields and placed themselves between the Texas Rangers and the farm workers in the picket lines.[18] They also worked with Ernie Cortez, the sixth significant recruit, in organizing food banks in Austin for the farm workers. At the time, the UFW's campaign to unionize field workers symbolized the momentous struggle. Chicano activists saw themselves waging a war against an unfair system. Despite its pacifist leader, the UFW presented a rather radical image to many. Its motifs were nationalistic and its working-class roots were devoid of Angloism, making it an attractive symbol of *La Causa*.[19] Velásquez, more the urban activist, involved the group in calling *Raza Unida* (People United) unity conferences, throughout Texas. These gatherings were to play an important role in the development of the Chicano Movement in Texas. Prominent Mexican American scholars and activists came from around the country to speak to the students and community people and to motivate them to get involved in the social revolution raging in some parts of the Southwest. Being on the same stage with these figures helped legitimize the six in the eyes of Mexican Americans. It also allowed them to make contact with some militant elements of the political middle class.[20]

The first Raza Unida Conference took place in El Paso in October 1967 to counter President Johnson's cabinet hearings on Mexican American affairs. The hearings had been called to placate protesting Mexican American leaders who felt left out of the Democratic administration and who envied what they perceived to be Johnson's partiality toward blacks. When the list of invitees became public, it revealed that the administration sought to deal only with moderates who had an extensive history of loyalty to the Democratic Party. Though some of the invitees could claim to be legitimate spokesmen for the Mexican American community, a good number of them decided not to attend.[21]

One week before the hearings, Tijerina's Alianza held its annual meeting in Albuquerque. Several Chicano activist organizations met there and discussed the matter. A week before that conference, the five met and decided to push the idea of calling a counter-meeting in El Paso. Compean later explained their participation: "We talked about what was needed to be done. . . . It took us three sleepless nights to get a commitment from the people there . . . to go to El Paso. They had previously wanted to boycott the conference." At El Paso Velásquez, suggested "La Raza Unida" when the conference participants were looking for a name.[22] Ernesto Galarza, prominent scholar and union organizer, became the conference's first chairman.

A follow-up conference was held in San Antonio in January 1968, and several well-known Mexican Americans, including Galarza, attended and spoke to the participants about getting active in the movement that was sweeping the barrios. Two months later, another conference convened in Laredo.[23]

Shortly after coming together, the five concentrated on finding a name and a symbol and developing an organizational structure. They decided on the name Mexican American Youth Organization (MAYO) because it sounded "boy scoutish." According to Gutiérrez, the other names considered included Liga de Estudiantes y Obreros Nacionalistas (LEON), Partido Unificador Mexico Americano, (PUMA), and even, La Raza Unida. In fact, for a short time they were known as the Raza Unida, mainly because of their Raza Unida conferences. In the end they decided that a generic name like MAYO would take some of the heat off when they became militant and abrasive. The symbol that became synonymous with MAYO—the Aztec warrior inside a circle—was copied from Aeronaves de Mexico, the Mexican national airline.[24]

On paper a board of directors, made up of one representative from each chapter, directed the organization's activities. The board met on the last Saturday of January and the last Saturday of June. The first meeting was devoted to planning strategies and programs and the second to evaluating the programs and electing officers. The elected positions were those of chairman, vice-chairman, secretary, and treasurer. The MAYO founders decided to avoid the personification of the organization by not allowing anyone to serve more than a one-year term and by not emphasizing authoritative titles. They did not want MAYO to become dependent on one person who could be targeted for pressure by political opponents. Nonetheless, the organization was far from being democratic. Gutiérrez later said:

> [MAYO] was not democratic at all. I remember, for example, that Mario [Compean] pretty much handpicked who were the leaders he was going to work with, because they were already naturally emerging as leaders in gangs or other groups in the west side [of San Antonio]. I picked Carlos [Guerra], Efrain Fernández, and [Alberto] Luera because they were people who were working with groups in areas I knew. [Juan] Patlán did the same, Willie [Velásquez] did the same, and Nacho [Pérez] did the same. It was more like mentoring ... as opposed to electing. You were there as the organizer and that was not subject to election, that was a confirmation from me, Mario, Willie, Nacho, or Juan.[25]

MAYO was incorporated and by-laws were established. The membership requirements, though, were of a different nature than those of the usual nonprofit entity. They were meant to attract idealistic youth and to alienate moderates. They read like the creed of an ethnic, political movement, which is what MAYO intended to be. Members were expected to "put La Raza first and foremost"; to be alert but with a closed mouth; to have a desire to study, learn, and articulate, yet be ready "to attack"; and to support fellow MAYO members in time of crisis.[26] These rather simplistic requirements had the aim of developing a cadre of fiercely loyal members with a basic knowledge of the Chicano student movement and an obsession with cultural pride. They were to be militant in their fight against the gringo and respectful toward La Raza, thus making them modern-day political Robin Hoods. The preamble of the MAYO constitution read: "The purpose of the Mexican American

Youth Organization is to establish a coordinated effort in the organization of groups interested in solving problems of the Chicano community and to develop leaders from within the communities."[27]

To maintain a political movement, the MAYO leaders knew economics would be an important consideration. Velásquez, better versed in fundraising than the rest, became the prime fundraiser, getting money from local chapters of LULAC and the G.I. Forum. He acquired MAYO's first headquarters rent-free, atop a westside drugstore.[28] In its initial stage MAYO's aggressive style was admired even by established Mexican American political leaders and some barrio businessmen, who made small contributions and invited the young "militants" to lunch.

MAYO'S chance for a larger financial base came through the efforts of two acquaintances of Gutiérrez and Compean, Gonzalo Barrientos and José Urriegas, who helped them become involved in the founding of the VISTA (Volunteers in Service to America) Minority Mobilization Project in Austin. This self-help organization was funded to recruit and train two hundred young volunteers to work in four depressed areas of South Texas and in El Paso. Through his contacts with Urriegas and Gil Murillo, the project director and a sympathizer, Compean was hired as a recruiter and trainer. "I went to recruit people to be VISTA volunteers and many members of MAYO became volunteers," Compean said later.[29]

With the assistance of this patronage, MAYO grew from one chapter in San Antonio to more than thirty—of a few members each—in South Texas in one year. Compean later boasted: "MAYO had two hundred people loose. We had a budget. We had salaries for people. We had transportation. We had telephones. We had travel monies. So consequently that really allowed MAYO to expand."[30]

MAYO leaders, however, envisioned more than getting jobs for their members. They were interested in developing a financial base for their activities while creating an economic stimulus for the Mexican American community in San Antonio and, later, South Texas. That led to the founding of the Mexican American Unity Council (MAUC), an economic development corporation funded by a grant from the Southwest Council of La Raza, another Mexican American agency, which received money from the Ford Foundation. MAUC was the brainchild of Gutiérrez and Velásquez, who knew Julian Samora and Galarza, two prominent scholars with close ties to several funding agencies. Velásquez wrote the proposal and became MAYO's first employee earning five dollars a week.[31]

First Velásquez and then Patlán took the reigns of the development agency and made it a successful entity that served, into the 1980s, as a model for other Chicano economic development efforts. Initially, the Unity Council funded neighborhood associations and similar groups that worked with young drug addicts, advocated for better police protection in the barrio, and provided outreach services to the poor.[32] From there, the council went on to funding small businesses and training young Chicanos and Chicanas for jobs in the private sector. Through grants from the U.S. Office of Economic Development, they began to buy struggling, poverty-area businesses, either completely or partially, to infuse them with money, and to provide managerial help to get them on their feet again. Within four years of its existence, the agency's budget totaled millions of dollars and became the largest and most successful economic development agency in the city and the state. Eventually, it became involved in buying franchised firms.[33]

Notwithstanding its business orientation, the council continued to be involved with issues of health, particularly mental health. It received funds to train health para-professionals and other professionals oriented toward social work. MAUC became a successful source of employment, but more importantly, it served as a conduit for a one-time Ford Foundation grant of $8,500 in 1968 to MAYO, which allowed it to hire one staff member.[34]

One year later Pérez headed the founding of the Texas Institute for Educational Development (TIED), which received federal and state funds to provide health care to farm workers and other disadvantaged groups. Through TIED, free clinics and other health agencies directed by Chicanos began to appear in South Texas. Several years later, the agency turned its attention to health education rather than direct services. The concept behind the agency was original, and it brought praise from federal officials, who later attempted to duplicate the program nationally.[35] Like MAUC in its first years, TIED was used to employ MAYO members as well as to organize, around health and economic issues, the communities they served. The long range-effects on their localities nonetheless transcended and outlived their political purposes.

While MAYO was able to use federal and private dollars to sustain itself and its foot soldiers, it also provided services to Mexican American communities, at the same time claiming that it did not receive or accept direct money from the federal government. Yet for all their economic successes, MAYO leaders knew that their good fortunes were only a one-time deal. They had been able to surprise the Anglo power establishment the first time, but eventually the funds would dry up.

In the meantime, as VISTA volunteers the MAYO activists engaged in polarizing communities and in organizing study sessions and neighborhood advocacy groups. Polarization was, according to Gutiérrez, the best way to organize people.

> We felt that it was necessary to polarize the community into Chicano versus gringos. . . . After the gringo was exposed publicly, the next step was to confront their security-status. . . . Once the Chicano community recognized the enemy, then he [*sic*] had the power to eliminate gringo attitudes by not voting for the gringo and not buying from the gringo.[36]

MAYO organizers tried to get involved with neighborhood groups and agencies that worked with low-income people and disadvantaged children. Through these students and agencies they attempted to reach parents and other adults. This strategy did not prove successful at first. Most parents did not relate well to the militant talk, the revolutionary garb of some of the organizers, or their youthfulness. Consequently, many of the less ideologically oriented activists concentrated on the youth almost exclusively, a mistake that later haunted MAYO.

Since many of the youths were best attracted through fiery speeches and confrontational politics, special effort was made to taunt the Anglo structures that had long governed without opposition in these communities. MAYO's strategy sought to exasperate Anglos into overreacting or showing their "true colors." Press conferences became a major way of keeping MAYO in the headlines, impressing the Mexican American youth with nationalistic rhetoric, and riling the Anglo community. MAYO's press conferences were lively, name-calling affairs. On one such occasion Gutiérrez said:

> MAYO has found that both federal and religious programs aimed at social change do not meet the needs of the Mexicans of this state. Further, we find that the vicious cultural genocide being inflicted upon La Raza by gringos and their institutions not only severely damages our human dignity, but also makes it impossible for La Raza to develop its right of self-determination.

For these reasons, top priority is given to identifying and exposing the gringo. We also promote the social welfare of Mexicanos through education designed to enlarge the capabilities of indigenous leaders.

We hope to secure our human and civil rights, to eliminate bigotry and racism, to lessen the tensions in our barrios and combat the deterioration of our communities.

Our organization, largely comprised of youth, is committed to effecting meaningful social change. Social change that will enable La Raza to become masters of their own destiny, owners of their resources, both human and natural, and a culturally and spiritually separate people from the gringo. . . . We will not try to assimilate into this gringo society in Texas nor will we encourage anybody else to do so. . . .[37]

Whenever MAYO members could confront an Anglo politician, a law enforcement agency, or any other representative of authority, they reveled in it. They wanted opportunities to prove to the Mexican American community that Anglo racists were vulnerable and could be confronted and beaten down.

Newspapers became an effective medium for introducing MAYO'S philosophy to the people in the barrios. The first MAYO newspaper was *El Deguello* in San Antonio. Three others in circulation by 1969 were *Hoy* in the Rio Grande Valley, *El Azteca* in Kingsville, and *La Revolución* in Uvalde.[38] In naming the newspapers, the activists exhibited their ardent nationalism, which was vividly captured in an editorial explaining why MAYO had chosen the name *El Deguello*, which, signified, in the old Mexican Army, that no quarter was to be given.

Just as that bugle rang out [at the Alamo] that quiet morning, so, too, must it ring in every Chicano's ears.[39] As Chicanos we have given the gringo pleas, requests, and even demands. The gringo refuses to hear our voices just like Travis did. Obviously, gringos didn't learn much in 120 years. So, *El Deguello* must again shout out its war cry to tell all Chicanos that we must rise up against the gringo again. He has had his last chance.[40]

Extemporaneous events proved to be beneficial to MAYO. Police harassment, indiscriminate firings of Mexican Americans, controversial school suspensions, electoral intimidations, and similar events brought immediate response from the MAYO activists, either through their own initiative or by invitation from community groups. Each incident brought organizing opportunities that often led to the formation of more MAYO chapters.

One major media event occurred when the U.S. Commission on Civil Rights decided to hold hearings in San Antonio from December 9 to the 14, 1968. One of those subpoenaed was Captain Alfred Y. Allee, a thirty-six-year veteran of the Texas Rangers, the state's most famous law enforcement agency. No commission hearing on the Mexican American community could end without looking into the area of police brutality, and no law enforcement agency had a more controversial and negative reputation among Mexican Americans than the Texas Rangers. Only a year earlier the Rangers had ruthlessly suppressed a strike in the Rio Grande Valley by arresting hundreds of farm workers, with no pretext other than the fact that the farm workers were being unionized by Chávez's United Farm Workers.[41] The Rangers' reputation for intimidation, harassment, and violence, however, had not been acquired in contemporary times, but rather had been developing since the mid-1800s.[42]

When first summoned, Allee refused to attend. He claimed that his life had been threatened, and he blamed MAYO for those threats. Gutiérrez responded by challenging Allee to come and face the commission and many of his former victims and other Chicanos who were not afraid of him. Allee replied that if they had any guts, "they would face me in my own home." Gutiérrez rebutted that MAYO would meet him "anywhere and on any terms" and then he called him an animal. An infuriated Allee shot back that he would be there but with an escort of Texas Rangers.[43] When Allee arrived in San Antonio, he was met by hundreds of young MAYO-led Chicanos from across the state who had surrounded the auditorium where the commission was meeting. The Texas Rangers and their leader were forced by the crowd to enter the proceedings through the back door, and once inside, Allee was grilled by commission members who knew of his past activities.[44] MAYO came out of the confrontation looking like an organization of valiant youths willing to face danger for their Raza. The event signaled, they maintained, the end of subservience to the gringo.

These confrontational tactics brought a stern reaction from both Anglo and mainstream Mexican American politicians, as well as editorial writers from the state's newspapers. Said one newspaper editorialist in describing MAYO members: "[they are] a handful of apparently frustrated young men who have yet to discover their goals. . . . Meantime racism gets a new fuel at a time when nearly everybody else is trying to move in another direction."[45] Texas Governor Preston Smith did more than talk. He ordered VISTA volunteers to leave Val Verde County after county commissioners there accused MAYO of creating racial tension. In ordering the program ended, Smith said: "The abdication of respect for law and order, disruption of democratic process, and provocation of disunity [sic] among our citizens will not be tolerated." MAYO responded to this action by staging a large demonstration in the town and nailing what they called the "Del Rio Manifesto" to the courthouse door.[46]

U.S. Congressman O. C. Fisher of San Antonio continued the attack. He urged the House Committee on Internal Security to undertake an investigation of MAYO. Fisher accused Gutiérrez of being "deeply involved" in the grape strike at Delano, California, and "a prime agitator" in the "Rio Grande Valley disorders which erupted two years ago." He wrote to the committee, "Since this is a relatively new organization, it would seem to me that your committee may be interested in exploring the nature of its objectives and involvement which would seem to affect the peace and security of the area involved."[47]

All these criticisms, however, did not measure up to the attacks levied on Gutiérrez, Compean, and the other three leaders and their organization by Congressman Henry B. González, Texas's most famous mainstream Mexican American politician. González, a liberal Democrat who once ran for governor of Texas and barely missed getting his party's nomination, lambasted what he called MAYO's racism.

> MAYO styles itself the embodiment of good and the Anglo-American as the incarnation of evil. That is not merely ridiculous, it is drawing fire from the deepest wellsprings of hate. The San Antonio leader of MAYO, José Angel Gutiérrez, may think himself something of a hero, but he is, in fact, only a benighted soul if he believes that in the espousal of hatred he will find love. He is simply deluded if he believes that the wearing of fatigues . . . makes his followers revolutionaries. . . . One cannot fan the flames of bigotry one moment and expect them to disappear the next.[48]

For three days he blasted MAYO on the floor of the House of Representatives. He criticized "older radicals who lend their assent and even support." The Ford Foundation, which had funded MAUC and thus MAYO indirectly, also did not escape González's fury, nor did the Mexican American Legal Defense and Education Fund (MALDEF) or the Southwest Council of La Raza, which were friendly to MAYO. González blamed the Ford Foundation for wasting taxpayers' money in order to support "brown thugs" who were bent on using racist tactics to divide Anglos and Mexican Americans.[49]

González was especially indignant about a MAYO press conference in which Gutiérrez called for the elimination of the gringo. What Gutiérrez actually said was, ". . . some Mexicanos will become psychologically castrated, others will become demagogues and gringos as well, and others will come together, resist and eliminate the gringo. We will be with the latter." He went on to say that a "gringo" was "a person or institution that has a certain policy or program, or attitudes that reflect bigotry, racism, discord and prejudice and violence." When he was asked by a reporter what he meant by "eliminate the gringo," Gutiérrez responded, "You can eliminate an individual in various ways. You can certainly kill him but that is not our intent *at this moment*. You can remove his base of support that he operates from, be it economic, political, or social. *That is what we intend to do*" (author's italics).[50]

Although the threats and subsequent explanations were enough to incense most Anglos, the way the newspapers played the story created a furor. Gutiérrez's qualifiers and later attempts to retract some of the militancy of his words were lost in the public debate over the "killing of the gringo." González labeled MAYO leaders "Brown Bilbos"—a reference to Theodore Bilbo, segregationist senator from Mississippi—who were practicing a new racism.[51] His was a vicious attack, and it opened the flood-gates for more scathing criticisms of MAYO from both Mexican Americans and Anglos. It also guaranteed that a segment of Mexican American liberals would not only resist MAYO overtures, but work to destroy the organization. A weak congressman in Washington, D.C., González nevertheless wielded enormous power in the twentieth Congressional District, which included much of the west side of San Antonio. His speech became a albatross around the neck of Gutiérrez and the organization.

The immediate impact of the assault on MAYO was the eroding of the organization's economic base. Governor Smith's charges forced the national VISTA organization to clamp down on MAYO's activities, and many of the organizers were soon purged from their jobs. Congressman González's denunciation ended the possibility of any more direct funds for MAYO. MAUC survived and prospered because Patlán moved the organization away from politics and eventually away from MAYO control, but TIED barely managed to hang on with small grants that were never large enough to hire much of a staff.

Political consequences notwithstanding, MAYO had no intention of abrogating its agenda, and prominent among its objectives was educational reform. While media events and public debates increased MAYO's notoriety, another strategy became a trademark for which the organization would be known and feared: school boycotts. From day one the leadership gave education a high priority. In their constitution MAYO leaders unequivocally stated, "We seek to control local school districts or individual schools in order to make the institution adapt itself to the needs of the [Chicano] community rather than ... making the ... student adapt to the school."[52] They sought to gain control over the curriculum, the hiring of administrators and teachers, the financing, and the schools' relationship to the community. MAYO leaders realized that even middle-class Mexican Americans had rallied to the issue of education in the past.[53] It was also an area in which schools were vulnerable. Few Anglo educators could seriously defend the education system in the barrio. In San Antonio 98 percent of the teachers without degrees were concentrated in schools that served the barrio. And these poor schools, like many others in the Southwest which served Mexican Americans, received much less money— three hundred dollars less in San Antonio—per pupil than the predominantly Anglo schools.[54]

When the MAYO leadership elected to challenge the educational system, it chose methods other than litigation or quiet diplomacy. Boycotts, they decided, would be the strongest weapons because funds were based on how many days of school a child attended during the year. The more absenteeism, the less money. Through their networks, MAYO activists identified students who were natural leaders and who could rally others to their cause. They oriented these students to "boycott politics," assisted them in writing a list of demands and in setting up press conferences, and then let them take over the frontline leadership while the MAYO leaders from outside the locality remained in the background. In two years MAYO initiated numerous boycotts—the estimates run from eighteen to thirty-nine—from Lubbock in West Texas to the Rio Grande Valley and San Antonio in the south.[55]

Sidney Lanier High School, on San Antonio's central west side,

Sidney Lanier High School, on San Antonio's central west side, was MAYO's first target. Velásquez led the effort to create a student coordinating committee which presented a number of grievances to the school administration. The demands centered on three major points: the instituting of college preparatory courses, the establishment of culturally-relevant courses, and the elimination of the "No Spanish" rule forbiding the use of Spanish on the school grounds. That rule was seen as particularly demeaning by some of the more nationalistic students. The more moderate students strongly advocated the college preparatory courses.

Lanier seemed the wrong place to start a student revolt because it had a Mexican American student population of nearly 97 percent, was located in a stable working-class neighborhood, had a large number of Mexican American teachers, and was recognized as academically the best high school in the barrios of San Antonio. Violence, vandalism, and absenteeism, so often associated with urban, inner-city schools, were not major problems at Lanier.[56]

Judging from appearances, the school did not seem a good place to organize, but MAYO activists were looking beyond appearances. They saw that there were few college preparatory courses, a large dropout rate, and that students were being punished for speaking Spanish. Most of the graduates were getting low-paying jobs, while graduates of the city's Anglo high schools were going on to college. Possibly just as important, they saw that Sidney Lanier student leaders were well respected by the Mexican American community because they tended to be more articulate and came from more stable families than students in other west side high schools, which were worse off financially and located in less stable neighborhoods.

The protest movement within the school created a rift between the students and the Mexican American principal and many of the Mexican American teachers, who sided with the Anglos. Even the nearby neighborhoods were divided, with some parents charging that the student leaders were communists and others defending the protesters' courage and willingness to stand up for their rights. The student leaders, some coached by MAYO organizers, others encouraged by more moderate activists, were able to gather support from a number of the Mexican American politicians in the city and this gave legitimacy to the protest. Support from several Catholic priests also helped to divert some of the criticism.

The climax of the student controversy came when school officials held a meeting with the parents and the student leaders in a

Catholic parish hall adjacent to the school. More than five hundred people attended, including a group of Anglo sociology students who came to study the event. In a dramatic confrontation between students, led by José Vásquez and Homer C. García—both non-MAYO activists—and school officials, the parents and other interested persons were able to hear both sides and to meet the conflict's protagonists.[57]

The student leaders came better prepared than the school officials, who underestimated the students' sophistication. School officials brought former students to testify in favor of the school's rules, particularly the one dealing with no Spanish on the school grounds. When one former student told the audience, in heavily accented English that the "No Spanish" rule sought only to help students learn English, and that he was an example of one student who circumvented it to his detriment, a student leader quickly rebutted, telling the audience that speaking Spanish had hurt the student a lot less than the bad instruction he had received.[58]

Playing to the nationalist feelings of a large number in the crowd, the student leaders continually pointed out rules and practices they described as humiliating and degrading to the Mexican American community. In a tone and style that exuded pride in their ethnic heritage, they repeatedly demanded respect for the culture and traditions they brought from home. Slowly they won the favor of the audience. Ironically, they did it by being more articulate, in both Spanish and English, than the "successful" students who were persuaded to speak on behalf of the school. Years later one former student wrote:

> The school was supposed to be the beacon of light that would lead us to a better life, but all that came from the school officials' defense was the offer of a stable life of hard work, limited mobility, and a traditionally well-played football schedule. It wasn't that the teachers did not teach about better things, it was just that no one in the school system did more than just teach. ... In contrast, what I was hearing from the student protesters were new challenges, new horizons, all the things that my parents and an occasional good teacher had taught me to believe in.[59]

Completely embarrassed in the meeting, the school officials capitulated. In its May 1968 edition the Chicano newspaper *Inferno* reported: "Nine of the demands were granted as they were proposed. The one most popularly received was the one dealing with speaking Spanish at school."[60]

Shortly after the Lanier victory, students at Edgewood High School and Junior High School walked out of their classrooms, complaining that the state had abandoned them to classrooms without window screens, water fountains without water, teachers without certification, and a host of other problems. The Edgewood boycott proved successful when the media began to investigate the charges and found that most of them were true. The Edgewood Independent School District ranked as one of the poorest in the nation and it became an example of the disregard that officials had for the Mexican American students.[61]

On November 14 another major walkout occurred in the Rio Grande Valley when one hundred forty students left the Edcouch-Elsa High School after two of their fellow students had been expelled for failure to cut their hair. MAYO organizers then helped other students write a list of demands for better facilities and the right to speak Spanish on the school grounds. This was a spontaneous boycott, but like others that followed, it had been prompted by the successes at Lanier and Edgewood. The school protest led to the striking down of the "No Spanish" rule as unconstitutional by a federal judge, and thus one of the most degrading school rules in Texas was eliminated.[62]

Numerous other boycotts followed the one in Edcouch-Elsa. The main demands in each case were the same: no punishment for speaking Spanish, establishment of a bilingual-bicultural program, the firing of racist teachers, the celebration of Mexican holidays, and availability of college preparatory courses for all students. The adoption of even half of these demands would have required major shifts in policies, so many administrators resisted, and thus many threatened boycotts turned into walkouts. Walkouts were not unique to Texas, for spontaneous walkouts occurred in California, Colorado, New Mexico, and other states. What was different was that these were being initiated, supported, or directed by a single organization.

One of the major beneficiaries of the boycotts proved to be bilingual education, which had become federal law in late 1967. Funds were not appropriated until 1968, and the programs in Texas did not begin in full until 1969. When they did, they had a groundswell of support from many high school-students and their parents and from some school officials and teachers who needed the funds to implement such programs to placate the protesters. The boycotts also changed the relationship between parents and the school districts. In supporting their children's confrontation with the school administrators and school board members, more parents became involved in school issues and in attending school board meetings.[63]

From these confrontations came many of the new leaders of MAYO. These leaders and their followers were not exclusively male, for women made up a significant part of the membership. They came from the larger pool of Mexican American women who were attending college, oftentimes away from their homes. The nature of the activities allowed women to become spokepersons and leaders, though never at the level of the men. MAYO's recruiting success, however, remained limited to students and young people. Even when the parents came out in full force to support their sons and daughters, they limited their involvement to the school conflict. Gutiérrez later recalled: "We were never able to get parents to join us. It was not until thirty-eight walkouts later, that we finally learned enough techniques to organize parents, teachers and students."[64] It was to be in Crystal City, Gutiérrez's hometown, that MAYO claimed its first major organizing victory.

Brown legs
are beautiful
too!

We demand
Chicana cheerleaders!

—Crystal City protest sign

CRYSTAL CITY REIGNITES

Destiny, it seems, had tapped Crystal City for a major role in Texas political history, particularly that portion dealing with Mexican Americans. Already in 1963 the small, rural, agriculturally based town had been in many of the state's newspaper headlines, and for a short time it had become a symbol of simmering social unrest. Not since the late 1800s, when Mexican Americans were still a significant majority in some southwestern states, had they been successful in winning an electoral victory as they had in Crystal City. Another small Texas town, Mathis, had followed the Crystal City victory by winning control with a majority Chicano slate, but this group was more assimilationist and made no effort to be a rallying symbol.¹ Few would ever point to Mathis and say that it was one of the precursors of the Chicano Movement, as they would say later of Crystal City.

The revolt of 1963 had a significant influence on Gutiérrez, who at the time was a student at a nearby community college in Uvalde. The electoral victory of "Los Cinco," as the candidates were called, was an example of repressed passions and fervent nationalism bursting into the open, and it impressed a young man who had grown bitter from his experiences at the hands of Anglos who controlled the political, economic, educational, and judicial institutions of Zavala County. He later described 1960s life in Crystal City as "suffocating" and "a tunnel without any light at the end."²

His views were in part inherited from his Mexican father, who as a young medical school graduate had joined the army of Pancho

Villa during the Mexican Revolution of 1910. He came to be one of Villa's medical officers and a member of the Mexican ambulatory corps. The elder Gutiérrez served as the military and then elected mayor of Torreón before he was exiled twice during political upheavals in Mexico. In 1929 he came to the Rio Grande Valley and moved to Crystal City. A fervent Mexican nationalist, he never became a U.S. citizen and asked to be buried in Mexico when he died. The younger Gutiérrez later laid claim to that nationalist fervor. He also maintained that his speaking abilities came from his father.[3]

Life for José Angel had not been difficult while his father lived. Though not rich, the family was one of the better off in the barrio. But when the father died at the age of seventy-four, the family found itself without any means of support and without the lines of credit they had enjoyed. Twelve-year-old José Angel saw his life change drastically. He became just another of the poor Mexican boys in Crystal City and his mother another of the poor women who had to perform menial jobs to feed her family. Gutiérrez later recalled this new life as a harsh one and said it was only then that he began to notice the disparities between the two communities that lived in Crystal City and to question why his people lived in such destitute conditions.[4]

Crystal City was one of many rural slums in Texas where most of the Mexican population either worked for extremely low wages in the nearby cannery and the surrounding ranches or waited for the harvest season to travel up north. Nearly one thousand of the town's families earned less than three thousand dollars a year, which was below the poverty level for a family of four. More than half the homes had no toilets and one-third had no plumbing. One section of town did not even receive water. A reporter for the *Washington Post* wrote of the town, "The Chicano neighborhoods are a collection of wooden shacks and unpaved muddy streets." In contrast, "the Anglo neighborhoods [have] concrete sidewalks and roadways [that] weave past modest middle class homes and high-priced ranch style structures."[5]

This kind of past had rallied hundreds of Mexican Americans in 1963 to register to vote and to cast their ballots for a slate of five uneducated, working-class Mexican Americans who ran for the city council. When the vote total was released, the reaction was euphoric: people hugged each other, some cried, some got drunk, and others honked their car horns for hours until the Texas Rangers cracked down on them.[6] The rallies, the pamphleteering, the voter-registration drives, and the political fundraising were activities new to most Mexican Americans in Crystal City. For many, it had been the first time they had united for a cause at the risk of losing jobs or getting physically abused. The period leading up to the election had been one of *orgullo*, pride of being *mexicano*.

Six years had passed, and Gutiérrez knew that not much had changed in Crystal City and the neighboring communities. The dream of a Mexican social revolution had died in 1965.

When Gutiérrez arrived in Crystal City in June 1969 with his wife Luz[7] and their first child, he came for two reasons, one economic and the other political. Only three months before, he had been released from the army reserves after six months of active duty. There he had had time to write down some of his political ideas and to affirm in his mind that partisan politics were essential for Chicano empowerment.

On his return to San Antonio, he tried to regain his job as a field researcher for the Mexican American Legal Defense and Education Fund (MALDEF) but was refused. It seems that the pressure Congressman Henry B. González had put on the Ford Foundation had reached MALDEF.[8] Gutiérrez threatened to sue, and the legal agency paid off his contract rather than rehire him. Without a job and with few possible prospects in San Antonio because of his reputation, he decided to visit Reies López Tijerina in New Mexico and Rodolfo "Corky" Gonzales in Colorado, and then return home to Crystal City to live rent-free with relatives.[9]

Before he left, though, he attended MAYO's semiannual state meeting in San Antonio, where Compean won the election for chairman and where new, more specific organizing goals were agreed upon. Gutiérrez presented his concept of a third political party. This had been one of MAYO's original goals, but little had been done to carry through with the idea. When Gutiérrez first mentioned it in 1967, the other activists had told him to "write up" the idea and send it out for reaction. He studied the state's laws dealing with political parties, wrote a proposal, and sent it out to farm-worker groups and to activists in El Paso, Crystal City, and other places, but he received no response and the idea was shelved.[10]

The MAYO meeting of 1969 seemed the right time to resurrect the third-party concept because the organization had just completed its first electoral activity, a race for the San Antonio city council. Compean and two other candidates had run under the banner of the Committee for Barrio Betterment and challenged the powerful Good Government League, which had dominated San Antonio politics for more than two decades.[11] Although the committee did not run strictly as a MAYO front, Compean nonetheless expounded the concept of La Raza Unida and even placed that slogan in all his campaign literature. He talked of Chicano self-determination and called for the development of alternative political models to the Republican and Democratic parties even though the election was nonpartisan.[12] He limited his campaigning to the west side barrios but still came within a few hundred votes of getting into a runoff with the incumbent mayor. He captured a number of the Mexican American precincts and became convinced that the idea of a third party would attract support in the barrios.[13]

Unfortunately for Gutiérrez, he could not find many other enthusiastic supporters besides Compean. Luz later recalled that most of the MAYO activists did not consider the program feasible and some of them thought it ludicrous. Instead, they were more inclined to support a program designed to win control of a particular area in rural Texas.[14] They were interested in taking over existing institutions rather than continuing to use confrontations and protests as strategies for change. Through they were in essence talking politics, the nonpartisan nature of local elections in Texas allowed them to have electoral designs without considering the need for a new party.

The MAYO delegates discussed four possible target areas with large concentrations of Mexican Americans. The areas were chosen because they were poor, they were controlled politically by Anglos who could easily be accused of being racist, there had been MAYO activities in them before, and the chances of success were considered good. The four targets contemplated were the Winter Garden Area, a seven-county stretch in South Texas that included Crystal City (Zavala County); the Plainview and Lubbock area in West Texas, which had a significant number of former migrant workers and field hands; the Kingsville area, where Texas A&I University was located; and the Rio Grande Valley, an area close to the Mexican border which had the largest concentration of migrant workers in the state and which ranked as one of the poorest parts of the country.[15]

The MAYO delegates decided on the Winter Garden Area and agreed to focus on three of the seven counties: Zavala, Dimmit, and La Salle. Gutiérrez was born and still had family in the first county, Patlán was from the second, and MAYO had a strong chapter in the third. The main reason for choosing the Winter Garden Area, though, was that Gutiérrez had decided to go back home to organize. Compean consequently appointed him head of the Winter Garden Area Project.

By deciding to head the MAYO project in his hometown, Gutiérrez adhered to a rule of the organization which stated that each organizer had to return home and agitate in his own community. Gutiérrez wrote in his diary his strong feelings about that MAYO principle: "Our young Chicanos must learn and accept the fact that to not return [is] in effect saying, My people and my town are not worth going back to ... I wonder how our young, educated and bright Chicanos can think of joining VISTA or the Peace Corps or the army and not see that the struggle is where they come from."[16]

When Gutiérrez made a preliminary trip to Crystal City, the Zavala County seat, he found a controversy already brewing among the high-school students. Chicano students were upset over the de facto quotas the high-school administration had when it came to extracurricular activities. In the spring of 1969 they became particularly angered over the selection of the baseball sweetheart and the cheerleading squad. In both instances, the Mexican American students felt that the small Anglo minority received a better deal.[17] Chicano students, led by Libby Lara and Diana Palacios, presented the principal, John B. Lair, with a petition asking that the students be allowed to elect the cheerleaders. Lair refused to accept it, so the students went to the school superintendent, John Billings. By then the petition had grown to seven demands and had three hundred fifty signatures. It insisted, among other things that teachers stop expounding their political beliefs to the students and that the school implement bilingual and bicultural education.[18] Gutiérrez could easily identify with the protesting students, as he had graduated from Crystal City High School in 1962 and had encountered the same kind of blatant discrimination.

He vividly remembered two incidents that were to influence the way he felt about Anglos for the rest of his life. The first occurred when as junior class president he conducted an election for twenty pairs of servers for the senior prom. The students elected thirty-four Mexican Americans and six Anglos. Gutiérrez took the list to John B. Lair, who quickly dumped it in the trash can and proceeded to develop another list that had ten Mexican American couples and ten Anglo couples. He told Gutiérrez, "This is who won," to which Gutiérrez responded, "No sir . . . why are you changing the names?" Gutiérrez would always remember the reply, "Because we live in this town and this town wouldn't put up with Mexican boys . . . with these white girls and we're not going to start no trouble, are we?"[19]

The second instance came during the election of the most handsome boy and most beautiful girl. With the Anglo students bloc voting and the Mexican American students having a larger choice, six Anglo students and four Mexican American students became the nominees. Their pictures were taken and then sent to well known Hollywood movie stars Troy Donahue and Kim Novak.

Time passed and there was no answer. Gutiérrez, along with several other anxious students, decided to break into the journalism office and check to see if any results had come back. In one of the files they found letters from the actors excusing themselves as judges and indicating that they felt the local community would best be the judge of who was beautiful. "We thought, 'No winners'," Gutiérrez later commented. "We asked the following day . . . [and] they said they hadn't heard. Within ten days they announced they had received word. They had a letter from both people (Donahue and Novak) saying who won—they were white [students]. We knew they had forged the letters. That was how far they went. I, for one, said, 'This people will never willingly change.'"[20]

After the students presented Billings with the petition, he agreed to meet with some of them and several parents. In the meeting he promised the protesting students that there would be an explicit quota of three Anglos and three Mexican American students in the cheerleading squad. He also pledged to deal with the other issues with either more quotas or by finding out what other communities in the area were doing. The superintendent's solutions proved that the administration would be pushed no further than the policy of separate but equal.

Gutiérrez and Patlán, who was temporarily staying in nearby Carrizo Springs, advised the students to accept the arrangement because the school year was winding down and students would have little leverage in a walkout. The seniors were sure to be flunked, and the school board would have the summer to let things cool down. The students accepted, but they were not truly happy, and that left a smoldering nonconformity that Gutiérrez quickly sought to take advantage of. In June the school board added more fuel to the controversy when it decided that the superintendent's actions were "pandering to the hot-headed students" and over-turned his decisions.[21]

By midsummer Gutiérrez had initiated several discussion groups in which he brought together a group of men to drink beer and talk about the lot of Mexican Americans in Crystal City. There was no agenda, but the discussion always drifted to politics and the need to make changes. The 1963 electoral revolt was often rehashed, at times heatedly because there were still many bitter feelings about the experience. Some thought Mexican Americans would always be second-class citizens. The emotional scar of the Anglos' reaction to that election lingered in the minds of several of the men. Gutiérrez found that some of the men had major inferior-ity complexes when it came to dealing with Anglos. He later noted: "The defeat of the 1963 effort in 1965 caused a cynicism and pes-simism to develop. It was very vicious because people would say things to me like 'You are crazy trying to do it again. We already did it once and it didn't work. We are just incapable of self-govern-ment.'"[22] Others did not totally trust Gutiérrez. They were not sure whether he had come to Crystal City to establish his own little political empire or whether he even had the capacity to be a leader. They questioned him on subjects dealing with history, science, and any other topic they could imagine to test his knowledge and his ability to think.[23]

Victoriano "Nano" Serna, who owned a convenience store, became Gutiérrez's best ally. He provided the meeting place and most of the beer and snacks. Julián Salas, who had been elected justice of the peace in 1968, also became an early convert. Salas shared Gutiérrez's dislike of the Anglo. Even though he served as a county official, he did not have an office, a telephone, or supplies, and he did not receive any cases to try.[24] The Anglos had isolated him and diminished any influence he could have had.

Both Serna and Salas became facilitators for Gutiérrez's mes-sage and provided legitimacy for his cause in the eyes of many Mexican Americans in Crystal City. Their network of family and friends offered a natural constituency to organize into a study group. With the help of these two, Gutiérrez spoke to many with-out having an obvious public image that would have attracted at-tention from the Anglos in town.[25]

Besides a community network, Gutiérrez needed a staff and he recruited Bill Richey and Linda Harrison, who had been fellow students during his stay both at Texas A&I University and St. Mary's University. Through his connection in the VISTA program, he had Richey and Harrison hired and transferred to Cotulla in La Salle County. In the fall of 1969 he recruited María Ynosencia and two students, Severita Lara and Beatriz Mendoza. In Carrizo Springs, a neighboring community in Dimmitt County, he recruited David Ojeda and his wife Rosa.[26]

In moving to organize in the Winter Garden Area, Gutiérrez decided to change some of MAYO's tactics. He realized that the rebellious, loud approach would do more to alienate the poor and tradition-bound Mexican American community than it would to unite it, especially since the community, having seen the chaotic manner of "Los Cinco," sought legitimate leaders who knew what they were doing and had the ability to succeed. Because of MAYO's insistence that no one could straddle the fence on the issue of Mexican American rights, and because it chose to confront rather than negotiate, polarization resulted from most of its activities. In time, MAYO made as many enemies as it did friends. Gutiérrez later recalled: "We failed in making friends. We were so bad . . . We would rather be hated than liked. Pretty soon there were more people hating us than liking us. . . . Our image was terrible . . . Regrettably this was being seen by the Chicano community much more so than the *gabacho*."[27] By 1969, an element within MAYO had made a move to change the organization's public image from that of a group of rebellious, sloppily dressed, often times foul-mouthed youth to that of an organization of articulate, undivisive activists with close ties to the community.

Compean and Gutiérrez led the fight for a new image, but they were outvoted by those who felt that their dress was irrelevant to their activities. The opponents won the debate by stressing discipline in lieu of a change in wardrobe. Interestingly enough, Compean and Gutiérrez remained the most militant of the group, Compean with his cultural nationalism and Gutiérrez with his verbal attacks on the gringo and his use of profanity. Although numerous MAYO activists saw a need for change, most who were recruited in the urban centers and expected to stay there did not alter their style much. A number of those in the rural communities realized they had no choice but to make some changes if they were to succeed in their organizing activities.[28]

Gutiérrez presented an image of a young, educated Mexican American who had returned to live and work in his hometown. He avoided being seen as a leader in the traditional sense and sought instead to be a motivator and an adviser to the natural leaders of the rural community. His organizing tactics were proving fruitful but slow when a major new conflict arose at the high school.

In October the Crystal City High School Ex-student Association decided to choose a queen and her court for the homecoming activities. To be eligible, the candidates had to have at least one parent who had graduated from the high school. Of the twenty-six applicants, only five were Mexican American and this brought an outcry from students who did not qualify. With an average median educational level of 2.3 years, the Mexican American community could not claim many graduates.[29]

Severita Lara, now a recognized student leader because of her work with Gutiérrez, published a pamphlet criticizing the requirement. She was quickly suspended for three days, though she returned after the second day with the help of a MALDEF lawyer.[30]

Gutiérrez and Luz moved quickly to organize support for the students and to expand the demands. In this effort they were assisted by Virginia Músquiz, a long-time activist and friend of Gutiérrez, as well as other men and women who had captured the vision of a town in revolt. Some had been part of the 1963 campaign; others were new to this kind of activity. Most were women, and they proved to be tenacious and untiring in their efforts to gain support for the student walkout. The work was divided by gender, Gutiérrez and others working with the men and the students, and Luz, Múzquiz, and other women with the students' mothers. They were able to convince more than one hundred parents and family members to attend the school board meeting on November 3, when the issue of choosing the homecoming queen was placed on the agenda.

The women and students were anxious to attend, but the men were either afraid or simply did not feel it was their role to argue before a school board. Gutiérrez well understood the men's inhibitions and decided to wait until they had a few beers at the local bar before he went over and began to denounce the school board for discriminating against the students and then for threatening to throw out the women because there was no room in the meeting hall for so many people. Some of the men, already partly intoxicated, cursed and made idle threats against the school board. After getting them riled, Gutiérrez led them to the board meeting.[31]

At the meeting hall Luz had already carried out her part of the plan by getting the women and students to occupy the back, thus forcing the men to move up front. Since the board had refused to move the meeting to accommodate the large crowd or even to bring more chairs, the men stood around the board members' table. The board found itself surrounded by rough-looking men with a strong smell of alcohol on their breath. When Gutiérrez and Jesse Gámez, a native of Crystal City with a law practice in San Antonio, brought up the issue of the coronation activities, the men became loud and boisterous.[32]

The board, overwhelmed and intimidated by the large, angry crowd, turned down the Ex-student Association's request to use the school grounds for its ceremony. They took the other grievances under advisement after a contentious, three-hour meeting.[33] Rather than defusing the students' momentum, the board's action simply made it more determined. The students and the parents viewed the board's capitulation as a sign of weakness and resolved to press for the other demands.

The protesting students and parents were not the only ones to view the board's actions as buckling down under pressure, however. The Anglo community saw the school board as too cowardly to confront the "disturbed young men," and the more militant Anglos began harassing the school board members and other Anglos they considered too lenient in their view of the protest. One member of the Ex-student Association even expressed the feeling that it might be time to "change the crew" in the school's administration.[34]

The hostile attitude of the Anglo residents prevented any serious effort to compromise on the demands. The board members, assailed from both sides but conscious that the Anglo community had already once turned back a challenge from the barrios, decided to reject all the demands. In an extremely short meeting on December 8, a board spokesperson announced that the grievances had been found to be unsubstantiated and that no more time would be spent on them.

The board's action cemented the polarization between the two sides of town and dispelled any notion that the Anglos were now more willing to negotiate than they had been in 1963. The blatant insensitivity was particularly appalling to the small middle-class element that had expected some concessions from the Anglos in return for support against Los Cinco in 1965. They felt despised by the lower-class Mexican Americans and ignored by the Anglos. A number of them became susceptible to Gutiérrez's persuasions.

Gutiérrez had counted on the board's rejecting the demands and creating more hostilities. He knew that anger was the one emotion that could break the fear the Mexican American community had of the Anglo. In anticipating the negative decision, he had prepared plans for a school walkout that would gradually grow stronger and would involve parents from day one.

As soon as the decision was announced, Gutiérrez, Luz, and several leaders went to work. All that night they went from house to house recruiting the first one hundred students to walk out the following day. They identified the students less likely to be intimidated and the ones whose parents were supportive.[35]

At this time Gutiérrez's previous organizing work proved to be crucial. Parents who had met him through the discussion sessions sensed that he knew what he was doing and came out in support of their sons and daughters. By the second day two hundred fifty students failed to show up to class; by that afternoon the boycott had spread to the junior high school, and nearly five hundred fifty school-aged children had stayed home. On the third day four hundred sixteen of six hundred seventy-three high-school students failed to attend school.[36]

Sensing that the boycott would not blow over, the board asked an investigative team from the Texas Education Agency (TEA) to mediate. The two-person team from TEA stayed in Crystal City for two unsuccessful days and left with the recommendation that the school close early for the holidays in order to avoid violence. School officials rejected the advice and attempted to defuse the situation by agreeing to develop a course on Mexican American history. But they would not budge on the other requests, so the students refused to negotiate and simply vowed to outlast the school administrators.

After the first week the parents became involved at the decision-making level. Along with numerous other individuals who had participated in the discussion groups, they banded together to form Ciudadanos Unidos, a grassroots political organization that intended to stay together after the boycott issue was settled.[37]

The Ciudadanos Unidos and the student leaders sponsored a rally on Sunday of the first week, and it attracted more than one thousand people who came to hear Gutiérrez, the Rev. Henry Casso—head of an organization of Mexican American priests—and Albert Peña, Jr., an old friend of Gutiérrez's who had been a prime supporter of the 1963 revolt.[38] The publicity of the rally and the boycott strengthened the students' hand. At the start of the second week student leaders Diana Serna, Severita Lara, and Mario Treviño were invited to Washington, D.C., to meet with Texas Senator Ralph Yardborough, who introduced them to Senators Edward Kennedy and George McGovern. They also spoke to officials of the Departments of Justice and Health, Education and Welfare (HEW).

Meanwhile, the board could feel the pressure mounting, so it again requested mediators from TEA. The board members stated that they were ready to negotiate but would do so only with the parents of the students. Gutiérrez quickly advised the students and parents against this type of meeting. He knew that the school officials would attempt to intimidate the parents, some of whom would be fearful of losing their jobs or feel uncomfortable speaking English and thus be no match for the more assertive board members. When the TEA team arrived, they found that no meeting could be arranged. An interdenominational church committee also attempted to mediate, but it, too, failed when infighting broke out among its own members over which side was right in the boycott issue.[39]

Near the Christmas holidays the school officials were handed a major blow when the Texans for the Educational Advancement of Mexican Americans (TEAM), a group headed by Josué González, announced that it would send teachers to instruct the students during the holidays so they would not fall behind in their studies. Some of those teachers were sympathetic to MAYO and, with the help of the organization, which had now gotten involved, began to establish "liberation" classrooms outside the school grounds to teach not only the regular curriculum but other lessons on Mexican American history.[40]

Just behind the TEAM members came a two-person mediating team from the Community Relations Service of the U.S. Department of Justice. Gutiérrez had left nothing to chance. He knew from experience that with pressure from Anglos the school board would not give in easily. He also felt that it would be willing to engage in questionable tactics in order to win the confrontation. He needed only to remember 1963 to know that intimidation and violence were weapons often used against Mexican Americans. His own experience at the hands of the Texas Rangers reminded him that if the confrontation was contained at the local level, local "remedies" would be applied very effectively.[41] With the media and federal mediators present, the few hotheaded Anglos could be kept in check.

Gutiérrez defused the accusations of radicalism by toning down the public statements so common during his leadership of MAYO. To avoid the charges of "communist" and "subversive," he organized pledge-of-allegiance and flag-raising ceremonies on the morning before the students took their places outside the school with their signs.[42] Gutiérrez had prepared well for the boycott and later proudly recalled:

> The rallies of Christmas of 1969 provided the happiest times for La Raza. Since the boycott La Raza had maintained the upper hand in media, in tactics and in morale. The mood of imminent victory was exemplified by speaker after speaker during the rallies.
>
> During this time the Mexicanos of Crystal City were one in thought, action and goal—they were La Raza Unida. No longer did the slogans for unity need shouting; nor did the songs of solidarity need heeding—la Raza had gotten it all together. . . . The farm workers opened their modest homes to the strangers from TEAM . . . the members of TEAM came to teach the boycotting students; the truckers provided the bus service for liberation classes; and the parents joined their children at the daily marching around the school and through the city's white business sector.[43]

With nearly 65 percent of the student population boycotting classes and with pressure mounting from the Department of Justice, TEA, and HEW, the school board finally decided to negotiate a way out of the crisis. The school board, five students, five parents, and two mediators from the Community Relations Service met in three lengthy sessions and worked out a compromise that gave the students most of what they had asked. On Tuesday, January 6, 1970, the walkout ended, and the students returned to school the following week.

The board attempted to save face by stating that some changes were contingent on available funds, but neither side ever believed that the agreement was a true compromise. The students had won a dramatic victory, and the school officials and their strongest supporters had been humiliated. The victory had been made possible by the discipline the students exhibited and because they had waited for the right time to walk out. In neighboring Uvalde the following year, students did not heed Gutiérrez's advice and they left school near the end of the term. The school board and school officials ruthlessly crushed the protest by expelling most of the students involved. The selective service board, working in conjunction with the school officials, drafted the oldest students, some of whom ended up as casualties of the Vietnam War.[44]

The Mexican American community knew this triumph was well deserved, and it encouraged them in a way that the 1963 election had not. They realized that they had won because they had prepared and had remained united. They also recognized that in Gutiérrez they had a bona fide leader capable of anticipating the Anglos' moves and knowledgeable enough to bring the required help from the outside. Most of his supporters felt that this would be a lasting victory, though a few must have thought about what the Anglos would do to retaliate.

Gutiérrez had no intention of waiting for a backlash or of giving up the offensive. Even before the walkout ended, he initiated a selective boycott through Ciudadanos Unidos of stores owned by Anglos who had threatened retaliation against the students and their parents. They also boycotted the store of one Mexican American school board member who had not been supportive of the school walkout. This action surprised and frightened some of the Anglo businessmen and added to the disarray of the Anglo community, which felt humiliated by the turn of events.[45]

The celebration had not yet subsided when Gutiérrez moved toward organizing an electoral challenge to the Anglos in the upcoming city and school board elections. Ciudadanos Unidos had emerged from the conflict a strong organization. At first some of its members had been afraid, and so they met in parks, in cars at night, and in homes away from where they could be seen. But as the boycott became more intense and popular, they began to meet at the Campestre, a popular dance hall, and assumed a more public role.[45] To this group Gutiérrez expounded the idea of a third-party political movement that would run candidates for the school board and the city council. By January Gutiérrez had received an endorsement from MAYO during its December national meeting to promote the building of a third political party that would carry out the organization's program of Chicano empowerment. By mid-January Crystal City's electoral passions had reignited, and they would not be contained at the county limits.

El partido Democrata
es el partido de los pobres
si quieres seguir siendo pobre
sigue votando Democrata.

The Democratic Party
is the party of the poor.
If you want to stay poor
continue voting Democrat.

—*La Lomita* newspaper

LA RAZA UNIDA
BECOMES A PARTY

It was a determined group of MAYO activists that came together at a Catholic seminary building in Mission, Texas, to discuss the future of the movement in the state. Everywhere else, it seemed, the *movimiento* clearly headed toward a more militant posture, and different groups were consolidating their constituencies and jockeying for control or at least leadership of the social upheaval. It was also clear that mainstream Mexican American politicians and activists had already gone or been pushed as far as they were going. In addition, MAYO leaders were being besieged with invitations to join the Democratic Party and change it from within.

The national meeting at Mission proved significant because there MAYO made the break with the traditional modes of nonpartisan civil rights agitation. It split with the more mainstream elements in the Mexican American community. As long as MAYO remained nonpartisan, its members could move in and out of Democratic Party circles. Interestingly, several months after the national meeting, Compean ran for district chairman of the Democratic Party in Bexar County and came in a surprisingly strong second. Compean and others also worked on the Albert Peña, Jr. campaign in San Antonio, and Gutiérrez worked on a Democrat's campaign for county commissioner in Uvalde, but those activities only bought time until the party could be established.[1]

Once they opted for a partisan alternative, they went at it alone. This, it would seem, was something that involved a great deal of reflection and discussion, and there was some during the early years of MAYO, but by 1969 momentum and circumstances took over.

The organization made a definite resolution to stay outside the traditional channels of American activism. By this time, MAYO leaders had become "pragmatic radicals." They placed importance on getting immediate results by being resilient, adaptable to shifting political winds, and sensitive to the process of action and reaction so as not to be placed in a position they could not control. They shunned the dogmatic approach of sectarian groups in order to avoid ideological limitations on their freedom of action and choice.

Their political philosophy was based on what they did not like as much as it was on what they sought to achieve. They attacked Anglo institutions as having been founded on institutional racism, propagated to keeping minorities on the outside. MAYO questioned the moral fiber of American society, accusing it of using democratic and religious demagoguery to keep whites in charge and minorities exploited. "We feel the system is neither ours nor for us," said Gutiérrez. "We are political prisoners neither allowed to participate nor able to participate."[2] By using the seething rhetoric and trying to delegitimize the political system, MAYO activists were saying that they wanted no part of the system either then or in the "idealized" future of the Texas liberals, who were at the time also trying to gather momentum.

The Chicano power leaders wanted a new system based on a cultural nationalism that was not as yet defined in terms of political processes and economic institutions. They were in truth inching toward a segregated, if not separatist, political ideology. This move toward a more fervent nationalism was spurred by Gutiérrez's rhetoric and Compean's leadership in MAYO. Gutiérrez, by his own admission, was an integrationist.[3] Those who heard him, though, thought of him as a separatist. Compean, on the other hand, though not an avowed separatist, did lean heavily toward that view. This duality of thought gave rise to a rhetoric of fervent nationalism among activists who were not necessarily seeking such drastic action. By this time, the concept of Aztlán was popular, especially among activists from California. Aztlán, according to Mexican mythology, was where the Aztecs had originated before they came to conquer the central valley of Mexico. All that was known about

Aztlán was that it was north of Mexico. Some Chicano nationalists began claiming that the American Southwest was Aztlán and that Chicanos were called by destiny to recover the homeland. Although few Chicano scholars and intellectuals ever gave more than lip service to the concept, many political organizers used it as a recruiting aid. There were some in MAYO who accepted the concept of Aztlán as real and preached it to their followers.

Notwithstanding their strong militant tendencies, MAYO leaders avoided the stringent sectarian ideologies fashionable at the time. They lambasted capitalism, as most activists did in those days, but they never overtly advocated socialism, which at the time had gained popularity among other Chicano groups as well as in the white youth movement. In terms of homegrown Chicano ideologies, only Rodolfo "Corky" Gonzales's Chicano liberation thesis was prevalent, and it avoided sectarian tendencies.[4] MAYO leaders were not inclined to bring more attacks on themselves by advocating a socialist system that could be implemented only nationally and not regionally. Socialism versus capitalism was one battle they anxiously avoided, as they realized that there were no organizing advantages to it. When pressed on the matter of prevailing ideologies, though, most MAYO leaders echoed Alberto Luera, who espoused a combination of political democracy and economic socialism.[5]

MAYO organizers learned the hard way that their ideology had to conform to their organizing practices, which in turn conformed to the issues current in the barrio. Gutiérrez lamented the early mistakes. "You don't come in with your own agenda; we tried that. We tried coming in and telling the people to fight against imperialism, colonialism and capitalism—that was like talking moon talk."[6]

At the national convention two major resolutions were voted on and passed, channeling the organization's future efforts. One stated that MAYO would support and, whenever possible, promote alternative educational systems such as Colegio Jacinto Treviño, a university without walls and without certified instructors to be administered by Chicanos for Chicanos.[7]

This issue became a point of contention, as several MAYO leaders felt that politics should be the top priority and not pseudo-educational enterprises, no matter how noble. Narciso Alemán, a MAYO organizer from the Rio Grande Valley, led the fight for the alternative education emphasis. He wanted to drop or minimize the boycotts, and he lobbied hard. With resources so limited, most delegates saw a need to galvanize them in one direction. But to avoid a split they supported two directions instead of one. Although they voted to support alternative educational systems, however, the organization never did become engrossed in them.[8]

The other resolution called for the formation of a third political party, which involved a concerted redirection of effort. MAYO leaders and activists became concerned with registering voters, developing party platforms, and raising funds for electoral campaigns. Ironically, at the height of its activity, MAYO began to decline, giving way to the all-consuming process of partisan politics. MAYO would exist for a couple more years but without any of its major founders and with few of the trained cadre.

For those who were ready to make the transition—and not all were—they could look back satisfied at their work. They had established a different Mexican American organization that had changed the mood of the barrios. The "sleeping giant" image was being replaced by one of an energetic, active community engaged in self-determination.

After the meeting in Mission, the activists left with unusual confidence and a high level of contentiousness. Before leaving the old seminary building, they committed what some Catholics considered a sacrilege. Angry over the Church's refusal to give them the building for their university without walls, they spray-painted brown a statue of Our Lady of the Immaculate Conception that stood on the grounds. This action only enhanced the negative reputation MAYO had among some elements in the Mexican American community.[9]

Shortly after the conference Compean was interviewed on Spanish television and he came out swinging, lambasting the two political parties, Anglo justice, and the Catholic Church. The tongue-lashing was meant to serve notice that MAYO stood even more determined to take on the Anglo institutions and that Chicanos on the sidelines were going to have to choose whether to be part of the movement or part of the problem.

By late January 1970 the Ciudadanos Unidos were ready to form the basis for Gutiérrez's political party. The Ciudadanos Unidos organization had opted for calling the party El Partido de la Raza Unida, despite objections from Gutiérrez, who felt the much-used slogan would alienate the middle class because it was closely tied to MAYO and sounded radical. The name was later changed to

Raza Unida Party (RUP) to accommodate the word-limit requirements of the Texas Election Code. Luz was elected county chairman, and on January 23 an application was filed for the formation
of the Raza Unida Party in Zavala County. Similar applications were
submitted in Dimmit, La Salle, and Hidalgo counties. Dimmit and
La Salle were part of the Winter Garden Area, and Hidalgo lay deep
in the Rio Grande Valley.[10]

At the conclusion of the school walkout, Gutiérrez quickly
moved to get the parents and students ready for the elections to be
held that spring. With educational issues being such an integral
part of MAYO's political activity, the school board elections became
the first battleground. Mere representation was not enough; Gutiérrez wanted control of the institution. The school board already
had some Mexican Americans, and few changes had been made. It
was MAYO's philosophy that reforms would come when the Chicano community had not only the votes to implement changes but
also the strength to resist outside pressures to rescind them. Empowerment also called for a shake-up of the organizational structure and a changing of the guard in the school's administration.

With the support of Ciudadanos Unidos, Gutiérrez recruited
Mike Pérez, a dance-hall operator, and Arturo Gonzales, a twenty-
one-year-old gas-station attendant, to run with him for the three
positions on the school board that were up for election. Gutiérrez
had decided that he needed to take a more public role in order to
build the party. For the city elections scheduled one week later,
Pablo Puente and Ventura Gonzales were chosen to run for the two
spots. Gonzales worked at the Del Monte packing and cannery
plant outside the city, and Puente managed an auto-parts store.[11]
Gutiérrez was lucky to get two running mates, as most Mexican
Americans were reluctant to run for fear of retaliation from their
Anglo employers. Most Mexican Americans in Crystal City could
not afford the luxury of radicalism or independent thinking, at least
not in 1970, when political reprisals were common and usually
unchallenged.

Almost immediately, the city attorney disqualified Puente because he did not own property, as the city charter required.[12] It
took strenuous efforts by the Mexican American Legal Defense and
Education Fund to get him back on the ballot barely in time for the
election and only after he agreed to forfeit the absentee ballots.
Puente was willing to do this in order to stay on the ballot (the

election process had already begun) and because few Mexican Americans voted absentee, so the votes lost would have little effect on the outcome.

The courts were only one of several ways Anglos in Crystal City tried to head off a Gutiérrez victory. First, the Anglo organization, Citizens Association Serving All Americans (CASAA), which had helped defeat the first revolt in 1963, chose Mexican American candidates, mostly middle-class citizens they considered "safe."[13] This strategy had worked before, and Anglos knew it might be the only thing to work again. The candidates got financial support and volunteers to man the telephones and pass out literature. At first, CASAA's Anglo members worked discreetly, but by the end of the campaign they were the most visible of the supporters.

A second strategy to head off defeat was an attempt by the Anglo board members to make changes that were inevitable in the school system. Their efforts were given a boost when John Billings resigned as superintendent, effective that summer. The board quickly moved to hire John Briggs, a former school superintendent who had adopted two Mexican American children. He took over as assistant superintendent until the end of Billing's term. The board also refused to renew the contract of the besieged high-school principal, and the junior-high principal resigned to go back to teaching. By election time the main targets of the students' wrath were gone. Unfortunately for the school board, Chicanos in Crystal City recognized that the moves were political decoys. They knew that the board's action had come only after months of negotiation and a bitter walkout, and only after the Anglos realized they were in danger of losing control.[14]

As the elections neared, the political maneuvering and the rhetoric became intense. The Anglo-Mexican American coalition kept hammering away that the rural community needed "responsible men for responsible jobs." Poor migrant farm workers, dance-hall operators, gas-station attendants, and young radicals were not the right people to govern the city. One day before the school board election, the CASAA campaign workers dropped two thousand leaflets by plane over Crystal City. The leaflets contained the text of a militant speech Gutiérrez had given in Odessa, in which he attacked the Catholic Church, called himself an atheist, and blasphemed.[15]

In the leaflets were also warnings that a Chicano victory would cause economic stagnation and the loss of many jobs. No business would consider moving to Crystal City if it was governed by radicals and the schools were teaching communist notions. It was a subtle message to the Mexican Americans dependent on Anglos for their livelihood that their votes would be closely watched.

In the end, the CASAA strategy served no purpose other than to heighten tensions and to cement the distrust that Mexican Americans had long felt toward the Anglos. Though not all Anglos were racist, nor did they all agree with the intimidation tactics, most went along with the CASAA strategy. They seemed to fear a backlash from the same people they had employed or associated with for many years. Their own actions reaffirmed that Mexican Americans and Anglos had lived side by side for years but had never learned to live together.

As it turned out, all the political strategies of Ciudadanos Unidos's opponents proved fruitless: the Gutiérrez-led ticket swept the three seats with 55 percent of the vote. That victory was followed by an even more impressive win by Gonzales and Puente in the city council elections several days later. They received 60 percent of the vote. It was an important triumph for Chicanos in South Texas, and it gave them control of the city.[16] This was accomplished when two Mexican American incumbents, one on the school board and the other in the city council, became sympathetic and shifted allegiance, a result of the strength Ciudadanos Unidos had gained in Crystal City. Their campaign had focused on discrediting any Mexican American in the Anglo camp, and their boycott of small businesses owned by Mexican Americans who did not support the student demands brought an economic hazard to those perceived to be on the wrong side of the fence.[17]

Fewer than six years after the Anglos had recaptured Crystal City from Los Cinco, they were again out of power, but this time to a better organized and more astute opponent. Anglos realized soon after the election that the situation was different from the one in 1963. Although most of the voters were still illiterate and poor, they no longer seemed so afraid, and without doubt they were better led. The Chicano revolt of 1963 had been an uncontrolled flood of passions, but this one was a calculated barrage of blows from a wide-awake and power-hungry giant.

The victory in Crystal City reverberated throughout Aztlán, in communities similar in size, in urban centers, and in universities where Mexican Americans came together. The successful revolt symbolized what Chicanos everywhere could achieve with hard work and well-planned strategies. Within days of his election, Gutiérrez received several hundred calls from Chicano activists nationwide, congratulating him and asking him to come tell them how they could do the same in their localities. Crystal City became a sort of political mecca for Chicanos, a symbol of what brown power could do. Back home the electoral victory made converts of MAYO members who originally were lukewarm to the idea of a third party. "No one could argue with success," Gutiérrez later recalled.[18]

One who could argue, and did, was an old nemesis, Henry B. González. In a meeting of the Southwest Political Science Association in Dallas, he criticized the third-party approach as a wedge between the population groups of Texas.

> The unfortunate thing about MAYO's approach is that an appeal to race pride is a slender and volatile glue upon which to build a political power base. . . . The rhetoric for the MAYO tactic is inflammatory. There is a constant stress on the "gringo" as an enemy to be removed, one way or another. The hints of violence by MAYO speakers are unmistakable and constant. As real as the danger of violence may be, the more likely danger lies in the fact that the MAYO tactics are designed to polarize the community.[19]

González labeled the ethnically based organizing a "game that can be played by more than one party." He was referring to the American Party of George Wallace, which was organizing then for a second run at the presidency. He added that the "Wallaceites" had 70 percent or more of the state's population on which to build, while the La Raza Unida Party could count on only 15 percent of the state's people.[20]

A similar perception was shared by the most influential defector from MAYO, Willie Velásquez. As one of the founders of the organization, he had been the moving force behind the La Raza Unida conferences, one of the chief fund-raisers, and the leader of the Mexican American Unity Council in its first year. Along with Nacho Pérez, he involved the organization in the farm-worker movement. An individualist with a flair for the dramatic, Velásquez did not share Compean's and Gutiérrez's enthusiasm for the more ideological goals. While dedicated to working at the grassroots level, he believed in pluralistic participation rather than Chicano empowerment. An avid student of history, he concluded that ethnic movements and third parties were ill-fitted to survive in American politics. Velásquez later described himself as a Jeffersonian Democrat who believed in the system.[21]

To Compean, Velásquez was a "do-gooder" interested in providing helping hands to local organizations rather than developing political strategies to combat the system statewide. During the first year of MAUC, Compean, who served on the board of directors, made a motion to fire Velásquez, but Gutiérrez, a close friend of both, worked out a compromise that eventually led to a resignation.[22] In Velásquez's version of the story, he quit because of constant bickering in the board meetings. After a year he felt burned out and decided to take a job with the Southwest Council of La Raza in Phoenix, Arizona.[23] Before leaving, he told Gutiérrez that the party was a mistake and that he did not want to spend his time trying to raise funds for something that was bound to fail. Velásquez felt that the MAYO leaders' ignorance caused them to make rash decisions. "We didn't read enough," he said later. He also believed that there were provocateurs, some probably on government payrolls, who pushed MAYO toward a more militant role, one that took it away from any possible compromise with middle-class Chicanos, who tended to be dyed-in-the-wool Democrats.[24]

It was the potential of success, however, rather than provocateurs or ignorance, that pushed the party idea to move at a faster rate than even Gutiérrez had envisioned. Crystal City had gotten the biggest headlines, but there were several other victories in the Winter Garden Area which contributed to a sense of groundswell in favor of MAYO and the La Raza Unida Party movement.

In Carrizo Springs two candidates backed by the party, Rufino Cabello and Jesús Rodríguez, became the first Mexican Americans to be elected to the city council. Both had started the campaign as Raza Unida candidates but changed to independents when the campaign became bitter and divisive. Since the elections were nonpartisan, they could do it without alienating their Raza Unida supporters.[25]

In nearby Cotulla the party-supported candidates did even better, winning two city council seats, two school board positions, and the mayorship. One Chicano candidate lost but by only forty-five votes. The efforts there were coordinated by Juan Ortiz, Arseno García, and Raul Martínez, the La Raza Unida Party chairman for La Salle County. The party had prepared well by registering nearly two thousand voters in the county during the month of January.[26]

Alfredo Zamora, Jr., a school teacher, defeated incumbent mayor Paul Cotulla, a descendent of the town's founder, by a count of 587 to 554. Enrique Jiménez, Jr., received 636 votes against the incumbent's 493, and George Carpenter, Sr., another party candidate, got 667 votes against his opponent's 439. The only loser in the city council race was Alfredo Ramírez, who received 530 votes to the incumbent's 575 votes. In the school board race Reynaldo García won 667 to 537, and Rogelio Maldonado, 693 to 524.[27]

Only in Robstown, where Guadalupe Youngblood had gone to organize, did the party fail to come up with a victory. The RUP candidate for the city council finished fourth in a field of five.

After the election the priority became the consolidation of control in Crystal City and the further development of the Ciudadanos Unidos organization. Shortly after the spring victories in the school board races, the school attorney, R. A. Taylor, was replaced with Jesse Gámez. Taylor's dismissal, though one of the first, was by no means the most important. A wholesale change of teaching faculty began with the simple process of changing the school environment. Anglo teachers felt uneasy serving under a "radical" school board that implemented such things as a free lunch program, courses in Mexican American history, and bilingual education. They were also upset by what they perceived to be hostility from their Mexican American students, many of whom were sympathetic to La Raza Unida Party. When the fall semester began in 1970, nearly 40 percent of the teachers were Mexican American, an increase of almost 100 percent. This new group of teachers proved to be more supportive of the school's new direction. Even the new Anglo teachers tended to either be sympathetic or unequivocally neutral.[28]

To counteract some of the economic retaliation from the infuriated Anglos, Gutiérrez and his majority began to use school-district jobs for patronage to the party faithful. The number of cafeteria jobs increased, and all of the new jobs went to Mexican Americans. The number of teacher aides before the new board took office had been twenty-four, with Anglos holding thirteen of those positions. By the start of the new school year the number of positions had jumped to sixty-seven, and all but three went to Mexican Americans. In a matter of a few months Mexican Americans began receiving two-thirds of the total monthly salary of $40,000.[29]

The new administration's first priority was halting the alarming rate at which Chicano youth were dropping out of school.

Teachers and counselors were encouraged to use innovative techniques and acquire contemporary materials to retain the students. The Mexican American became the focus of civics, history, journalism, drama, and literature classes. Even the agricultural classes changed direction, as students began discussing problems of migrant farm workers. The school library acquired more books on Chicanos and by Chicanos. The new school board was more willing to accept and to seek government funding than the previous one. In one year federal assistance to the school district increased from $417,000 (1969–70) to $720,000 (1970–71).[30]

In a short period of time the school became a breeding ground for "Chicanismo," where army recruiters were unwelcome, only UFW lettuce was eaten, and the band played "Jalisco" as its fight song and went on and off the football field with raised clenched fists. In less than a year the school, once a symbol of Anglo control, became the first exhibit of La Raza Unida Party's blueprint for the rest of South Texas.

The transformation of the city paralleled that of the schools. Once it took office, the new city council hired Bill Richey, one of Gutiérrez's first recruits to the Crystal City campaign. He proved to be an efficient administrator while carrying out the party's agenda for Crystal City. He quickly moved to fill city posts vacated by Anglos with qualified Raza Unida supporters. And he also set out to attract federal and state funds. In this effort he was as successful as his counterparts in the school district.

The victory celebrations were not yet over when the maneuvering began for the November elections. The party had filed to run candidates in Dimmit, La Salle, Zavala, and Hidalgo counties for positions that were selected through partisan elections. Raza Unida banners had been prevalent in the city and school contests, but the November elections would be the first "real" races of El Partido de la Raza Unida.

The party filed for sixteen positions in the four counties, confident that it could win the majority of them since its candidates would be running mostly against Anglos in areas where Chicanos were the majority and where Anglos had already been beaten. Many of those who voted for the Raza Unida in the spring would be voting again and would be assisted by other Mexican Americans in the counties' outlying areas. Also, the party had organizations in the four counties which were registering new voters who were likely to support La Raza Unida. Party leaders believed that migrant workers could be trained to vote absentee while they were away. The party machinery prepared to use every tactic to get the voters to the polls, and once there, there seemed little doubt about their preference.

The Raza Unida leaders were not the only ones to think that way. Shortly after the school elections, board president E. F. Mayer had these words of warning: "The other communities better wake up or they'll be facing the same thing."[31] Zavala County Judge Irl Taylor also cautioned that the Chicano party looked capable of sweeping all its candidates into office. But he added that the "better thinking Mexican Americans are not going to let" José Angel Gutié-rrez make such a clean sweep. He also advised that Gutiérrez had to be met "head on" and predicted that the RUP leader's "line" would not sell. If it did, said the judge, the Democrats would go "down the drain."[32]

Fortunately for the Democrats, they controlled the county government and quickly moved to keep La Raza Unida confused and, if possible, off the ballot. The judges in their counties told Richard Clarkson, the party's lawyer, that they did not know what to do with the petitions calling for ballot status for RUP and that they would decide in September or October, when it came time to print the ballots.[33]

The judges, the chief administrators in the county, pointed to contradictory statements by the state attorney general, and the secretary of state to justify the confusion. The attorney general, Crawford Martin, reacting to an inquiry by Hidalgo County District Attorney Oscar B. McInnus, stated that the Raza Unida would not be eligible to be on the ballot because it had filed its application on January 19, too early to be within the voting year, which began on March 1.[34]

This was a revised opinion from one he gave earlier. In the spring he ruled that the new party could nominate candidates even though it had no state organization and planned only to run candidates in Hidalgo County. The only requirement was that the party present signatures of at least 3 percent of the number of voters in the last election.[35]

The secretary of state, Martin Dies, Jr., ruling on the same inquiry from Hidalgo County, disagreed with Martin and instructed county officials to accept the petition. County Judge Milton Rich-ardson accepted Dies's ruling and placed the party on the ballot. The party leaders attempted to use Dies's ruling as a basis for obtaining ballot status, but the other county judges were just as adamant about using the contradictions to keep them off the ballot. The initial statement led to a series of court fights that went on almost until election day in November.[36]

The party filed suit in the Fourth Court of Civil Appeals in San Antonio to force the county judges to place the RUP candidates on the ballot. In court the counties' lawyers challenged the party's nominating activities and its filing procedures. Attorneys for La Salle County argued that no precinct elections were ever held to elect delegates to the party's county nominating conventions, as required by the state's election code. Attorneys for Judge Harold Dean of Dimmit County claimed that there were not enough signatures on the party's petitions and that precinct conventions were held in only two of the seven election precincts.[37] The Zavala County attorney pointed out that the petition, or application, for ballot status carried the year 1969 instead of 1970.[38]

The Fourth Court of Civil Appeals denied the party's writ of mandamus. The panel of judges was unanimous in the case of Zavala and La Salle counties, but split in the case of Dimmit County. The judges ruled that there had not been substantial compliance with Provision 13.54 in holding precinct conventions. The article read:

> Any political party without a state organization desiring to nominate candidates for county and precinct offices only may nominate such candidates ... by primary elections or by county conventions held on the legal primary election day which convention shall be composed of delegates from various precincts in said county, elected therein at primary conventions held in such precincts between 8:00 A.M.–10:00 P.M. on the dates set by law.[39]

Associate Judge Carlos Cadena dissented on the specific case of Dimmit County, where the party had been disqualified because some of the petitioners had voted in the Democratic Party primary. He stated that the election code did not explicitly forbid a member of one party from signing the petition for ballot status of another party. "Language expressing such disqualification is absent" from the Texas Election Code, he added.[40]

Alfredo Zamora, RUP mayor of Cotulla, was the first to react, calling the decisions a great disappointment. He added:

> The decision is a pity. We tried to do everything necessary to comply. We went to hearings, but no one—not judges, lawyers, not anyone—seemed to know what needs to be done to get a third party on the ballot. I think our party should have been allowed on the ballot—at least until someone comes up with some guidelines covering such a situation.[41]

After hearing the verdict, the RUP party's lawyer filed for a hearing with the Texas Supreme Court.

The first judicial setback came on September 28, and it was followed two days later by another legal defeat. On September 30 the Texas Supreme Court upheld the lower court's ruling. It took the high court only half an hour of deliberation to reject the party's arguments. But again it was a split decision, and the split was also over Dimmit County, with Associate Judge Jack Pope ruling that La Raza Unida had fulfilled the requirements for getting three candidates on the Dimmit ballot.[42]

Chief Justice Robert W. Calvert reiterated the three shortcomings found by the Fourth Court. Petitions filed in Zavala County, ruled the court, carried the date January 1969 instead of January 1970. In La Salle County inadequate records failed to show that precinct conventions had been held at the time required. Finally, in Dimmit County, petitions calling for placing candidates on the ballot fell five signatures short after ten signees were ruled ineligible for having voted in the Democratic primary.[43]

In responding, Clarkson stated that the "January 1969" date was a typographical error but that the voter registration numbers as set out on the petitions were current for 1970. He added that the precinct conventions in La Salle County were held just before the county nominating convention and all who attended were made delegates. Finally, Clarkson contended that the secretary of state had declared that Democratic voters were not disqualified.

Clarkson then declared that the party would be willing to forfeit the absentee ballots if it could be placed on the ballot by November 3.[44] The court did not sway from its position, so Clarkson immediately moved to file in federal district court. This time, though, the suit entered the docket as a civil rights case. Clarkson told Chief Judge Adrian Spears of the Western District of Texas that the civil rights action distilled into "whether all Anglo candidates or all Mexican American candidates will be elected." Spears remarked, "That's a pretty sad choice for the court to invoke."[45]

Forty-one people were subpoenaed to testify as the lawyers and the judge tried to get the case resolved before the absentee voting started on October 15.[46] While waiting for the court action, the party asked the U.S. Fifth Circuit Court of Appeals in New Orleans to force the counties to print the names of its candidates on the ballot before the conclusion of the trial. Clarkson stated that the move was made to keep the case from becoming moot. But the court denied the request.[47] On that same day the Texas Supreme Court released its written denial of the party's request for a writ of mandamus.

Chief Judge Calvert noted that the party lawyer had admitted that the party's applications in the three counties were signed and filed with county judges before its county conventions were ever held. Therefore, said Calvert, the petitions were obtained even before the candidates were known or certified by the county clerks. He added:

> The statute does not expressly provide that the application . . . shall be signed and filed after the names of the nominees have been certified to the county clerk, but that seems to us to be the only logical and reasonable interpretation. Otherwise party leaders could foist upon the signers totally unacceptable candidates and then defeat the purpose of the application . . . our interpretation serves the further beneficial purpose of assuring that persons asked to sign an article 13.54 petition will . . . have available to them the names of all other candidates for the same office, and will be in a better position to make an intelligent decision as to whether they should sign.[48]

Two days later the party suffered yet another legal blow. Judge Spears, in a conference with lawyers from both sides, questioned whether the party had any case on the civil rights issue. Clarkson had no time to argue the point and so he requested time to file an amended pleading challenging the constitutionality of the Texas Election Code. This new tactic, however, required a three-member panel of federal judges and thus the hearing was delayed one more week while the judges were selected. Spears was designated head of the panel, which also included U.S. District Judge Jack Roberts of Austin and U.S. Circuit Judge Irving Goldberg of Dallas.[49]

Their hopes already fading, the party leaders were finally dealt the death blow to their ballot chances. On Monday, October 12, the Odessa law firm of Warren Burnett, which had been providing the party legal services free, withdrew from the suit. Clarkson said he was forced to withdraw because Burnett, a prominent West Texas lawyer who headed the firm, had become ill and was hospitalized. The illness, coupled with the law firm's heavy workload and the lack of time before absentee balloting, left the firm no choice. "We fought the good fight," said Clarkson. "I sincerely believe this will be the established parties' last hurrah in these three counties."[50] A quick flurry of activity to get another lawyer for the case ensued, but nothing came of it. No action was taken, and Judge Spears dismissed the case.

Gutiérrez and the candidates conferred and decided to run a write-in campaign rather than let their momentum die. With such a high illiteracy rate in Crystal City, the write-in campaign was a gamble, but failure to run would have diminished the people's enthusiasm for the party. Consequently, Ciudadanos Unidos, as well as volunteers from as far away as California and Wisconsin, set out to teach the Mexican American voters of the three counties how to write a name on a ballot.

Ever the optimist, Gutiérrez soon came to believe that the party could win. "Have your headlines ready," he told newsmen. "We're going to win some." He stated that the best possibilities were in La Salle County, followed by Zavala and Dimmit. Hidalgo County was questionable, as the party had almost no organization there.[51] A federal court had ruled that the illiteracy provisions of the Texas Election Code were unconstitutional but declined to order election officials to provide any help for illiterate voters, adding that it was up to the legislature to rectify the situation. Judge Taylor of Zavala County quickly announced that he would enforce the code as it stood, meaning that no help would be available to the uneducated Mexican American voter.[52]

On the Sunday before the election, hundreds of Mexican Americans in Crystal City rallied in La Placita, a small park in town, where the voting procedures were explained in detail in both languages. Posters had been hung all over town showing the names and the ballot lines of the write-in candidates to remind the citizens about the challenge that confronted them in trying to take power from the Anglos. Those who could not read were instructed to measure the distances in the ballot to know where a candidate's name was to be written. Then they were drilled to memorize the writing of the name.[53]

Without the benefit of the absentee ballots, the party was confronted with a major obstacle. It had planned to provide absentee ballots to the migrant farm workers who left town to follow the harvests. Without its name on the ballot, the party had to send out a call to the migrant workers to come back home to vote. Some came, but others could not afford the trip and the lost work time. Nonetheless, the high level of campaigning and the rhetoric made for an environment that seemed to indicate that a victory was attainable. It is quite possible that if the write-in campaign had started earlier, there might have been several victories.

On election day the Anglo opposition struck back. Although RUP party leaders had expected some problems, most were not prepared to face the obstacles placed in their way. In Cotulla the election official started out the day giving literacy tests to all those who came to the voting places. Many of the Mexican Americans did not understand or speak English and could not pass the test or were simply too frightened to try. The testing was illegal, but it persisted until RUP voters protested vigorously and threatened to contact state officials. When they were forced to cease that activity, Anglo officials began to harass campaigners within sight of the polling place, and arrested one woman who had set up a table well away from the one-hundred-foot radius where electioneering was prohibited.[54]

In Dimmit County the election fraud began even before the elections. County officials printed a sample ballot with the candidates in the wrong order. This was done purposely to confuse the illiterate voters who were being instructed by RUP activists to determine where the write-in candidate's names would go. Consequently, many of the write-in names were not placed next to the offices for which they were running. Election officials also intimidated the voters by not placing voting booth partitions as required by law and by looking over the voters' shoulders to see for whom they were voting. It was an act of courage for Mexican American voters to add the RUP candidates' names to the ballot.[55]

In Crystal City things were even worse. In one precinct RUP poll watchers were prevented from entering the polling station because their credentials carried the wrong precinct number. It had been the correct number until election officials changed it just before the election. When they insisted on entering, the sheriff threatened to arrest them. Then the sheriff forced a sound truck that was urging Chicanos to vote to cease its activities, even though it was within the prescribed limits. In other precincts the judges entered the booths and looked on as the voters wrote in their candidates' names. They also searched voters to make sure none of the Mexican Americans were carrying hidden papers with the candidates' names. In one case they forced open an old lady's arthritic hand to make sure she had not written the names on her palm. Still in other precincts, some voters were turned away because they had supposedly already voted and their names were checked off. Only if they insisted were they allowed to vote.[56]

Some Anglo campaigners made threats, insinuating that Raza Unida voters would be taken off welfare rolls and would no longer receive surplus commodities. The Ciudadanos Unidos newspaper, *La Verdad*, charged that the head of the county's welfare office, Bruce Ivey, had visited welfare recipients and informed them that voting for Irl Taylor was a way to get an increase in welfare payments. This created fear among the voters because it meant that the Anglo officials were ready to retaliate economically against anyone known to have aided the new Chicano party.[57]

The most flagrant violations, though, came in the vote counting. Here was an area where Mexican Americans were powerless and they paid a heavy price. The election judges screened the votes with an eye toward magnifying any potential problems with the write-in votes, and they found many opportunities. The illiterate voters misspelled the names of the candidates, and those votes were counted for someone else. Even though the law permitted them to use their judgment in accepting the voters' intentions, the election officials refused to give La Raza Unida the benefit of the doubt. A vote for Isaac Juárez, a vote for Isaac Juáres, and a vote for Isac Juarez were counted as votes for three different people. In the case of Ramón de la Fuente, who was running for county commissioner of Precinct 1, the election judge took one hundred and nine votes from his column because voters forgot to write *Jr.* at the end of his name.[58]

The write-in campaign had been a long shot with only a small chance of success, but the obstacles thrown in the way of the Mexican American voters made it all but impossible for the Raza Unida Party to win. Fifteen of the sixteen RUP candidates were defeated by safe margins. Only Roel Rodríguez, of La Salle County, who ran for county commissioner, won—just barely.[59] Nevertheless, the candidates averaged nearly 40 percent of the vote, a significant percentage, given the traditional non-participation of Mexican American voters. Had the party leaders not been so shell-shocked from the election fraud, they would have immediately seen that their campaign had had a great impact on the people of the three counties. Mustering up some enthusiasm, Gutiérrez told reporters: "We are capturing the imagination of the Chicano voter. This is the party that is finally opening up an avenue so they [Chicanos] can express themselves, their frustration, anger and aspirations . . . with the 18-year-old vote and a place on the ballot for our party, the gringos can kiss South Texas good-bye."[60] Gutiérrez added that the work on the 1972 state elections would begin in January 1971. And he vowed that the party would be ready and on the ballot.

By the fall of 1971, though, Gutiérrez seemed to have changed his mind about going statewide. He began talking to his closest associates about staying at the county level, which had been the original intent of the Winter Garden Area Project initiated by MAYO. He apparently recognized that the rhetoric had gotten out of hand and party leaders had made grandiose statements that were far from realistic, among them his own claims of a strong state party. It is also possible that the amount of work necessary to consolidate the party's power in the 1971 city and school elections in Crystal City made him reevaluate the party's resources, leadership, and chances.[61] In any case, when the party called its first state convention, he felt that going statewide would be a serious mistake. There simply were not enough trained leaders to mount a state drive. Most of the potential leaders were either in college or had dropped out of school, were unmarried, and had little economic security. The few elected officials were men who lacked the skills to handle the job and consequently needed to be monitored and assisted in most of the complicated decisions they were to make.

The organizational structure in Crystal City was an exception to the rule. Most of the Raza Unida chapters in the state had no money, no hierarchy, and few committed voters. By choosing to organize first among those who had been left out of the political mainstream both in South Texas and the urban Texas cities, the Raza Unida activists had taken on a long-lasting electoral burden. Their constituency consisted of poor, uneducated, and, up to that point, electorally apathetic citizens. Although the campaign would attract many of the best and the brightest in the population, they would be coming into an organization not equipped to handle, much less train and indoctrinate them.

In his politically sober moments Gutiérrez realized that to establish what he constructed in Crystal City in other South Texas towns would take most of the decade. Crystal City's successful 1970 revolt had actually started with the first Chicano electoral victory in 1963. And most of the organizing had begun among friends and acquaintances who respected him because of his education and his family. Few organizers could claim the same conditions existed elsewhere. Gutiérrez must also have known that most of the MAYO leaders had not yet shown they possessed comparable skills in organizing. In his master's thesis, where he laid the groundwork for the social revolution to come, he wrote that the young militants of his era would not see the fruits of their labors. In another instance he remarked that it might take thirty years before the political and economic situation really changed in South Texas.[62.]

Unfortunately for Gutiérrez, he had done too good a job of selling the state party in his jubilation after the Crystal City victory. *Partidarios* from all over Texas came together in San Antonio on October 31, 1971 to discuss the future of El Partido de la Raza Unida, which they believed had much to offer them in the way of assistance for their areas.[63] Some were also naive about the amount of effort necessary to recreate a Crystal City type of revolt. Gutiérrez lined up support for his point of view from the rural delegates who were also leery of a state organization, but he quickly discovered that Compean had done the same thing among the urban delegates and that there were more of them.

The discussions were heated, though not divisive, and they went on for hours, as Gutiérrez pointed out the weaknesses of the party structure, the lack of resources, and the sure-to-come opposition from Mexican American Democrats, who would see themselves threatened by a third party. Compean rebutted just as emphatically that a statewide party would rally Chicanos and give impetus to the movement. It was a way of gathering resources and recruits and avoiding a county-by-county certification process that could be derailed by any small-town judge. More important, he argued, getting on the state ballot might become harder if there was a large turnout in the 1972 presidential elections because the number of signatures needed would be greater. For the keyed-up delegates, the clinching argument was that a statewide party meant the possibility of establishing little Crystal Cities all over the state. When the voting proceeded, Compean and his supporters won, 21 to 15.[64]

After the vote a platform committee was established, Compean was elected temporary state chairman after Gutiérrez declined, and a search began for candidates. The search lasted nearly up to the filing date in February 1972. Several prominent Mexican American leaders, including some who were not close to the party, were queried about running for governor. In attempting to recuit a mainstream Chicano, Gutiérrez sought to mend the rift between La Raza Unida and the middle class. He asked Carlos Truan of Corpus Christi, a state representative, but Truan said no. Also asked was Hector García, the founder of the American G.I. Forum, who also refused. One of the last to be considered was Joe Bernal, state senator from San Antonio and a strong supporter of MAYO. Gutiérrez had worked as an intern in the legislature with Bernal and he considered the Democrat one of the better politicians in office. Bernal also declined to run.[65]

Once they realized that no one outside MAYO or the party would volunteer, Compean, Gutiérrez, and the other party leaders began to look to the membership to find a candidate. Most of the party cadre quickly bowed out of consideration, so the searching went into the second layer of party members. The next choice was Ernesto Calderón, a war veteran from Waco who was contemplating joining the Raza Unida Party but was still an active participant in local Democratic circles. He said no but suggested a young lawyer from Waco who was an administrator in the Model Cities program. He was Ramsey Muñiz, an active local member of MAYO. Gutiérrez later said that Muñiz had come to file for the state board of education race when he was approached to run for governor. He was reluctant but ended up filing for both positions. Later that day he withdrew from the state board of education race. Compean remembered it differently. Two days before the filing deadline he called Calderón and told him to show up the next day with someone to run for governor or to come dressed in a suit to file himself.[66]

Considering the major step it was taking in its political infancy, the party's choosing of a candidate was very chaotic. Without fully knowing Muñiz—Compean had spoken to him only once before—party leaders allowed him to become the candidate. It is probable that three factors were responsible for the seeming laxity of the selection process. First, for the party leaders, getting on the ballot—not selecting the candidates—was the higher priority. None of them actually expected La Raza Unida to win the governor's race, though by being on the ballot they expected to win local races in several South Texas counties. Most of the party's leadership had little or no campaigning experience and lacked the overall perspective of a state election. Second, the party activists were more interested in presenting the issues than in selling personalities and believed that a good platform was more important than a good candidate. With a naive dogmatism, they set out to find people who were faithful to the party philosophy regardless of their looks, speaking ability, or political experience. This approach was, after all, consistent with their desire to be a party for all of those who had been excluded in the past and who did not fit the Anglos' model of a candidate.

The third factor was the party members' limited ties outside their political circles. Although Gutiérrez and the other leaders had received support from several prominent Mexican American political and educational leaders in the past, most of these individuals were either too involved in the Democratic Party or not committed enough to the rhetoric and militancy of the Chicano Movement to want to volunteer for what they deemed to be political suicide. Consequently, the party leaders jumped at the chance to lure a young lawyer dedicated enough to the Raza Unida philosophy to put his future on the line for the good of the party and its platform.

We are the people who have been made aware
of the needs of many through our suffering,
who have learned the significance of *carnalismo*,
the strength of *la familia* and the importance
of people working together . . . recognizing the
natural right of all peoples to preserve their
self-identity and to formulate their own destiny.

—From 1972 RUP platform

RAMSEY MUÑIZ
AND THE 1972 CAMPAIGN

Ramsey Muñiz, by his own account, had been active in MAYO since 1968 and had even served as an organizer for the group in northern Texas.[1] Yet he was not well known in party circles. Compean remembered having met him only once, when a small group of Waco activists had come to discuss an issue affecting that university town. Muñiz wrote in the area's Chicano newspaper but otherwise was not prominent in the movement before he became a gubernatorial candidate. Gutiérrez met Muñiz when visiting Waco to speak to the local MAYO group. When he arrived at the agreed-upon place, he found no one there but an "Anglo-looking," muscular young man. After waiting for several minutes, Gutiérrez realized that no one was going to show up except the fellow who sat there waiting. Gutiérrez, always one to fulfill his obligations, began his speech—in English. The fellow kept looking around and finally said, "Párale, ¿a quién le estás hablando?" ("Hold up, who are you talking to?"). At that moment Gutiérrez realized he was speaking to a fellow Chicano. They talked for hours that night and became mutually admiring friends.[2]

Once he became a candidate, Muñiz demonstrated a tenacity and a reservoir of energy and enthusiasm that astonished the party leaders. At twenty-nine, he still possessed the physical strength that had earned him the 1963 Mr. Corpus Christi trophy and an honorable mention in the Southwest Conference's 1965 all-star selection for his play as a lineman for the Baylor University football team. His athletic prowess and his good looks had also gotten him elected Mr. Baylor for two consecutive years.[3]

After graduating from Baylor, Muñiz entered the law school there and paid his way by serving as an assistant student coach for the varsity team. When he received his law degree, he served first as a law clerk for a local attorney, then as an administrative assistant, and finally as director of the Urban Community Development Corporation of Waco. At the time, he and his wife, Albina Peña, had a one-year-old daughter.[4]

When Muñiz filed to run for governor, there was no state campaign committee and no money, the platform was not complete, and no communications existed between him and the candidate for lieutenant governor, Alma Canales, who lived in Austin.[5] In fact, their relationship proved to be shaky throughout the campaign. Despite being in the same party, they were a contrast in style and approach. Notwithstanding his militancy, Muñiz represented middle-class respectability with his law degree, nice clothing, and attractive spouse. Canales was the radical, poorly dressed, married to a MAYO activist, and a less articulate candidate. Her name on the ballot was a result of the women's strength in the party caucuses, and she remained on the ballot, despite efforts to remove her by the Waco chapter, because Compean became her strongest supporter.[6] Early on, Muñiz was Gutiérrez's candidate and Canales represented Compean's leanings.[7] Eventually, this situation caused friction between Muñiz and the party's state chairman.

On February 9 Muñiz was unveiled at a press conference in San Antonio along with Canales and a list of fifty-two other RUP candidates. Immediately, two questions arose in regard to the party's candidates and its ballot status. Reporters quickly pointed out that Canales, at twenty-four, could not legally take office if she won because the state constitution required a lieutenant governor to be at least thirty years old. Compean responded that the party would go to court if necessary to fight the age limitation. Reporters also asked Compean if he felt that raising the 22,358 signatures needed to get on the state ballot would be a problem. He answered that he saw no difficulty in getting them and warned the party's opponents that RUP stood ready to go through the long court process again to gain ballot status.[8]

When it came her turn, Canales declared that the party had

no interest in playing the same political "games" as the Democrats and the Republicans. "We're not going to replace a system that oppresses people with a brown system that oppresses people," she said, indirectly opening ground between Mexican American politicians and the RUP.[9] For many, Canales proved to be a direct, gut-level candidate who expounded the MAYO and Raza Unida philosophy. Her candidacy signaled that women would play a major role in the party. Muñiz was more aggresive in his remarks. He challenged the reporters to compare his credentials to those of two of his Democratic opponents, Lieutenant Governor Ben Barnes, who at the time seemed the favorite of the Democratic Party leadership, and Dolph Briscoe, a South Texas millionaire rancher. "Ben Barnes is the only candidate to have been a dropout from several colleges. He never worked a day in his life. And the other guy [Briscoe] raises cattle."[10]

Also present at the press conference were Flores Anaya, a lawyer, running for U.S. senator; Rubén Solís, candidate for state treasurer; Fred Garza, of the United Farm Workers Organizing Committee, running for state railroad commissioner; and Robert Gómez, candidate for land commissioner. Compean told reporters that the party also had candidates for such offices as state representative and county commissioner in nine counties: Hidalgo (Edinburg), Zavala (Crystal City), La Salle (Cotulla), Starr (Rio Grande City), Nueces (Corpus Christi), Victoria (Victoria), McLennan (Waco), Tarrant (Fort Worth), and Bexar (San Antonio).

Shortly after the announcement Muñiz went on the road to rally support for the petition drive. Armed with a red 1962 Plymouth and a Texaco credit card, he toured the Rio Grande Valley, South Texas, West Texas, and cities such as Houston, Dallas, Austin, and his hometown of Corpus Christi. Everywhere he went he hammered away at both parties, although the Democrats, who controlled the state legislature and the governor's mansion, received the brunt of the criticism.

In a speech at Pan American University in Edinburg, deep in the Rio Grande Valley, Muñiz urged the audience of mostly Mexican American students not to vote in the primaries so they could sign the petitions to put the party on the state ballot. He also accused Preston Smith, the governor, of remembering the Mexican American only at election time.[11] At Del Mar College in Corpus Christi he blasted both parties for making false promises.

Mexican Americans have had it with the lies. *Ya basta*. Raza
Unida offers the people an alternative and the days of being
led to the polls to vote straight ticket for these two other
parties are over. . . . it is not a revolt of guns or violence, but
by the vote. . . . if it's not done this year, it will come next year
or the next. . . . as long as there are Mexican Americans there
will be persons to replace people like me.[12]

There and everywhere else he stopped he was greeted by chants of
"Viva la Raza!"

In a short time Muñiz became comfortable as the lead man
for the party. At first he felt nervous speaking in front of an audience
and relied on prepared texts, but soon he discovered that his
strength was in speaking extemporaneously, drawing in his audience by asking them questions, leading the chants, and joking. His
mingling with the crowds after his speeches proved particularly
effective. Said one of the party leaders about him: "Ramsey had a
likable personality. People fell in love with him when they met him
because he was so personable, so down to earth . . . straightfor-
ward, unpretentious. He was a perfect choice as a candidate. He
was good at door to door. He worked long hours. He was sincere
and he spoke from the heart."[13] In a rhetoric-conscious community,
he not only said many of the things people had been wanting to
hear for a long time, but said them in Spanish and in a way that
assured people he would not recant them even under Anglo pressure. Young Chicanos, students, and dropouts liked his direct style,
his militancy, and some of his salty language. The older Mexican
Americans liked him because he carried good credentials, dressed
nicely, and could be the perfect gentleman. Wherever he went,
Muñiz picked up the signatures.

It was a stroke of good luck for the party that Muñiz was so
effective, because the signature gathering did not proceed as well
as the leadership had hoped. There were not enough volunteers to
carry the petitions, and too many of the registered voters were committed Democrats. Even when they were not, many of them felt
uneasy about passing up the primaries, in which they could vote
for a Mexican American or two, to sign a petition for an unknown
party. Despite the publicity that MAYO and the Crystal City takeover received, many Mexican American voters were uninformed.

The idea of a third party seemed to catch on faster among
those who had not participated in electoral politics before. As

Muñiz said at a rally: "The Mexican American and the black communities ... don't vote because in the past they didn't have a real choice. ... Our connection with the Democratic Party has been nothing more than a cheap marriage ... they have lied to us and betrayed [us]. ... Now we are divorcing ourselves from the Democratic Party."[14] Although many of these unparticipating Mexican Americans were enthusiastic about the new party, it became a big chore to qualify them to sign the petition. These people had to register to vote before they could sign, and the party did not have enough qualified registrars. The petition-gathering effort had been divided by region, and though the South and West Texas chapters had been able to pick up signatures at a fast pace, the big-city chapters in Houston, Dallas, Austin, and San Antonio were not keeping up with their quotas.[15] By June 15, 1972, a month after the primaries, Muñiz told a crowd in San Antonio that the party had fifteen thousand of the twenty-three thousand signatures needed.[16] This, the party leaders realized, was not exactly the groundswell they had expected.

Support began to increase rapidly, however, after the Democratic primaries when Briscoe won the nomination in a close race with Frances "Sissy" Farenthold, a maverick liberal from Corpus Christi who had attracted significant support from mainstream Mexican Americans. To many moderates and liberal Democrats, Briscoe recalled earlier times, when rural conservatives rode from out of their ranches to the state capital, where they maintained a status quo that excluded blacks, Mexican Americans and poor whites. The disappointment and frustration with Briscoe's nomination was made more acute by the fact that liberals had felt this was the year that they would sneak into office because of the disarray in the ranks of the conservative Democrats.

On January 18, 1971, one year before, and one day after Preston Smith had been sworn in for his second term, the Securities and Exchange Commission (SEC) had filed a civil suit against several of the top Democrats in the state for involvement in manipulative and deceptive practices.[17] The "Sharpstown Scandal," as it became known, entangled the governor; Waggoner Carr, the state attorney general; Dr. Elmer Baum, chairman of the Texas Democratic Executive Committee and interim appointee to the three-man State Banking Commission; Tommy Shannon, chairman of the House Administration Committee; William Heatley, chairman of the House Appropriations Committee; Gus Mutscher, Speaker of the

House; and Frank Sharp, a Houston millionaire who contributed heavily to conservative Democrat campaigns.[18]

Governor Smith, according to the SEC, had called a special session of the state legislature in order to have State Representative Shannon introduce the Texas Depositor Protection Act. That act would insure deposits of up to one hundred thousand dollars for state banks and would make them exempt from inspection by the Federal Depositors Insurance Corporation, which had cast a leery eye at Sharp's financial dealings. With the knowledge that the bill would pass, the seven individuals had obtained a loan from the Sharpstown Bank in Houston and bought stock in the National Bankers Life Insurance Company owned by Sharp, one of the insuring companies most likely to benefit with this change of law. The bill passed in the House on September 8, 1970, and in the Senate on the following day. With its passage, the SEC charged, the seven made profits in the thousands.[19]

When the scandal broke, the credibility of the top Democrats suffered, and the gubernatorial race opened up. Briscoe decided to run, and Farenthold promised the voters she would clean up Austin if elected. Claiming the voters were still with him, Smith decided to go for reelection; Carr also threw his hat in the ring, though he did not prove to be much of a factor. Barnes, who only a year before had seemed to be the heir apparent to Smith, also filed for the governorship but quickly found that people considered him part of the tainted group of establishment Democrats. Early in the primary season it became a two-person race between Briscoe and Farenthold.

The Democratic primary developed into a classic confrontation between a conservative and a liberal, a symbol of what had been going on in Texas for several decades at every level of the political spectrum. This time, though, it was a fair fight because both candidates were millionaires and Briscoe was not part of the in-group and consequently did not have the conservative Democratic machinery firmly behind him. When the top Democrats sputtered, Briscoe and Farenthold slipped ahead and into a runoff. Conservative Democrats, deprived of their top politicians, swallowed hard and quickly lined up behind Briscoe, who managed to hold off a furious finish by Farenthold.

Going into the state convention on June 10, Muñiz saw a golden opportunity to recruit disenfranchised Democrats into the Raza Unida fold and move a little more toward the center, where he could attract many Mexican American Democrats. Shortly after the runoffs he called on the liberal Democrats to support his campaign, saying "we're talking about the same things. Liberals have always talked about helping minorities. How much more can they help than by voting for us. What we are saying to liberals is 'how liberal are you.'"[20] Muñiz also offered his sympathies to Farenthold, whom he had helped in legislative races as a college student.[21]

At the convention Muñiz quickly established himself as one of the leaders of the party. He did it with his natural charm and through the number of people he attracted to the convention. In half a year Muñiz had traveled more, met more people, and been interviewed more than anyone else in the party except Gutiérrez and Compean. To many people outside the movement, Muñiz was the party. Whereas Compean prompted association with MAYO and Gutiérrez with Crystal City, Muñiz symbolized the state party, principally because he was its standard-bearer but also because he found himself a dynamic campaigner among a less-than-charismatic group of candidates.

While party activists were still defining the role of the party, its ideology and methodology, Muñiz already had a pattern to follow—that of a politician stumping the state for votes. Deeply conscious of La Raza Unida's premises, he brought to the campaign a militancy not seen since the days of the populist movements in Texas, but it was nevertheless a traditional campaign. He simply added a Chicano and personal twist to it. It was not hard, then, for him to come to the convention radiating confidence and feeling that momentum was on his side. In personal charisma he towered above most of the party cadre, and the less ideological delegates quickly became attracted to him.[22]

At the convention Compean was elected state chairman, a confirmation of the action taken the previous October, though this time he encountered token opposition. Muñiz and the other candidates were also officially nominated, without opposition, although a few of the original candidates had dropped out by this time.[23] After the formalities of nominations the party delegates debated and then approved a party platform.

> Contained in the various sections of this document are the hopes, ideals, and the future of many people. . . . Those who understand the full meaning of this document cannot deny that the course of history will be affected by the ideas con-

tained herein. For the first time, a political party will exist
which was started by Chicanos for Chicanos. The momentum
that Raza Unida Party has started will continue, however, not
only for Chicanos but for all who see the need for the people
to once again have control of the government so . . . the voice
of the people will be heard.[24]

As might be expected from activists who concentrated so much
time on educational issues and who gained their militancy through
school boycotts and protests, the RUP platform committee made
education its top priority, devoting fourteen pages to it.[25] After
decrying the large dropout rates in Texas schools, the cultural
genocide practiced in them, and the unfair school financing system, the platform called for specific measures that at the time were
radical. The party demanded that all school districts develop multi-
lingual and multicultural programs at all levels from preschool to
college; that state funds be distributed equally to all school districts; that school officials and school boards be proportionally representative of the community; that free early-childhood education,
including daycare and preschool activities, be provided for all children; that schools without walls be created; and that standardized
tests be eliminated as a measure of achievement until they accu-
rately reflected the language usage and culture of those tested. And
finally, the platform called for aid to private Chicano and black
schools and colleges.[26]

Aside from education, there were thirteen other sections dealing with politics, welfare, housing, justice, international affairs, natural resources, transportation, and health. In all areas the party
platform followed a leftist-liberal line. It called for free education;
lowering of the voting age to eighteen; giving the right to vote to
foreigners; breaking up monopolies; fair distribution of wealth; im-
plementation of equal minority representation in the judicial system; abolishment of capital punishment; passage of the Equal
Rights Amendment; removal of trade embargoes and economic
sanctions against Cuba; and the reduction of U.S. forces in Europe.
The abolishment of the Texas Rangers was a popular resolution at
the convention. The platform also called for the recognition of the
new state of Bangladesh.[27]

For a party representing the vanguard of Chicano separatism,
its governing document was only mildly nationalistic. It reflected
both an effort to attract liberal groups outside the Mexican Ameri-

can community and the influence of the antiwar movement. The quasi-ideology of the platform also revealed that most of the party activists were not as sophisticated as Gutiérrez in this area. It was evident in the document that party leaders recognized their own communities' conservatism in economic and social matters. They purposely avoided much of the socialist rhetoric fashionable at the time.

Immediately after the convention the signature gathering intensified, and the party leaders worried. Most of the rural areas were doing well, and Muñiz was picking up signatures wherever he went, but the goal of thirty thousand names did not seem realistic with less than a month to go. At that moment some members of the San Antonio RUP took the matter into their own hands and set up what they later called petition-signing parties. A select group of party faithful began to sign petitions with phony names and addresses, staying up late at night to fill out as many forms as possible. In a matter of weeks the RUP had enough signatures to submit to the secretary of state, and the San Antonio chapter was credited with making a face-saving, monumental effort. More than 70 percent of the signatures from San Antonio were false, but few party members ever knew it during the life of the party.[28] One activist later said that the falsifying of names was done after Gutiérrez hinted that the secretary of state, Robert D. Bullock, a neo-liberal loyal to Governor Smith, had implied that he would not scrutinize the signatures.[29]

Bullock was a boisterous maverick with conservative credentials but a flair for taking unorthodox stands. He proved to be supportive of the Raza Unida Party effort because he saw no threat from it. Gutiérrez later recalled with a chuckle the day he gave Bullock the petitions. The secretary of state asked him the name of the party, to which Gutiérrez replied "La Raza Unida." Bullock remarked angrily that he wanted the "English" name, to which Gutiérrez again replied "La Raza Unida." Bullock exploded with several expletives, whereupon Gutiérrez asked him his name. Bullock pointed to the plate on his door and said, "Bob Bullock—can't you read?" Gutiérrez then asked, "What's your name in Spanish?" After loudly answering "Bob Bullock," the angry state officer cracked a smile and then started laughing. "I like that," he kept repeating and laughing as he gave Gutiérrez a receipt for the names.[30]

Ironically, campaign workers for Senator Joe Bernal, who had been an outspoken supporter of MAYO and Gutiérrez, accused the

Raza Unida of being responsible for his defeat in the primaries. They argued that petition signers had abstained from voting in order to help the party get on the ballot. Though not bitter, Bernal made the same claim many years later.[31] Ironically, few of the legitimate signatures came from that district. Unable to tell the senator or the public about the way some signatures were gathered, party leaders simply responded that such was life in politics. After all, Bernal had been asked to run for governor under the party banner.

After the convention, party leaders came out swinging, mostly at the Democrats. Briscoe was perceived to be vulnerable, and some party activists were angry because Farenthold had refused to support Muñiz, whose views were closer to hers. Muñiz avoided criticizing Farenthold, choosing instead to woo her supporters by pointing out some of the similarities of his campaign with that of the defeated liberal. He suggested to liberals that they initiate a "Democrats for Muñiz" movement. In the same vein he told black leaders in Austin that any demands they would make, he would sign.[32] He also announced that in Houston and Dallas several black activists were organizing a "blacks for Muñiz" drive.[33]

In seeking black support, Muñiz received two major boosts. The first came at the Democratic National Convention in Miami, where Briscoe, following the lead of numerous southern delegates, voted for George Wallace for the presidential nomination. After Wallace's apparent defeat Briscoe quickly shifted his vote to George McGovern, but most Texas liberal delegates left the convention sure that Briscoe was not going to do anything to help the Democrats carry the election in the state. Muñiz quickly announced that through his action Briscoe had given the RUP campaign "at least $300,000 worth of free [media] time." He had come out and shown his true colors on color television, said Muñiz. He added that if Wallace's supporters launched another presidential campaign, as they had four years before, it would give the party a better chance of winning, because moderates and liberals who would vote against Wallace might also vote against Briscoe. Sarcastically, Muñiz offered to help Wallace's American Party find a candidate to run for governor of Texas.[34]

The second major boost for the campaign came when the Reverend Ralph Abernathy, head of the Southern Christian Leadership Conference, the organization led at one time by Martin Luther King, Jr., endorsed Muñiz for governor.[35] It was a major triumph for the RUP candidate, who was groping for big-name and liberal support. His black support was bolstered even more when a former high-school teammate, who had played in the National Football League, joined the campaign as a state organizer in the black community.[36]

On August 8 the party was certified to appear on the state ballot. With the party legitimate, Muñiz, who up to this time had been without an official campaign manager, named Gutiérrez to direct his electoral effort. In announcing Gutiérrez, he criticized the Republicans and Democrats for hiring out-of-state, big-name public relations agencies to handle their campaigns. Briscoe had hired a Tennessee firm and Henry Grover a New York company. Said Muñiz: "I don't have to go to New York City and I'm not going to have to go to Tennessee to run my political campaign. All I'm going to do is go to Crystal City. There is a firm right there and it has a staff of 10,000 people . . . and José Angel is going to be my campaign manager."[37] Muñiz rejected the reporters' notions that because of his reputation Gutiérrez would be a hindrance to the campaign. He added that already the organization was picking up support among conservative and older Mexican Americans.

The reference to Grover indicated that even La Raza Unida could see that the Republican candidate's campaign was picking up momentum. Grover had not been the choice of the Republican leadership, but he had won the primaries, had millions to spend, and excelled as a campaigner. Some political observers also believed that a McGovern-led Democratic Party meant a sure victory in Texas for Richard Nixon and a strong coat-tail effect. Middle-level party officials and campaigners seemed to understand this, but unfortunately for Grover, the top Republicans did not, and they dragged their feet almost until the end in throwing the party's manpower and money behind him.

In Houston, a few days before naming Gutiérrez his manager, Muñiz lashed out at the Republicans, who had just concluded their national convention. He accused them of talking through both sides of their mouths because they promised to recruit minorities but had only one Mexican American in the Texas delegation and no blacks. Talking about both parties, he said, "We've put them in the state house, we've put them in the White House, but we stay in the dog house. We don't want to stay there anymore." Muñiz predicted that RUP and not the Republicans would be the second majority party in the state and added that he offered an alternative to the look-alike conservatism of Grover and Briscoe. He also denied that the party was trying to help elect a Republican to get back at the Democrats.[38]

On August 28 some liberals who had remained silent, sulking after Farenthold's defeat, spoke cautiously about Muñiz and the RUP. In a cover story in *The Texas Observer* entitled *Ya basta!* they introduced Muñiz to their readers in this fashion: "If you can't stomach Dolph Briscoe and Henry Grover is unthinkable, the name of the Raza Unida candidate is Ramsey Muñiz." They went on to give some details of Muñiz's background, highlighting his assistance to Farenthold's legislative races. Then, in an almost melancholic reflection of their own party's failure to provide a better alternative, the editors wrote:

> Among many black, chicano and liberal Democratic leaders to whom the *Observer* has talked, it seems clear that as John Kennedy once said, "Sometimes party loyalty asks too much." For their own political sakes, they cannot support Muñiz against Briscoe. However, they are planning to telegraph to their supporters, in various ways, the equivalent of McGovern's great line from the Democratic convention, "Vote your conscience, folks, just vote your conscience."[39]

It was at this juncture, with momentum seemingly building, that Muñiz and the rest of the party took a break to attend the National La Raza Unida Conference in El Paso. For those not interested in the moderate tone of the campaign, this was a chance to go back to radical rhetoric and militant posturing. It also meant meeting thousands of other radicals and activists nationwide and taking part in a historic moment.

There is a monster
with two heads [Republican and Democrat]
that feed from the same trough.

—Rodolfo "Corky" Gonzales at the 1972 RUP Convention

UNIDOS GANAREMOS:
The Party Goes National

If Gutiérrez was leery of a state party, he was even less committed to a national organization at a time when the only victories RUP could claim were in Crystal City and in La Salle County. A three-month-old statewide party already took most of the resources, and two months before an election seemed the wrong time to begin a national La Raza Unida Party. But by the summer of 1972 Gutiérrez did not have much choice but to call a national conference, because if he did not, Rodolfo "Corky" Gonzales would.[1]

Gonzales headed the Crusade for Justice, a Denver-based militant nationalist organization that by the late 1960s had become the vanguard of the Chicano Movement. Among militant Chicanos, Gonzales represented the new leader, having surpassed in stature the softspoken César Chávez and the once-feisty Reies López Tijerina, who had just finished serving two years in federal prison.[2] Gonzales was a toughened product of the barrio streets of Denver and the harsh work of the fields. As a young man, he became a boxer and eventually was ranked third in the world in the Featherweight division.[3] After leaving the ring, he opened a bail-bond business and became active in the Democratic Party circles of Colorado, where he headed the Viva Kennedy Clubs during the 1960 presidential election. He became a one-man self-help agency as a

91

member of numerous local and national boards that coordinated poverty programs throughout the Southwest.

While serving as chairman of the board of Denver's War on Poverty, however, Gonzales was accused of discriminating against whites and blacks. When his supporters organized a picket against the *Rocky Mountain News* to protest the newspaper's reports, the mayor asked him to resign or be fired.[4] Gonzales resigned not only from his job but also from the Democratic Party, charging the politicians with insensitivity and outright cultural genocide against Chicanos. His letter of resignation to party chairman Dale R. Tooley was a scathing condemnation of the American political system:

> The individual who makes his way through the political muck of today's world, and more so the minority representatives, suffers from such an immense loss of soul and dignity that the end results are as rewarding as a heart attack . . . or cancer! . . . You and your cohorts have been accomplices to the destruction of moral man in . . . society. I can only visualize your goal as a complete emasculation of manhood, sterilization of human dignity, and that you not only consciously but purposely are creating a world of lackeys, political boot-lickers and prostitutes.[5]

Like a born-again Chicano, he plunged into a study of his people, their culture, and their struggle. Convinced he had found the way to unite his people, he established La Crusada para la Justicia (Crusade for Justice), a self-help community organization that sponsored Chicano theater, dances, fiestas, and political discussion classes. It was a place for the barrio people to come together and feel at home in a Chicano environment.

To express his new political philosophy, Gonzales wrote a poem that became the epic story of the Chicano Movement. "Yo Soy Joaquín" expounded what it was to be *la gente de bronze*—a people caught in a frightful duality of being the oppressed and the oppressor, of having heroes while being the defeated, of helping build a country but not sharing its fruits.

> I am Joaquín.
> I am lost in a world of confusion,
> Caught up in the whirl of
>   an Anglo society,
> Confused by the rules,

Scorned by the attitudes,
Suppressed by manipulation,
And destroyed by modern society.
My fathers have lost
      the economic battle
And won the struggle of
      cultural survival.
And now!
. . . We start to move.
Mexicano, Español, Latin, Hispano, Chicano.
I look the same.
I feel the same.
I cry and
Sing the same.
I am the masses
Of my People
and I refuse to be absorbed.
I am Joaquín
The odds are great,
But my spirit is strong.
My faith unbreakable.
My blood is pure.
I am an Aztec Prince
And Christian Christ.
I shall endure!
I will endure![6]

Gonzales took center stage when he sent out a call to congregate the first Chicano Youth Liberation Conference in March 1969 in Denver. Held at El Centro de la Cruzada, the conference focused on social revolution and cultural identity and addressed the question, "Where do the barrio's youth, the student, the rural Chicano, the campesino fit into the Chicano Movement?" In the area of social revolution, panel discussions were held on organizational techniques, Chicano politics and philosophies, methods of self-defense against the police, and planning protests and demonstrations. In the sessions on cultural identity, talk centered on Chicano literature, movimiento newspapers, and music.[7]

The conference served as a sounding board for Gonzales's new philosophy and as a means of propelling him into the leadership role of the movement. At the time, Chicanos lacked a charismatic national figure who could speak the language of the new militancy. Rhetorically more impressive than Chávez and Tijerina, and more

"Chicano-looking" than the unknown Gutiérrez, Gonzales seemed right for the role.

Attending the conference were representatives of all the major Mexican American activist groups in the country such as United Mexican American Students (UMAS, which had more than two thousand members); Mexican American Youth Association (MAYA); the Third World Liberation Front of the University of Berkeley; the Brown Berets, a paramilitary group with chapters throughout the Southwest; Mexican American Student Organization (MASO), from Arizona State University in Tempe; the Young Lords, a Puerto Rican group from New York and Chicago; and several other groups. Nearly fifteen hundred activists came.[7] The conference created a breeding ground for the development of an ideology that would take many of their ideas and rhetoric and place them within the context of the national role of the Chicano.

Chicanos were to be seen no longer as a minority group, but as a people with a distinct name, language, history, and homeland. Gonzales gave a new meaning to the word "Chicano," which had been for years a derogatory term in "respectable" Mexican American circles. It had been part of the rhetoric of resistance of the *pachucos* (zoot-suiters) of the 1940s and the youth gangs in the southwestern inner cities who fought assimilation and discrimination.[8] These youths had developed their own language, a mixture of English and Spanish, plus new words that had meaning only to them.[9] The new militancy added a political twist to words like *carnal* (brother) and brought into use the terms *Tío Taco* (Uncle Tom) and *vendidos* (sellouts).[10]

Gonzales's major accomplishment at the conference was to convince the activists that the Southwest was their homeland, that it was Aztlán, where legend said the Aztecs originated. Chicanos, he insisted, had a psychological and spiritual attachment to the land and the Anglos had stripped them of it to induce a cultural genocide that all the barrios were now facing. Divested of their land and their dignity and prevented from making economic gains, Chicanos remained easy to oppress. Aztlán became a battle cry, a legitimizing force for a people discriminated against on the Anglo side of the border and resented and ridiculed by Mexicans.[11] From the conference came the most important document in the early history of the Chicano Movement, one that set the tone for the next several years. *El Plan Espiritual de Aztlán* (The Spiritual Plan of Aztlán) declared:

In the spirit of a new people that is conscious not only of its proud ... heritage but also of the brutal Gringo invasion of our territories, WE, the Chicano inhabitants and civilizers of the northern land of AZTLAN from whence came our fore-fathers, reclaiming the land of their birth and consecrating the determination of our people of the sun, DECLARE that the call of our blood is our power, our responsibility, and our inevitable destiny.

We are free and sovereign to determine those tasks which are justly called for by our house, our land, the sweat of our brows, and by our hearts. Aztlán belongs to those who plant the seeds, water the fields, and gather the crops and not to the foreign Europeans. We do not recognize capricious frontiers on the bronze continent.

Brotherhood unites us, and love for our brothers make us a people whose time has come and who struggles against the foreigner *Gabacho* who exploits our riches and destroys our culture. With our heart in our hands and our hands in the soil, we declare the independence of our *mestizo* nation. We are a bronze people with a bronze culture. Before the world, before all of North America, before all our brothers in the bronze continent, we are a nation, we are a union of free *pueblos*, we are AZTLAN. POR LA RAZA TODO. FUERA DE LA RAZA NADA.[12]

El Plan in essence called for a separate nation, even if only spiritu-ally in the beginning. The plan exhorted the young Chicanos at the conference to go back home and design the way in which they could become socially, culturally, economically, and politically in-dependent. And it summoned all classes, from farm workers to professionals, to unite in a nationalist ideology transcending reli-gion, politics, class, economics, and borders.[13]

Accusing the Republicans and Democrats of being the "same monster with two heads that feed from the same trough," Gonzales called for independent political action. "Where we are a majority, we will control; where we are a minority, we will represent a pres-sure group; nationally, we will represent one party: *La Familia De La Raza*."[14]

A second liberation conference was held the following year, also in Denver and sponsored again by the Crusade. The delegates unequivocally called for the building of Aztlán, a Chicano political party, and support for a national moratorium against the war to be held on August 29, 1970, in Los Angeles. This time, two new groups appeared: the Socialist Workers Party (SWP), which later played a divisive role in the movement and the La Raza Unida Party of Texas, represented by Jesús Ramírez of the Rio Grande Valley. MAYO had also sent a representative to the first conference. At the conference Gonzales announced the formation of the La Raza Unida Party of Colorado on March 30.[15] This was undoubtedly influenced by the presence of the Texas RUP.

Instead of holding one statewide party convention to nominate all the candidates, the Colorado RUP held a number of them throughout the state in order to involve more people. At the first convention, on May 16, the party delegates selected Gonzales as the chairman and nominated Albert Gurule for governor, George García for lieutenant governor, and Patricia Gómez for state representative. Nearly eight hundred people attended that convention. At the second meeting, in Denver, Juan Valdez was nominated for state treasurer, Bruno Madina for Pueblo County sheriff, and Mark Saiz for the University of Colorado board of regents. Two more candidates were selected at the third convention.[16]

The fifth convention, which attracted close to one thousand activists to Boulder, proved to be the most successful. There the Colorado candidates, like their Texas counterparts, lashed out at the two political parties. Gurule set the convention's tone when he declared:

> The Democrats and Republicans are getting very concerned. When they go to speak, they will tell the people they have come to hear the friendly voice of the Hispano. Well, I think . . . the people are tired of listening to the friendly voice of the Hispano. They are now going to listen to the more aggressive voice of the Chicano.[17]

The convention delegates took a strong stand against the war in Vietnam. Said Valdez, candidate for state treasurer, "When our people are going out there and being used as cannon fodder, then I say we have to speak on that issue."[18] This was a far different attitude than the one MAYO took on the war during its early years. The Colorado party, however, had a charismatic leader uninterested in what others had to say. This strategy hinged on arousing anger among Chicanos, not winning elections or even influencing legislation. Gonzales had no desire to appear legitimate except to the vanguard of the Chicano Movement.

Unlike the Muñiz campaign of two years later, the Colorado party did not concern itself with attracting liberal support or being seen as a liberal alternative. Gurule, speaking to a reporter of *The Militant*, the Socialist Workers Party's newspaper, said:

> The Anglo who is sympathetic, who is sincerely interested in La Raza ... must be able to respect us when we say ... we want to do this on our own. If we say we are going to have a meeting and we are going to keep the Anglo out, they ought to respect that point of view. What's happened with some liberals I have known is that when I tell them we're having a meeting that they can't come to, they get all uptight. And the next thing you know you have an enemy. And they were probably enemies to begin with.[19]

Instead of concentrating on a campaign, Gonzales traveled, gave speeches, and planned conferences. He became involved in the Chicano Moratorium, a large, antiwar protest to be held in Los Angeles. Nearly twenty thousand people turned out, carrying signs, singing, and chanting antiwar slogans. Nothing like this had ever been seen before, and it signaled that the Chicano community, long known for sending its men off to war, was questioning the U.S. role in Vietnam.

Gonzales and Gurule were scheduled to speak, but they never reached the podium; they were detained, along with twenty-seven others, by Los Angeles police officers and arrested for robbery and for carrying a concealed weapon. They were later acquitted of the charges, but the detention may have been a lucky thing, because shortly after the arrest the police attacked the demonstrators. A full-blown riot ensued in which forty people were injured and Ruben Salazar, a well-respected *Los Angeles Times* reporter, died after being struck by a policeman's projectile fired into the lounge where he was relaxing after finishing his shift.[20] Gonzales's arrest and subsequent trial took energy and resources away from the campaign.

Consequently, without money, organization, or political tact, and without a strong voter-registration effort in a state with few Chicano voters, the Raza Unida Party did not come close to winning any races anywhere in Colorado. Gurule received 12,211 votes, 1.8 percent of the total; Valdez, 18,728, or 3 percent; and M. Avila attracted 14,540 votes, 2.3 percentof the total, as candidate for secretary of state. Two RUP candidates for the Colorado board of regents, Mark Saiz and Marcella Trujillo, received 4 and 5 percent of the vote, respectively.[21]

Colorado ran the first statewide Raza Unida campaign, but it was not the only state outside of Texas to have a party. After the second Youth Liberation Conference, some of the panel participants from California went back home and began their own quest for a Chicano third party. On November 22, 1970, shortly after California's gubernatorial elections, Chicano activists met in Berkeley to establish the Oakland-Berkeley chapter of El Partido de la Raza Unida.[22] By this time Gutiérrez had been on an organizing tour through California, Washington, and Oregon, so the party idea was not totally new. From the Berkeley meeting came a founding document whose preamble became the model for the rest of the state's chapters:

> We, the people of La Raza, have decided to reject the existing political parties of our oppressor and take it upon ourselves to form La Raza Unida Party which will serve as a unifying force in our struggle for self-determination.
>
> We understand that our real liberation and freedom will only come about through independent political action ... of which electoral activity is but one aspect. . . . Oppressive conditions that form the common denominator that unites us give rise to a spiritual cohesiveness, a collective consciousness, that forms the basis of RAZA NATIONALISM.[23]

Cultural nationalism was the impetus for unity among these Raza activists, but an additional line to the preamble implied a perception by the California leaders that nationalism was not enough: "We recognize that our culture alone cannot produce our freedom and that only an organized and protracted struggle, confronting our oppressors at every level and involving the greatest number of our people, can bring about our goal of complete self-determination and total freedom.[24] Because of the student movement in California, already four years old, the California organizers were more concerned with ideologies and with the use of such terms as "Third World," "working class," "struggle," "public ownership," and "political prisoners" than actually winning elections. Like their Colorado counterparts, they seemed ready to take a radical line regardless of its electoral perils.

On February 12, 1971, Gutiérrez attended the La Raza Conference on Community Colleges held at Merrit College in Oakland

and spoke about the party. He quickly addressed the question of ideologies by stating that he opposed "approaching problems by looking at ideologies. We [already] have one of the extremest ideologies and strongest alignments that we can use—*el carnalismo and hermandad. . . . En nuestra familia, cuando hay pedo, todos estamos juntos* (In our family, when there is trouble, we stand together)." He counseled the organizers to talk about the same things that the people were discussing. "We could not take the material from *The Militant* [SWP's newspaper] or the 'we-are-all-victims-of-the-same-oppressor' approach ... we tell the people 'never forget that *una mano no se lava sola*' (one hand does not wash itself). This is something that can be understood rather than 'we got to get our sh—together.'" He added: "We spend energy in saying that we are going to beat the gringo. But people ask 'When we beat the gringo, then what are we going to do?' So we [in Crystal City] try to address ourselves to actual problem solving. And the only solutions that you are going to come up with are solutions you find at home."[25]

Fifteen days after Gutiérrez spoke, a convention was held at California State College in Los Angeles, where two hundred and fifty people gathered to discuss the formation of the party. Simultaneous meetings were held at Riverside and San Bernardino. This particular meeting came about through the efforts of Bert Corona, long-time union activist with a reputation of being involved in Chicano issues. As an instructor at Cal State, he arranged for some of his students to work on party activities through an independent studies course. At the time, Corona was an influential member of the Mexican American Political Association (MAPA). He first summarized the history of the Democratic Party among Chicanos, and then he told the conference participants, "Our job is to unmask the Democratic Partly. We must clear this [party] out of our mind. Democrats have always put nails in our coffin."[26]

Corona turned out to be a strong catalyst for the party in California in its first year and a half. He was a powerful speaker with a dominating presence and a reputation of involvement in liberal and radical politics that went back to the 1940s. He had helped to found the Community Service Organization (CSO); he had been an organizer of the United Cannery Agricultural Packing and Allied Workers of America (UCAPAWA), one of the few unions to organize Chicanos in the 1930s; and he had served as a member of the U.S. Civil Rights Commission in 1967, resigning the following year after announcing that the "whole thing [Commission] was a ... waste to our people."[27]

As a founding member of MAPA, Corona represented a valuable link to the state's Mexican American middle class. In a political manifesto distributed statewide by Hernán Baca, San Diego County organizer, entitled "MAPA and La Raza Unida: Political Action of Chicanos," Corona outlined a new direction for Chicanos. He wrote it particularly for those Mexican Americans active in the state's political arena and in liberal causes. As an organization, MAPA had been supportive of the farm workers' movement and other labor causes. It had also been active in assisting undocumented workers and in electing Mexican Americans to office. It was they who had to make sure La Raza Unida would become a reality.

> MAPA must help in every way possible to create and maintain a strong La Raza Unida Party. ... Because of its eleven years of history, experience and know-how, MAPA is the Chicano organization that can contribute the most to La Raza Unida efforts. ... La Raza Unida will be and is a mechanism ... for ... political control ... for maximum bargaining power ... and shall have the power ... to deny our votes to the lesser-of-two-evils candidates and parties of the Anglo establishment ... all this is MAPA and Raza Unida work.[28]

He repeated this theme on January 22, 1972, at the Mi Raza Primero Conference in Muskegon, Michigan, a gathering of militant Chicano liberals, where he delivered the keynote speech. "On the basis that these two parties [Democrats and Republicans] have been nothing but promises—purely a love of words and not deeds—there is only one way out, and that is to form our own party."[29]

Although Corona was a formidable spokesman for the *partido*, his enthusiasm for this brand of third-party politics did not hide any ambitions for leadership. In fact, he never made any serious attempt to become a leader of the party, and his actual participation was short-lived, as he became immersed in the issues of the undocumented worker. He founded another organization, CASA-Hermandad General de Trabajadores, which dedicated its efforts almost exclusively to battling the regressive immigration bills circulating in the California state legislature and the U.S. Congress. Ironically, the organization, but not Corona, became a bitter enemy of La Raza Unida Party and most of the Chicano Movement organizations.[30]

Unlike the case in Texas and Colorado, California *partidarios* did not have anyone to look toward for leadership. Party chapters sprung up throughout the state but quickly divided into southern, northern, and central regions, each with its own leadership, and even these regional organizations were fragmented. The ideological leanings varied among and within the three groups. The chapters away from the large coastal cities, as well as some of the Los Angeles chapters, were nationalistic and reformist, while the northern chapters were leftist-oriented: some nonsectarian left, some independent socialist, some Trotskyite, and a significant number Marxist.[31] The first year, political debates were tempered in the name of *unidad* and because "Corky" Gonzales's brand of leftist nationalism provided a common denominator, but by the start of the second year, polemical conflicts became a serious hindrance to the party's development. With such diverse opinions it was difficult to find a leader acceptable to the majority. Even efforts to structure the California party into one state organization failed, as the three regions voted to reject such a notion.[32]

Another conflict that arose in California concerned the role of the party in the movement. The debate centered on whether the party should emphasize electing Chicanos to office or be involved in simply providing political education to prepare the barrios for the upcoming struggle for liberation. The ultranationalists and the Marxists favored the latter approach, and the cultural nationalists and reformists preferred electoral victories. This controversy originated in the diversity of ideologies, and it was fanned to flames by the seemingly clashing philosophies of the two giants in the party, Gonzales and Gutiérrez. Even before the party had a national structure, its members were debating an issue of national proportions. Ironically, neither man was a Marxist and both claimed to be cultural nationalists, although Gutiérrez later described his ideology as that of progressive nationalism. Yet their perceptions were based on different assumptions. Gutiérrez felt that La Raza Unida could gain political power county by county and region by region, winning in places where Chicanos were the majority and encircling the large urban areas where they were only a large minority. In building coalitions with other groups, even those areas could be influenced by the party's power. His vision was biased by the fact that he had grown up and lived in areas where Chicano majorities were common.

In contrast, Gonzales lived in a state where Chicanos were not a majority in any place, and even their barrio legislative districts were so blatantly gerrymandered that few Chicanos could hope to get elected to political office if they ran a nationalist campaign. Unlike Gutiérrez, Gonzales had years of experience as a mainstream politician and did not believe that Chicanos could work through governmental channels or would be allowed to systematically take control. The only alternative, then, was to develop La Raza's conciencia of its right to be free to a degree that it would force a break—in a manner as yet undetermined—between Chicanos and the Anglo nation in which they lived.[33]

This contrast in ideologies became acutely evident at a regional Raza Unida Party conference held in Pueblo, Colorado, on November 26, 1971. Speaking to a predominantly Colorado crowd, Gonzales urged that the party run a slate in the presidential elections of 1972. This would allow for the educating of the masses and the exporting of the nationalist rhetoric to all parts of the country where Chicanos lived. Though he did not suggest it outright, Gonzales wanted to be the candidate. But the Texas delegation had other ideas. Compean, leading the delegation in Gutiérrez's absence, questioned the party's strength and its ability to run a national campaign that would be taken seriously. He also chastised the meeting's organizers for failing to notify the Texas delegation of the meeting sooner so more delegates could attend.[34]

The following June, another regional conference took place, this time in Denver. Representatives from eight states—Washington, Nebraska, Texas, Idaho, Colorado, Michigan, California, and Illinois—gathered to discuss the party's philosophy and direction. Rubén Solís, the Texas RUP's candidate for state treasurer, chaired a meeting that continued the debate begun in Pueblo. The discussion arose about those who would use the partido's power to bargain with the Democrats and Republicans. This was a veiled reference to the Texas delegates, who were proposing a more flexible political line. Almost immediately, the speakers and debaters divided into two categories: those interested in espousing ideologies and those who wanted to talk about the mechanics of organizing and taking control. No fingers were pointed at the major proponents of the different approaches, but all of the delegates understood the inferences. No consensus resulted from the debate, and the party delegates left with a general resolution to break away from the two-party system and to meet for a national conference in September.[35] The delegates also voted not to endorse the Communist Party U.S.A. or the SWP because both parties were controlled by Anglos.[36]Unable to get the strong resolutions he wanted from the gathering, Gonzales called a press conference the day after the meeting. Accompanied by José Gonzales, a fellow Crusader, and by Arturo Vásquez, a delegate from the Illinois Raza Unida, he reiterated his familiar themes of nationalism and liberation and announced his party's intentions of destroying the Democratic and Republican parties. Acting as a spokesman for a still-nonexistent national party, he told reporters that party delegates would nominate a presidential candidate in their upcoming convention to run against incumbent Richard Nixon and liberal Democrat George McGovern, who by then had wrapped up his party's nomination.[37]

This arbitrary behavior reflected an obsession on the part of Gonzales to let the activists know that the concept of La Raza Unida was his. Gutiérrez had simply jumped the gun in Texas. Gonzales eventually claimed that before the Chicano Youth Liberation Conference in Denver in 1969—which Gutiérrez did not attend—no one had raised the issue of a Chicano third party.

The idea of a national convention had been Gonzales's from the start, though he had held several meetings with Gutiérrez and Tijerina to talk about strategies and agendas. Gutiérrez, being the youngest and least experienced, was assigned the task of coordinating the logistics, sending out the invitations, renting a meeting place, and setting up the various committees that would perform the necessary footwork. Gonzales quickly laid down the hierarchy: he would be the national chairman, Gutiérrez the vice-chairman, and Tijerina the elder statesman of the party.[38]

From day one, conflicts erupted between the Colorado and New Mexico leaders over who would be invited to attend and to speak and what would be the direction of the party. Gonzales was unshakable in his demands that no bureaucrats or politicians be invited and that Chávez could speak only if he endorsed La Raza Unida Party. Tijerina wanted a unity conference that would bring all elements of the Chicano community together and provide him a base for the continuation of his land-grant movement, which some in the Chicano Movement were already beginning to call reformist and self-serving.

Gutiérrez took no part in the conflict. He remained the disciple of the two political *caudillos*, who considered him a young novice with good skills but lacking the "anointment to be a major leader." Gutiérrez tolerated their condescension because he felt that he did not yet have the stature to claim equal ground. But his patience soon wore thin as he saw the two giants of the movement tear into each other for leadership of the convention and the party. The breaking point came shortly before the national convention convened, when Gonzales and Tijerina engaged in a virulent confrontation that almost turned into a fistfight. In the heat of the moment, Gonzales told Gutiérrez that he was choosing another vice-chairman more in tune with the future direction of the party. An angry Gutiérrez shot back that if that was the case he would place his name in nomination for the chairmanship and then added: "I'll win, too."[39]

The Texas leader was not simply letting off steam, he was convinced a victory was possible. He had, after all, coordinated most of the work for the convention, and most delegates knew him better than they did Gonzales. It was a simple matter to turn the convention staff into a campaign staff, ready to rip the chairmanship from one of the *jefes* of the movement. When Gutiérrez walked out of the room, it signaled the end of a united convention, and the beginning of a divisive struggle for the heart and soul of the national party.

The conflict between the two major figures in the party set the tone of the preparations for the conference scheduled for September in El Paso. The Texas and Colorado delegations went to the national meeting armed with specific agendas and ready to lobby every one of the delegates attending. All other issues took a back seat to the debate on leadership and ideology.

Notwithstanding this divisiveness among a few, the convention generated a euphoria among Chicano activists never before known in the history of the Mexican American people. People came to El Paso from every known Chicano community in the country, and from places of which southwestern Chicanos had never heard. Delegates from Minnesota, Illinois, Wisconsin, Nebraska, Washington, Rhode Island, Maryland, Washington, D.C., and other states joined delegates from the "traditional" Chicano states to form a mass of more than three thousand Raza Unida Party followers. They came in every conceivable way, hitching rides, carpooling, in buses, and in caravans. Some came alone; others brought the entire family. Some had money to stay in hotels, others had relatives or friends in El Paso, and still others hoped for a corner in which to place their sleeping bags.

Women comprised nearly half of those attending, and there were quite a few older people. The ideologies were as diverse as the financial and social circumstances. Nonetheless, most were drawn by the promise of unity and the hope that La Raza had finally come into its own. Nellie Bustillos, who had just run a close race for the school board in La Puente, California, under the party banner, later remembered being shocked to see so many "Mexicans" from outside the Southwest. She knew that many were coming from California, Arizona, and New Mexico because she had seen the cars with the Raza Unida bumper stickers pass her own caravan, their passengers cheering loudly. More than a political odyssey, it was a pilgrimage, and everyone the travelers met on the road represented a brother or sister in *La Causa*.[40]

Misfortune, though, struck even before the conference began, when Ricardo Falcón, a delegate from Colorado, was killed during an argument with a gas-station attendant in Orogrande, New Mexico, just fifty miles from El Paso.[41] The quarrel had ensued after the attendant, Perry Brunson, tongue-lashed Falcón and his companions for using the station's water to fill a leaky radiator. After he shot Falcón, Brunson refused to allow the other passengers in the car to use the phone to call an ambulance. Several of the town's citizens did likewise, preventing usage of even their pay phones. It was an ugly event that solidified the anger Chicanos had toward Anglo society. In their minds the killing manifested once more their alienation and subordination.

The episode was a tragedy for the Colorado delegation because Falcón was an articulate spokesman for the party. Only a short time before the convention he had explained his candidacy for the state legislature:

> I feel that it is my obligation, duty and God-given right to educate the masses of people to the living conditions that the Chicano, the poor and the unrepresented are forced to live under, and how we are exploited. ... I run as a Raza Unida candidate, not as a politician making false promises, but as an activist telling the truth.[42]

In an emotion-packed memorial address, José Calderón, a delegate from Greeley, Colorado, said of Falcón:

When we die, let us die as Ricardo did. Let us die fighting in the barrios, in the jails, in the college campuses, in the fields, in the streets for our raza. . . . And if we should die, let us die as Ricardo did and not like the many of us who die in Vietnam fighting for hate and imperialism; or those of us who die in some OEO [Office of Economic Opportunity] coffin wrapped up in the flag of bureaucracy and pacification; like those who die in some wall-to-wall carpeted asylum without ever knowing man's beautiful ability to give, share and sacrifice our lives for others as Ricardo did.[43]

Falcón became the party's first martyr, the first casualty of what many Chicanos believed would be a costly struggle.

During the convention the El Paso Del Norte Hotel served as the central lodging place; Gutiérrez and Gonzales stayed there, as did many other delegates. Others stayed in surrounding hotels, and still others "roughed it" in nearby homes, churches, and gymnasiums.[44] The hotel served as Gutiérrez's strategic lobbying area, while Gonzales used the aisles of Liberty Hall, where the convention convened, to do his politicking.[45] Salomón Baldenegro, who headed the Arizona delegation, was surprised on his arrival to find that the discussions, conversations, and gossip revolved around who would emerge as the leader of the conference and whose philosophy would prevail. Among the rank and file it was curiosity and anticipation; among the delegation leaders it was a much more serious concern.

The Southern California delegation had attempted to prepare for the conflict and to show a united front, but even it split between the Gutiérrez and the Gonzales factions. In a position paper sent to all the California chapters by the La Raza Unida Party Organizing Committees of the Southern Region, a call for neutrality and unity read:

We in the Southern Region are aware of the differences that exist between *el Partido* in Denver and . . . in Texas. . . . It is our belief that our state caucus should strive to be critical and independent of those perspectives. In other words, let us attend the convention with an open mind and let us not take sides until we have carefully weighed the merits of the pros and cons. We are of the opinion that in the final analysis the perspective of the vanguard party and that of the successful electoral party are not mutually exclusive. As far as Califas is concerned, we believe that the local situation must dictate the pragmatic orientation of the Partido. But either way, we are firmly agreed that the emphasis must be placed on collective leadership as opposed to individual leadership.[46]

Despite all the efforts to prevent it, the California delegation split, as did the Arizona and New Mexico groups. Only Texas and Colorado delegates seemed solidly behind their own leaders.

After an evening of getting together and introducing agendas, the conference began the following morning, a Saturday. By this time Gutiérrez had set down two rules that had some delegates fuming and others uncomfortable. He introduced a two-part loyalty affidavit that every delegate had to sign in order to vote in the convention. The form seemed designed to eliminate the Chicano delegates who were working as a front for other parties or organizations, particularly sectarian left groups like the Socialist Workers Party. The other rule affected Chicano newspapers and other for-sale periodicals. Anyone who wanted to sell any written materials in the Coliseum had to turn over all the proceeds to the convention organizers.[47]

Gonzales gave the first keynote address. Dressed in his movimiento uniform—black pants, black shirt, and a black armband— and speaking in his deep voice, he stood prepared to win the delegates over to his no-compromise position. Standing at the podium, Gonzales could see his dream unfolding, a personal dream that he hoped to turn into a national party with a presidential candidate and a revolutionary cadre. He felt that a majority of the delegation leaders, particularly those of New Mexico, California, Arizona, and a few in the Midwest, were solidly behind him. Still, he began with a friendly overture to the Texas delegation and its gubernatorial candidate. He presented a check from his wife to Muñiz's campaign and then offered to share the cost of the convention with the Texas Raza Unida.[48]

Gonzales then plunged into the substance of his speech. It was the message that he had expounded for two years: no compromise with the two parties.

To negotiate with Nixon is to negotiate with Spiro Agnew, with Laird, with ... the generals in the Pentagon, with the industrialists in the powerful corporate structure, with the golf partner ... of the Godfather, who is protecting the interests of the Cosa Nostra and the Mafia.

Then we have to look at McGovern who comes into a

candidacy, into a nomination arm in arm with Richard "the pig" Daley from Chicago. Who has given more power . . . to a racist white southern bigot. Whether he wins or loses, George Wallace will have more power [over McGovern] than fifteen million Mexicanos.[49]

Gonzales berated the Chicanos who opted for going with the two-party system:

> Everywhere across the country there are "Amigo committees" for every gringo candidate in the two-party system . . . and the politicos can have those type of amigos, because those amigos are working for their own personal jobs, their own personal financial interests; to liberate themselves . . . but they can never liberate themselves morally or spiritually . . . when they become the stooges, the puppets of the men who control this country and the world. . . . We can never be free. We can have $25,000 in our pocket, and if you're a . . . vendido, a tio taco, a *malinche*, you're not free, because you're licking the white man's boots.50

The speech played to the emotions of the delegates, and they responded, applauding, cheering, and chanting: "Viva La Raza Unida" and other Chicano power slogans. At the end Gonzales received a tumultuous ovation.[51]

Next came Gutiérrez. Most of the delegates expected him to promote his "balance-of-power" strategy, which had split the party activists since it first surfaced in an open letter to the National Chicano Political Caucus held on April 23 in San José, California. Before that meeting Texas RUP delegates had talked about "possibly" negotiating with the Democrats or Republicans for concessions, but doing it only from a position of power. In the open letter Gutiérrez had spelled out the four objectives of what he considered to be the Chicano agenda: (1) become the national balance of power; (2) win local elections; (3) defeat (electorally) the enemy; and (4) change the United States to be more sensitive to Chicanos and other minorities.[52]

To fulfill the first objective, the party had to unite the Chicano voters and influence their voting patterns to keep "white America evenly divided between Democrats and Republicans." This could be accomplished by shifting the Chicano bloc vote from one election to another as needed for "the maximum feasible benefit."[53]

Gutiérrez then proposed approaching Nixon and saying, "Show us how badly you want our vote," and then demanding:

> How about two Chicano federal bank charters for every state that has at least 10,000 Chicanos? How about 100 million dollars in governmental contracts for Chicano economic enterprises every year? How about two fully funded Chicano universities in every Southwestern state plus Michigan, Illinois, Wisconsin and Ohio? How about 10 million acres of federal land in occupied Aztlán? How about two Chicanos at the decision-making and money-spending level of every national and regional federal agency? ... this is only a partial list of requests. To the Democratic challenger we intend to say the same and much more.[54]

If the Democrats and Republicans refused to negotiate, the party members, according to Gutiérrez, would vote in local elections and forget about the presidential race.

To the surprise of most of the delegates, Gutiérrez never mentioned his balance-of-power position. Instead, he spoke of unity and the part the party played in achieving it.

> We must resolve our own problems with this political party. *Que va ser nuestro y de nadie mas.* (That is going to be ours and no one else's.) Some say it is impossible *y que nos vamos hacer garras* (and we'll tear each other up). Ask these same people if they saw fighting at the gringo conventions and they'll say "Oh, that was discussion, argument." In that case, he doesn't know Mexicans. We're not fighting, *Nos estamos poniendo de acuerdo.* (We are reaching a concensus.)[55]
>
> We will leave here a united party. We should have one priority ... to learn about each other—in public and in private—love, learn, respect and I hope, to fight for one another. ... .We should stop concerning ourselves with Chicano power ... and build power for Chicanos here today.[56]

Though less dramatic and militant than Gonzales's address, Gutiérrez's speech also played to the mood of the delegates. This was an occasion for unity and nothing he said could be interpreted as taking away from that. It is probable that Gutiérrez saw the sentiments of the participants as being against negotiation. He also realized that a number of the more articulate delegation leaders favored Gonzales's approach. A strong alternative to the Colorado no-compromise proposal would have torn the convention apart immediately and accomplished nothing. The new chairman of the party would be the ideological head, and Gutiérrez decided to concentrate on winning that position.

When Gutiérrez finished, there was a spontaneous clamor for Muñiz to speak. "We want Ramsey! We want Ramsey!" began with Ruben Sandoval of the Texas group, and it spread to members of several of the other delegations until it became a loud, coordinated cadence.[57] Of all the candidates running under the Raza Unida banner nationally, Muñiz was the best known because of his travels outside the state to drum up financial support, spread the party gospel, and persuade migrant workers to return to the state to cast their votes. He was also one of the few candidates seriously seeking to win and not just to make a political statement.

Gutiérrez was caught by surprise and it bothered him. Muñiz had not been picked to play an important role in the convention, and now the chanters were putting him under a more prominent spotlight. Gutiérrez tried to explain that Muñiz would speak later, but the chants only grew louder. Finally, Gutiérrez walked offstage and sent up Muñiz, who was instructed to tell the audience that he would speak that night at a rally of striking Mexican American workers of the Farah Manufacturing Company.[58] Many of the delegates were disappointed because he never got a chance to speak to them. Compean later told supporters that a Muñiz speech would have been opposed by the Colorado party and would have been viewed as an attempt by the Texas RUP to dominate the convention.[59]

The Muñiz incident revealed the difference between the gubernatorial campaign and the party conference. Muñiz needed exposure, a forum by which to attract voters, who would see the Raza Unida Party as an alternative to the do-nothing Democrats and Republicans. For liberals, it would be a party whose progressive platform fell more in line with the national Democratic Party's than the one Briscoe was running on. To Mexican Americans, *el partido* had to "feel" close to home. It had to take the best of the barrio and present it in a positive and sophisticated light. For the Mexican American middle class, in particular, it had to appear legitimate. Unfortunately for the Texas RUP campaign, the delegates from out of state had no interest outside of projecting a militant, radical, and ultranationalistic posture. Though they generally liked Ramsey, they did not share his high regard for suave politics and were convinced that la gente yearned for belligerent rhetoric.

Muñiz felt so out of place during the convention that he spent much of his time alone or in his hotel room, unable to take advantage of being in El Paso, where Mexican Americans made up almost 70 percent of the population. Upon arriving, he had told reporters that the convention and his campaign were going to "shake up this city like it's never been shaken." Roland Arriola, who did most of the campaign managing, had scheduled many appearances for Muñiz in the city. But the party leaders toned down the intensity of the effort, and consequently, it was overshadowed by the media coverage of the rambunctious convention.[60] On the third day of the conference, Muñiz left El Paso for a barnstorm in Lubbock, where he spoke at the state convention of the Cursillos de Cristianidad, a large, mostly Hispanic Catholic group.[61] The day before, he had spoken at a benefit dance for the striking workers of one of the country's major pants makers. In a rousing, extemporaneous speech he told the mostly middle-aged unionists:

> What we're saying, brothers, is that we're going to make a significant political impact, and we will become the balance of power in Texas and the Southwest. We don't care what the political pros say, because something needs to be done now. When you're hungry and when you're suffering, you need to get together real fast. And we don't care if you're brown, black or white.[62]

The strikers loudly cheered Muñiz's only chance to call attention to his candidacy.

Present at the convention, and attracting a lot of attention, was Tijerina, who had been out of federal prison for nearly two years. At one time the most rhetorically militant Chicano activist in the Southwest, Tijerina had mellowed in prison. He did not threaten violence anymore, and he sought to work through established channels. Although a strong supporter of the party from the start, having had his own third party in New Mexico in years past, Tijerina had never been a separatist or ultranationalist. He was more of a militant reformist obsessed with making the U.S. government honor the land grants that many New Mexicans had received from the Spanish Crown.[63] Nevertheless, Tijerina remained one of the fathers of the militant Chicano Movement even though he did not use the words "Chicano" or "Aztlán."

Tijerina steered away from endorsing any proposal, although his thinking approximated that of the Texas delegation. In his address he spoke of unity before ideals, organizations, and leaders, and cautioned the delegates not to get into a fight over political purity.[64] Later, at an impromptu press conference, he said: "I support Raza Unida, but I also work with millions of other Spanish-surnamed Americans who work for the Republican and Democratic parties." Commenting on Gonzales's no-compromise stand, Tijerina said the Colorado leader was simply frustrated with the two-party system. When questioned further on his own views, Tijerina responded that the issue did not merit a stand-off.[65]

After Tijerina finished speaking, Gutiérrez and Gonzales joined him at the podium, and the three of them stood with hands locked and in the air, a gesture of unity that brought the cheering delegates to their feet.[66] It was the last real sign of harmony until the final session, because fierce debates on resolutions began shortly afterward. Most of the discussion went on among the state delegations. Much of the disagreement on the resolutions revolved around their wording and on the procedures for voting, with most of the procedural objections coming from midwestern delegates. They dragged out the sessions even though they were a small group. In fact, California with 66 votes, Texas with 65, and New Mexico with 23 had 144 delegate votes; the other fourteen states shared the 297.[67] Actually, California had 65 votes but ended up casting 66.[68]

Raul Ruiz of California chaired the Saturday night session, in which resolutions and amendments were presented. Gutiérrez, as convention chairman, had the obligation, but he felt that the inevitable controversies would hurt his chances of being elected Congreso de Aztlán (Congress of Aztlán) chairman.[69] To avoid the dilemma, he took the microphone and nominated a shocked Ruiz to be the temporary chairman. Ruiz, a Gonzales supporter, found himself attracted toward Gutiérrez when the delegates became hostile and the Texas members came to his defense.[70] There were nearly five hundred resolutions up for consideration, ranging from bilingual education and redistribution of wealth to independence for Puerto Rico.[71] The first one, which called for support of the farm workers and their strikes, passed with an abstention by the Illinois delegation, which felt that the parliamentary procedures inhibited their freedom. On a second vote the same delegates accused Ruiz of trying to influence the vote. During discussion of the fourth resolution, the Illinois delegation again came to the forefront by moving that all the resolutions be approved and be amended later by the Congreso. Then it called for a vote to be taken on the party chairmanship. New Mexico's Juan José Peña amended the motion to read that the resolutions would be clarified by each state delegation and presented to the Congreso for final drafting. That wording proved acceptable to the convention.[72]

Ironically, the question of whether to support Nixon or McGovern in the presidential race did not become a major issue of discussion, even though group discussions had been going on during the conference on this topic. Muñiz supporters had, in a thinly veiled manner, courted the Democratic presidential nominee through an "endorse us and we'll endorse you" offer.[73] They felt that a McGovern endorsement could swing the liberal vote in Texas toward the party and make it possible to win. But the Muñiz loyalists were not the only McGovern apologists. Chicanos within the Communist Party were distributing free copies of the *People's World*, which carried an article entitled, "Which Way for La Raza Unida?" In it Juan López strongly advocated that the Raza Unida Party concentrate on stopping Nixon's reelection: "To fail to help defeat Nixon is to confuse the people and win their disrespect and scorn. The people will ask, and rightly so, what kind of party is this that while it talks good and does good work, when it comes to the decisive question of curbing the drive toward fascism, insists on yelling from the sidelines."[74] The issue never came to a vote because the Texas delegation found itself divided on the matter and because its chances of pushing through its balance-of-power strategy seemed remote.

The voting on most of the resolutions was lopsided because the convention had decided to call for a unit vote, which meant that each delegation would cast all its votes for the resolution that the majority of its members favored. The proposal gave the California and Texas delegations even more influence. The other states attempted to correct this imbalance by proposing that the Congreso be made up of three voting representatives from each state to ensure equal representation. This proposal was amended by the New Mexico delegation to give the three members proportional voting power. This meant that the individual votes of the representatives from California, Texas and New Mexico carried more weight than those of the other states.[75]

With the resolutions out of the way, the vote for the party chairmanship remained as the last item of business for the convention. The Texas delegation quickly proposed that the national chairman not be elected on the unit rule but rather on a straight delegate vote. This was a crucial point because of the five largest delegations three were badly split, and one vote could mean the difference between getting all of the state's votes or none. Gutiérrez's supporters knew that California leaned toward Gonzales and that the delegations from New Mexico and Arizona were a toss-up. A number of things worked in favor of the Texas proposal. First, many of the delegates were dissatisfied with the unit vote because it gave too much power to the large population areas in their states. Second, though Gonzales's supporters knew which states were solid backers, they were unsure about the numerous other state delegations, which were unknowns before arriving at the convention. Consequently, the Colorado group was caught undecided. Had they led a fight against individual votes and won—and it is uncertain whether they would have triumphed—Gonzales might have taken a one-hundred-delegate lead after the first three states voted. California had already voted during its caucus to cast its votes in a bloc. The majority, by a 48½ to 17½ count, favored Gonzales. This result caused California's pro-Gutiérrez delegates to walk out of the convention.[76]

The Illinois delegation, led by its chairperson, Magda Ramírez, argued that the Texas motion was out of order since each state had already voted to choose its own voting procedures. The question went to the appeals committee and delayed the convention until almost four-thirty A.M. At that time the appeals committee asked for a vote, and the states elected to accept the Texas proposal by 356 to 72.[77] The acceptance came after several delegations decided that the attempt to reach a consensus would have created too much tension among their members.[78]

The vote cleared the way for the election of the Congreso chairman. The nominations had actually been made at two o'clock A.M. but the appeals had delayed the voting. After Gonzales was nominated, Peña attempted to move for adjournment to allow tempers to cool, but Ruiz ignored the motion and allowed Gutiérrez to be nominated. Although the appellate committee agreed with him, Peña later withdrew his motion and the vote was cast.[79]

The election culminated an intense campaign by Gutiérrez and Gonzales, the only two candidates for the chairmanship. Their attempts to win support were a contrast in styles and personal philosophies. Ironically, both alienated a good number of delegates even as they were making new allies. Gutiérrez rented a suite at the El Paso del Norte Hotel, arranged a bar, and called in delegation leaders as well as other key activists for private conferences. He met every delegate in a suit and with a smile, a hearty handshake, and an invitation to get a drink. He had done his homework, according to Baldenegro. "He knew who I was and what I had been doing in Arizona."[80] It was a slick performance and worked with many delegates. It did not with Baldenegro and other militants, however, who compared Gutiérrez's style with what they had seen on television in the Miami Democratic Party Convention only a short time before. It smacked of traditional party backroom politics.[81] To his credit, though, Gutiérrez was never accused of promising anyone anything other than decisive leadership.

Gonzales did almost all of his campaigning on the floor of the Coliseum. It was not his style to lobby for support in a fancy hotel. Instead, he called a delegation leader, found or made a corner among the delegates, and chatted. His eleven husky bodyguards created a barrier around Gonzales and the person being lobbied.[82] While Gutiérrez sought the delegates's votes, Gonzales wanted their hearts and minds. He demanded them. To some of the delegates, Gonzales's approach was intimidating; to others it was inspiring.[83] Colorado delegates made much of their ideological alternative, but they were really banking on their leader's charisma.

Gonzales did not have a monopoly on charisma, however. Gutiérrez was also a spellbinding talker. More important, he had put together a delegation of shrewd political lobbyists. They were well organized and as a whole were a more dynamic group, with a number of them known beyond Texas. Gutiérrez and his delegation also brought something with them that no one else could claim: tangible results. Crystal City had a national reputation and, to a lesser extent, so did Muñiz. The Texas party had its name on the state ballot and had won several elections. Also, and more important, the Gutiérrez people had been the convention coordinators and had been lobbying and making friends even before the meeting. In the end, this combination proved too much for Gonzales's charisma.

The final vote count was not close at all. Gutiérrez received 256½ votes to Gonzales's 170⅚; there was one abstention and fourteen no-votes.[84] The outcome was a shock to the Colorado delegation, and several members threatened to walk out of the convention. But Gonzales quickly headed off a walkout by going to the podium, embracing Gutiérrez, and raising his hand in a show of unity. Behind them stood a banner that said *Unidos Ganaremos*

(United We'll Win).[85] The convention participants, many of them hoping to go home united, cheered boisterously. For all practical purposes the convention was over. The Congreso would have its first meeting on November 24th in Albuquerque.

Gonzales's backers made the most of their defeat. Said José Calderón, leader of the Colorado delegation: "We came down here with a very positive philosophy, and our number one priority was that we didn't endorse any of the presidential candidates, and we accomplished that."[86] Arturo Vásquez, of Illinois, said:

> I think you had here represented two contending forces. . . . The forces of those people . . . willing to adopt accom- modationist policies to the two parties which are presently oppressing us in this country . . . and the forces of people represented in persons like Corky Gonzales who want to maintain the independence of our movement at all cost. . . . And those forces clashed here and I think the forces represent- ing independence, . . . nationalism, . . . really won.[87]

Gutiérrez downplayed his victory and said that the issue had never been the contest between him and Gonzales, but rather the need for a national chairman. Nevertheless, the Texas delegation had won a major victory. The party had begun in the Lone Star State and its leader would remain there. And as far as the *Tejanos* were concerned, leadership of the Chicano Movement had moved from Colorado and California to Texas.

We have no way of publicly supporting this group [Raza Unida] without antagonizing Republicans and making La Raza Unida look as though they had sold out. At the same time, neither do we want to antagonize Raza Unida supporters and drive them back to their old position as Democrat voters.

—internal memo, Nixon staff

THE SIX PERCENT VICTORY

Muñiz was happy to get back on the stump at the end of the national meeting. Although he had been elected one of the three Texas delegates to the Congreso de Aztlán, his participation at the convention had done little for his campaign. A few delegates from outside the state had stayed to do some campaigning and some monetary assistance had been promised, though little if any ever came. Muñiz knew that the campaign's real constituency was far from El Paso's Liberty Hall. Even those Mexican Americans who lived in the border town were ideologically and politically removed from the radicals and militants who had congregated for three days to discuss and debate.

Fully aware of this fact, the Muñiz organization went back to the campaign in a traditional manner. The prime stops were in the Rio Grande Valley, South Texas, and the Winter Garden Area. As he traveled, Muñiz continued to build an organization. At the beginning of his candidacy he had campaigned alone because no one knew him and few were willing to take a risk with him. Now, with media exposure and some significant endorsements behind him, more people were willing to be active in his crusade, including some who were not interested in joining the party. Tony Bonilla, state director of LULAC, was one important middle-class supporter, especially in South Texas, where LULAC had long been active. At a banquet honoring Muñiz, he endorsed the entire Raza Unida slate: "I am here as a Chicano and a *carnal* to Ramsey Muñiz. There is no

119

question who should get the vote. One of his opponents has become rich by using the Mexican American and Mexicans and the other has ideas that run along with the John Birch Society. Briscoe and Grover are not different."[1]

At the banquet were several Mexican American mayors and ex-mayors who were taking a close look at La Raza Unida. Muñiz told the group that he respected all Mexican American groups. "We will not fight among ourselves. I don't have anything against Dr. [Hector] García [founder of the American G.I. Forum] or labor leader Paul Montemayor. We all want the same thing. And if they want to help us . . . here we are."[2] A short time later, Muñiz received the endorsement of the Hays County Independent Organization, a mostly Democratic group that also endorsed McGovern for president and "Barefoot" Sanders for U.S. senator.[3]

The weekend after the convention, Muñiz named Dr. George Treviño, an associate professor of physics at Del Mar College, the local campaign manager in his hometown of Corpus Christi. The appointment was another effort to get credible, high-profile people on the bandwagon. "He will have an impact with the students, the faculty and the community," said Muñiz. And he added that the party was already having an impact on the state. He quoted a "good source" from the Briscoe campaign that a survey done for the Democrats showed that Muñiz was leading in South Texas. Joking with the reporters, Muñiz told them he would ask Briscoe for a copy of the survey to show to a conference of student councils in Lubbock where they were both scheduled to speak.[4]

Ramsey was not the only Muñiz hard on the trail. Albina (Abbie), his wife, along with their two-year-old daughter Delinda, was also traveling the state seeking votes and attending receptions, rallies, and picnics.[5] She was often described by the media as "bouncy and zealous."[6] A former cheerleader and senior class president, Abbie seemed out of place among the Chicana activists, and she never really belonged to the party as much as she did to her husband's campaign.[7] She spent four-day weekends making speeches and traveling with and without him. The other three days she attended Our Lady of the Lake College in San Antonio, where she worked toward a master's degree in educational administration.[8]

Meeting up with Muñiz and his wife as they crisscrossed the state were the other RUP candidates. They got less exposure and for the most part much less support from nonactivists. Except for a few local candidates in South Texas, none could muster any momentum. Still, most were benefiting from Muñiz's appeal. On October 8 the AFL-CIO Local 180, Radio Electricians and Machine Workers Union of San Antonio, endorsed Muñiz and state assembly candidates Albert Peña III, Hector Rodríguez, and Rubén Sandoval. The union also endorsed Martín Sada for Bexar County sheriff.[9] Peña was one of the stronger candidates. Son of Albert Peña, Jr., the old hardline liberal Democrat and endorser of the La Raza Unida local slate, Peña seemed capable of beating Democrat Joe Hernández in a district that was 85 to 90 percent Mexican American.[10] The other real chances of victory were in South Texas, particularly in La Salle and Zavala counties.

Gutiérrez, who had not done any intensive campaigning before the convention, engaged in an all-out tour of the state, hammering away at the Democrats and Republicans and exhorting Mexican Americans to pull the lever for the whole party slate. In Dallas Gutiérrez referred to the other two parties' candidates as animals who were concerned only with self-interest. In Houston he put to rest any hopes liberals had that he or the party might opt to endorse McGovern. A *Houston Post* reporter wrote: "The Crystal City native said the party, in line with the position it took at its national convention . . . is discouraging Chicanos from voting for either President Nixon or Senator . . . McGovern. That will be the party's posture through the November 7 election."[11] Gutiérrez told the San Antonio-based *Chicano Times* newspaper that the liberal Democrats "are asking us to support McGovern, but they don't want to support the candidacy of Ramsey Muñiz."[12]

By this time the Democrats had begun responding to the Raza Unida's charges, with the liberals taking the lead in the attack. Representative Tom Moore of Waco called Muñiz a "con artist." Said Moore: "He's screwed us up from hell to hog valley, running around here getting the Mexicans stirred up, voting against their own best interests."[13] Moore was a member of the "Dirty Thirty," a group of liberal-to-moderate legislators, some whom lost close primary elections and blamed the defeats on La Raza Unida. A number of Farenthold's supporters also blamed Muñiz for her defeat. Said one of them: "Sissy [Farenthold] has done more for Chicanos than any of those guys [RUP candidates]. Who was there in Del Rio? Who was there after Celia? Christ, we had to drag her away from the Fernández trial in Pharr. Why don't they realize? They can't win, but they are willing to screw us up. How could they?"[14] State Senator Bernal, a former ally who lost a close bid for reelection to the legislature, chastised Muñiz mildly. "Ramsey ... made mistakes. I told him, 'how can you expect Sissy to support you? How can you even ask her when you slammed her so? You didn't slam anyone else, you didn't slam Briscoe, you slammed Sissy, to lead the young Chicanos out of her camp.' ... It was a mistake."[15]

Mark Smith, a lawyer from Lubbock, warned Chicano liberals that a vote for Muñiz would silence their already-muffled voice in the Democratic Party councils. It was a thinly veiled threat. Smith went on to put the future of the liberal wing of the state's Democratic Party on the shoulders of the Chicano community.

> A vote for La Raza Unida ... is nothing more than a vote for destruction of the liberal wing of the Democratic Party in Texas. It can only result in destroying any hope for a two-party state in which the Democratic Party is representative of the voice of the people and their aspirations for justice. Every Democrat must tell people why we cannot support La Raza Unida and the *vendidos*. This year we must hold our noses and vote the straight party ticket.[16]

In a letter to the editor of *The Texas Observer*, James Keller accused Gutiérrez of racism for having said, "We are pro-Chicano ... we want our own candidates ... we want South Texas." Such statements, said Keller, were tantamount to Anglos saying they wanted their own party. "It is unfortunate ... that the politics of racial division is still being practiced. If the raza is to be truly *unida*, then the raza must include us all, right down to the lowliest white liberal. *Viva la gente! Toda la gente!*"[17]

Some liberals, such as John Rhode of Irving, were supportive: "You bet I can't stomach Briscoe. You bet I'll vote for Muñiz. ... I hope to God there are thousands more like me."[18] Several university student-body presidents also endorsed Muñiz, along with Paul Moreno, state representative from El Paso, and Mickey Leland, a black Democrat running for state representative in Houston. Overall, though, Muñiz received little liberal support.[19] Most liberals chose to vote the party ticket or stay home. Even Chicano liberals who liked Muñiz chose the path of Paul Montemayor, well-known unionist from Corpus Christi, who said:

> Ramsey is a wonderful person, honest, sincere and intelligent. He is a fine, fine man and we're very proud of him. He is one of those who have become totally disgusted with the Demo-

cratic Party ... and all the crap we get from them. I think Ramsey will make a contribution ... [but] I myself will, of course, vote for the Democratic ticket.[20]

Montemayor's reaction was typical of most of the Chicano Democrats who held elective offices or who were integrated into the party structure. They liked a militant Chicano on the campaign trail who brought up legitimate concerns and issues, but they were not willing to sacrifice their own political futures to help. Most had gotten where they were through difficult struggles and only after paying their political dues for years. Many of them thought Muñiz would become a Democrat after he got the anger out of his system. It is possible that the Muñiz campaign would have been considered more seriously if it had been funded well. But Muñiz spent only a few thousand dollars statewide.

The funding of La Raza Unida Party, however, did become an issue in the campaign, with the Democrats charging that the Muñiz organization was receiving contributions from the Republicans. McGovern made the first major charge shortly after the national convention, as his supporters reacted negatively to the nonendorsement position of the national La Raza Unida Party. One rumor that circulated among Democrats was that La Raza Unida leaders had asked the McGovern campaign for a two-hundred-thousand-dollar contribution in exchange for an endorsement.[21] Another rumor said that the Committee to Re-elect the President (CREEP) had given Muñiz eight thousand dollars.[22] Muñiz denied it and so did Gutiérrez, but the charges resurfaced during the Watergate hearings in 1974 and throughout the 1974 gubernatorial campaign.

Gutiérrez did in fact meet with Republican officials on two or three occasions to discuss strategies of mutual benefit. He saw his balance-of-power approach as still the most beneficial, and he sought a guarantee from Republican officials that his grant proposals would be read and funded. He even got a team of Nixon administration bureaucrats to go to Crystal City and see the poverty there.[23]

Republicans had designs for La Raza Unida but were divided on methodology. One element in the GOP felt that Gutiérrez could be manipulated through bribes, and another believed that quiet, uncompromising support would prove the most fruitful. In a letter to Fred Malek, a member of the White House staff, Alex Armendáriz, of CREEP, wrote, "We have no way of publicly supporting this group [Raza Unida] without antagonizing Republicans and making La Raza Unida look as though they had sold out. At the same time, neither do we want to antagonize Raza Unida supporters and drive them back to their old position as Democrat voters."[24] The last sentence implied that Gutiérrez had already expressed his "wants."

This memorandum came one month after another Armendáriz wrote in which he reported being told by "various observers" that the issue of an eight-thousand dollar contribution to the Muñiz campaign had been brought up during a meeting outside the convention hall in El Paso. In return, the party would publicly condemn George McGovern. The memo did not specify who brought up the issue, who was in the meeting, or whether any arrangements had been made.[25] Yet it was this memorandum that was used repeatedly to accuse the party of having taken money from the Republicans. Even "Corky" Gonzáles eventually used it against the Texas party.

The Nixon campaign staff did attempt to bribe Gutiérrez. A member of the president's committee arrived in Crystal City with a briefcase full of money seeking not an endorsement but either neutrality or condemnation of the Democrats. "It was a lot more than the eight-thousand dollars I was accused of taking," Gutiérrez said later.[26] Gutiérrez rejected the money, probably because it would have been almost impossible for him to hide it and because in and of itself the money was not enough to do much for the poor county. Gutiérrez had no qualms about negotiating with the enemy, but only if it benefited la Raza.

What Gutiérrez did get was an assurance that Republican officials would help his grant proposals along. In the October 9, 1972, memo to Malek, Armendáriz recommended that an override of Governor Smith's veto of the Zavala County Health Corporation be sustained because, "should the poll gap tighten in Texas, the neutrality of La Raza Unida will be important." He then cited a Republican study indicating that nearly 70 percent of Mexican Americans in Texas approved of the party. He added:

> The fact that there are about 1 million Mexican American voters in Texas and that [Hubert] Humphrey won that state in 1968 by only 38,000 votes, substantiate the possible importance of La Raza Unida neutrality in this election ... The Zavala County grant provides us with an opportunity to support the party directly in a positive and legitimate manner.

Such an action is likely to strengthen their position of neutrality which is so politically beneficial to us.[27]

In another memo, dated September 14, 1972, Armendáriz noted that Gutiérrez had killed a "Dump Nixon" resolution introduced by the California delegation and which seemed to have had strong support among the delegates.

Ironically, the Raza Unida Texas Chapter had arrived at the convention ready to endorse McGovern if the Democrats agreed to several conditions. But McGovern made a mistake by first condemning the killing of Richard Falcón and then retracting his condemnation. It is unlikely, though, that the Texas chapter would have obtained the endorsement of McGovern from the national delegates.[28]

To the people in Crystal City, Gutiérrez explained that he had told both the Democrats and the Republicans what Mexican Americans needed, as was his responsibility as head of the national La Raza Unida Party. "Immediately after my visit [to CREEP]," he wrote in *La Verdad*, the party's local newspaper, ". . . they [Republicans] began to investigate our grant proposals that we had submitted to the government." Gutiérrez exonerated himself by implying that the Republicans had taken the initiative and sought to gain a neutrality which, he pointed out, was already there.[29]

Gutiérrez did do some serious negotiating. Shortly before the election, after the Zavala County Health Corporation had been approved but amended to include an advisory committee that would have brought some Anglos into the administration, Gutiérrez called Armendáriz and threatened to condemn the president publicly for insensitivity to the Mexican American community. The Republicans quickly responded to his demands by eliminating the advisory committee.[30]

Gutiérrez had kept his dealings with the Republicans quiet during the convention because of the large number of delegates who opposed any contact with the two parties. Gonzáles would have most likely been elected party chairman if the majority of delegates had known that Gutiérrez was dealing with the more conservative head of "the monster with two heads." For Gutiérrez, the negotiations with the Republicans were just one more step in his goal of Chicano empowerment. He saw no moral or philosophical conflict in condemning both parties and then opening fruitful dialogue with one of them. He also found nothing wrong with establishing agreements without letting the party leadership know.

The accusations of Republican support did not really hamper Muñiz's efforts. Lack of money proved to be the real problem. There were no funds for radio and television commercials, large signs, or massive mailings. Most of the traveling was done by car, and except for an occasional stop at a cheap motel, the campaigners stayed at supporters' homes. Every campaign stop had to pay for itself, and that meant a lot of tamales, beer selling, and passing around of the hat. Instead of large halls for rallies, Muñiz and the other candidates attended numerous backyard gatherings that drew as many as two hundred and fifty people. They were much like the *tardeadas*,[31] with music, food, and often performances by Chicano theater groups. At these gatherings the local party chapter had an opportunity to introduce its candidates or activists to a larger audience that Muñiz would attract. Often, professors or university students made educational presentations to *concientizar* (sensitize) the crowds about their history, their past, struggles and their culture. Participants received them well, particularly those in the lower classes, who saw their own lives lauded and glorified by young scholars anxious to organize them into a voting bloc. Muñiz was the main attraction at these backyard rallies, and he rarely disappointed the crowds.

By the end of the campaign Muñiz was frantically dashing from town to town and barrio to barrio. The other candidates were also blitzing the state, making sure that no part of it remained unattended. In one campaign day Fred Garza spoke in El Paso; Flores Anaya in Dallas, Fort Worth, and San Marcos; and Alma Canales in San Antonio and Waco. At the same time, Muñiz traveled to rallies in Odessa, San Angelo, and Dallas, a tour of three hundred miles.[32] At these stops the candidates passed out bumper stickers, buttons, leaflets, and party platforms. Nearly half a million pieces of political paraphernalia were distributed to try to make up for the party's inability to buy television and radio time for political advertisements.[33]

In the last two days before the election Muñiz made his final attacks on Briscoe. Talking to a crowd of about six hundred people in his hometown of Corpus Christi, he accused Briscoe of harboring "illegal aliens" in decrepit housing at the Catarina Ranch and paying them fifty cents an hour for farm labor. He also showed the crowd and reporters an affidavit from Luis Anaya, who delivered feed to the ranch three times a week. Anaya claimed that he "had seen a great number of illegal aliens from Mexico employed there as ranch hands." Muñiz showed photos taken by a Raza Unida free-lance photographer of the huts in which the workers lived. Said Muñiz, "All you have to do is go near the ranch and ask where the *mojados* (wetbacks) live and anyone will take you there."[34] In Laredo both Gutiérrez and Muñiz reiterated an earlier charge that Briscoe had undergone treatment for mental depression in 1971 under an assumed name. Gutiérrez challenged the Democrat to sue him if the charges were unfounded.[35]

On election day party leaders were predicting that Muñiz would receive seven hundred thousand votes. Gutiérrez, always the exaggerator, spearheaded the prophesying about the party's role in the election. They did such a good job that the morale of the campaign workers implied a possible victory, and some supporters actually believed that Muñiz could win. Emilio Zamora, a university student in Austin, later recalled that he and a friend were shocked by the possibility of a win. "What will we do if we win?" had been their reaction.[36] They would not have to worry.

The real worry belonged to the Democrats, who by now realized that they were in a fight for the governor's mansion. In the last three weeks of the campaign Grover's money and his hard-hitting television and radio spots had shifted momentum toward the Republicans. It seemed clear to the Democrats that Briscoe, a traditional, rural conservative, was going to have trouble keeping the urban centers in the Democratic column. It would be especially tough if Nixon's victory in Texas was an electoral avalanche, and most thought it would be. If the Republican took the cities, Briscoe would have to take the rural areas plus South Texas by a wide margin, and herein lay his fear of Muñiz and La Raza Unida Party. No one could predict Muñiz's impact on the race. The Chicano vote in South Texas could become the deciding factor in the governor's race, and no one knew how it would be divided.

On election day the voting results came in, as they usually did, with the Democrats taking an early lead. That trend lasted until nine P.M. when the returns began to show a move toward Grover, who caught and passed Briscoe before ten P.M. He kept that lead much of the night, which led to some early celebrating by Republicans and La Raza Unida supporters. Muñiz had said at the end of the campaign that he would either win or prove to be the balance of power in the state. Early in the night it became clear that he would not be a serious contender, but the chance for a Republican victory was encouraging. An upset would give the party a tremendous bargaining opportunity, regardless of the national convention's resolution not to negotiate. Unfortunately for the party and the Republicans, Briscoe made a surge at the end and slipped by Grover, capturing 47 percent of the vote total for a plurality of the votes cast. It was the lowest winning percentage in the state's history, and it made Democrats and Republicans take notice of the new Chicano third party.

Muñiz received 214,149 votes, or 6.28 percent of the vote, to Briscoe's 1,631,724 (47.8%) and Grover's 1,534,460 (45.08%).[37] When the disappointment over not causing an upset wore off, the party leaders were ecstatic about their showing. Muñiz told reporters, "The people . . . have experienced true democracy for the first time, a democracy they never experienced under the Republican or Democratic party."[38]

Some Mexican American politicians had predicted an insignificant showing for Muñiz and the other Raza Unida candidates. One even claimed that the party would not get 10 percent of the vote in the Mexican American districts. But Muñiz did get that and more. He received 51 percent of the total vote in Brooks County, 46 percent in Jim Hogg County, and 19 percent in Nueces County his home county. He defeated Grover in Duval, Kleberg, Jim Wells, Jim Hogg, Webb, Zapata, Kinney, La Salle, Maverick, Uvalde, Valverde, Brooks, Dimmit, and Zavala counties and lost to him by only fifty-four votes in Hidalgo County. Most of these counties were in South Texas and the Rio Grande Valley. Muñiz also won Zavala, Brooks, and Jim Hogg counties against Briscoe but lost the other twelve predominantly Mexican American counties in South Texas to him.[39] In the fifteen-county area Muñiz received 30,020 votes to Grover's 31,641 and Briscoe's 60,697.[40]

In the urban areas Muñiz's percentage was lower but his vote total was higher. In San Antonio he received 32,121 votes; in Dallas, 21,962; in Austin, 21,964; in Houston, 18,970; and in Corpus Christi, 15,281. In the eighteen major metropolitan centers outside the South Texas area, Muñiz garnered enough votes to claim 38 percent of the ethnic vote.[41] In some of the university towns, such as Austin (University of Texas), Waco (Baylor), Lubbock (Texas Tech), and Bryan (Texas A&M), he received support from young Anglo voters.

Notwithstanding the support Muñiz received, it was Briscoe who benefited the most from the Mexican American vote. He lost every major urban center in the state except San Antonio and El Paso, two cities with large numbers of Mexican American voters. Briscoe won El Paso and San Antonio over Grover by 25,000 votes and South Texas by 29,000. That was a 54,000-vote advantage. The other share of his 97,164-vote margin was provided by West Texas and East Texas rural areas.[42]

There are many reasons why Briscoe did well in those areas, but the primary one was that Texas politics had been dominated since the days of Reconstruction by rural conservatives. The legislative districts were gerrymandered in ways that gave the less-populated rural areas greater representation than the major urban centers. Most Texans lived in cities, but the rural populations had a larger share of the congressmen, state representatives, and state senators. The power of the large landholders and oil producers, as well as the ability of the rural areas to deliver solid votes for particular candidates or slates of candidates, were the major factors in their legislative imbalance. Small-town politics was an art in Texas. When Lyndon Johnson ran for the U.S. Senate, he won on questionable returns from South Texas. He trailed throughout the night but pulled ahead at the last minute. The last two counties to deliver the exact votes he needed to win were Jim Hogg and Duval.[43] Duval was literally ruled by the family of George Parr, a political ally of Johnson. The Parrs were known to deliver almost 100 percent of the Mexican American vote in any election. Though practically tyrants in their counties, they had befriended the Mexican Americans when other Anglos had not. This kind of vote delivery was characteristic of many all-Anglo rural counties as well.[44]

Conservative Democrats could count on the rural counties to come through for them in overwhelming numbers. That is one reason why many rural politicians held top positions in the legislature and the state government. With political power came the spoils. Not only could conservative Democrats give state jobs, contracts, and valuable "inside" information, but they could also take them away. And they were quick to retaliate, as Republicans and liberal Democrats found when they tried to force an investigation of the people involved in the Sharpstown scandal.[45]

It is surprising, then, that Muñiz received as many votes as he did. One reason might have been that the Republicans were also keeping an eye on the Democrats' questionable methods. Nonetheless, the powerful Democratic machine created numerous problems in the rural as well as urban voting polls. In some precincts paper ballots ran out as early as one o'clock P.M., in others evidence emerged that "dead people" were casting votes. In Crystal City two hundred absentee ballots, folded identically, were mailed from the same area and arrived the same day. In San Antonio, the lower Rio Grande Valley, and Dallas La Raza Unida's candidates were left off some ballots. And the usual intimidation tactics witnessed in the 1970 election were also evident.[46]

In the end, though, the biggest obstacle to the Raza Unida candidates proved to be the lever and the *X* at the top of the paper ballot. For years the Democratic Party had taught its members to pull the lever at the top of the voting machine or punch the *X* at the top of the paper ballot to vote for the entire slate. This was particularly effective as a strategy in San Antonio and El Paso. Mexican American voters first pulled the lever and then tried to vote for the few Raza Unida candidates on the ballot, not realizing that their vote had already been cast for the Democratic slate.[47] Said one Raza Unida candidate, "Many of our people would have voted for our candidates had we taken the time to educate them about that bastardly little lever on top."[48]

The conservative Democrats were not the only ones making the most of the lever. McGovern's supporters also took advantage of confused voters. They passed out leaflets urging a vote for the Democrat on one side and on the other a vote for La Raza Unida candidates. Since there were no instructions on how to split the votes, some Mexican Americans pulled the lever next to McGovern's name and locked in votes for the whole Democratic slate. This happened in San Antonio and South Texas.[49]

All these tactics lowered the party's vote total, but they could not account for the disparity of votes between Muñiz and the rest of the slate. Alma Canales received 88,811 votes to Bill Hobby's 1,734,835; Rubén Solis, Jr., 83,299 to Jesse James's 1,239,877; Fred Garza, 106,397 to Byron Tunnell's 1,392,552; and Flores Anaya, 41,946 to John Tower's 1,365,708. In Robstown, twenty-nine miles west of Corpus Christi, Muñiz received 33 percent of the vote, but the other candidates received less than 10 percent. In most areas with strong Mexican American voting patterns, the other candidates received less than 10 percent of the vote. The electoral thrashing of La Raza Unida appeared more evident in races involving Mexican American Democrats. In a Nueces County commissioner's race, for example, Democrat Solomón Ortíz defeated RUP's Lupe Youngblood nine to one. Paul Longoria, Democrat, defeated

Ricardo Molina in Molina's hometown of Brownsville by a margin of 17 to 2 for a state senate seat.[50] It was much the same in the other local races statewide that pitted Mexican American Democrats against Raza Unida candidates.

One bright spot was the race for state representative on San Antonio's west side, where Albert Peña III received nearly 35 percent of the vote. It is likely that his high vote total resulted from his father's prominence and the fact that he, like Muñiz, ran a more traditional race. As a lawyer with a private practice, he also seemed more credible than other RUP candidates.

In spite of the defeats of most of the local, regional, and state candidates, the party did consolidate its gains in Zavala and La Salle counties. In Crystal City the party won the sheriff's and county attorney's offices and two of three county commissioner seats, but it lost the tax collector's position and two of three constable posts. In La Salle it won two county wide races.

Although not the balance of power, the party, as far as the leaders were concerned, did become the tangible third force in Texas electoral politics. Mexican Americans now had a choice, and La Raza Unida activists were sure the people would choose them. In two years the party had obtained two hundred thousand votes, two counties under Chicano rule, a host of young and dedicated organizers, a rising political star, and the driver's seat of the movimiento. With these achievements, the party shifted its focus toward the community level. Local, nonpartisan, elections were in April, and party leaders intended to be ready.

We've been oppressed so long,
and been stepped on by so
many people, that we have too
many streams of prostituted
thought.

We have too many ideologies.
They range . . . from the
cultural nationalists who would
like to see us in Mayan and
Aztec dress, to the super militants
who wear buttons like boy scouts
wear merit badges.

—José Angel Gutiérrez, speaking in Houston, 1974

UNIDOS VENCEREMOS:
The National Party Falters

For those who left the national RUP convention unhappy over Gutiérrez's victory, the struggle for the leadership of the third-party movement had not ended. They had been outmaneuvered but not beaten, and they looked forward to the next confrontation at the Congreso de Aztlán meeting at Albuquerque in November. In the meantime, though, they took time to embarrass an old ally.

Shortly after leaving the convention Tijerina, anxious to smooth over the differences and head off any possible ideological split in the Chicano Movement, called for a Chicano National Congress for Land and Cultural Reform in Albuquerque on October 21–22. "Unity Before Ideas, Leaders or Organizations" served as the major theme, and immediately it became the first point of contention.[1] Gutiérrez attended, but Gonzales refused to go and sent a letter to Tijerina stating that his uncompromising philosophy prevented him from sharing the platform with government bureaucrats and other mainstream activists:

In the past years I have disassociated myself from those people who confuse and mislead the gullible members of our Raza. I can no longer bargain with despotic government representatives; I want no type of alignment with political prostitutes; I have no intention of creating reaction for the profitable benefit of the professional program managers. I agree on

135

total unity. Total unity based on the ideals of liberation of the mass of our people.[2]

Gonzales nonetheless wished Tijerina well. But some of his people were not so tolerant and they came prepared to resist any kind of coalition with the Chicano middle-class liberals who were invited to make presentations.

Tijerina did not see the movement as anyone's to control, at least not in a sectarian way, though he stood ready to regain the leadership that he felt he once had. In early 1972 he told a reporter, "There will be no doubt as to who is to lead the Indo-Hispanos in the Southwest. José Angel will tell you who. It doesn't have to come out of my mouth. It's a role that is developed around you. If history and the forces of nature put me there, how can I back out?"[3] Tijerina wanted to avoid politics at the conference in order to consolidate Chicano support on the land-grant issue, which he had championed for more than a decade. The Mexican government under Luis Echeverría Alvarez seemed willing to talk about its failure in dealing with the Treaty of Guadalupe-Hidalgo, and there were more middle-class supporters for Tijerina's Alianza. If he could unite the more militant activists with the liberal Chicanos in government, he believed he could force the nation's citizenry to feel the same remorse and sympathy for the Alianza it had felt regarding the black civil rights struggle and the farm workers' grape and lettuce boycotts. At the national RUP convention Tijerina had told the delegates in a fatherly fashion:

> There is a powerful expression of our yearnings. But now that we have the revolutionary spirit, we must not lose sight of the brotherhood awareness. Temper the revolutionary spirit. Cultural identification is needed, but we must not let it lead us to hatred. We can become intoxicated and lose sight of our real goal to fully participate in the political system of the United States.[4]

The Raza Unida activists who attended the conference in Albuquerque were not interested in being part of the political system of the United States, nor were they interested in sacrificing ideology for the sake of unity. The Raza Unida Party was a political party with the same aim as other political parties: to gain control. Party officials did not see any benefit in coalescing with Democrats, bureaucrats, or activists more interested in causes than political control. They wanted control of the Southwest to build Aztlán, and Tijerina had already rejected the notion of a brown nation while he was in jail awaiting one of his many court appearances. At that time he said angrily, "I am not for separatism from the United States. My motto is justice, but not independence from or revolution against the United States."[5] But for the Raza Unida activists the days of an ideologically heterogeneous movimiento were over. In their view the RUP stood as the only legitimate vehicle for Chicano empower-ment, and other Chicanos would have to choose between it and the rest of the movement.

From the first day the Albuquerque meeting became em-broiled in controversy. Many of the participants did not like the "let's-study-the-problem-approach" of some of the more moderate workshop narrators. They also resented the expensive conference programs and soft drinks and the new convention center, which Tijerina had rented for two thousand dollars. During the evening session a Brown Beret from California announced that David Sán-chez was no longer the national chairman for the Berets. Typical of many Chicano conferences, this one became a hodgepodge of divi-sive discussions on numerous issues rather than the well-organized meeting Tijerina had envisioned. By the late evening some of the party members had moved to pass several resolutions, one of which called for recognizing RUP as the official voice of the Chicano National Congress. The maneuvering by party activists of-fended some in attendance, and Tijerina moved quickly to block any take-over of the conference. He first tried to belittle them by calling them *niños [que] no saben nada* (children who know nothing), but when the debate at the platform got heated he de-nounced the party. "The Partido de La Raza Unida wasn't with me in Tierra Amarilla [where he made his famous courthouse raid]," he told them. Then he added, "If you want to take over, you can pay the $2000 for this place."[6]

Gutiérrez, who earlier had admitted some discomfort with the theme of "Unity Before Ideas" but who wanted to avoid offend-ing Tijerina, attempted to assure the New Mexico leader that the party had not conspired to take over the conference. Tijerina did not accept the explanation and walked off the platform and out of the Congress, leaving the party in charge. Juan José Peña of New Mexico, a friend of Tijerina before and after the conference, took over as acting chairman.[7] When Tijerina left, so did the majority of the people. By the Sunday session only a quarter of the participants remained. Tijerina called the Congress a failure and accused Gonzales of being responsible for the undermining. "I am disappointed in Corky. . . . I wouldn't be surprised to learn that he wanted the Congreso to fail."[8] After that conference the three main militant activists of the Chicano Movement—Tijerina, Gutiérrez, and Gonzales—never again met or stood together in a show of unity. In a span of two months Gonzales's sympathizers had "unwelcomed" César Chávez to the national convention and had driven Tijerina out of the party. In November they congregated again to do the same to Gutiérrez at the meeting of the Congreso de Aztlán in Albuquerque. Gonzales did not attend because he was not a member.

Two problems quickly arose in Albuquerque. Most of the delegates from the ten states that were able to send representatives wanted to establish a hierarchy of officers. The national convention had opted, because of a lack of time, to adopt Gutiérrez's idea of establishing a Consejo de Aztlán, a three-member board of advisers to the chairman. Gutiérrez appointed Peña, Salomón Baldenegro (Arizona), and Hernán Baca (California) to the Consejo. Colorado was deliberately left off, and the Corkistas came ready to change that at the first meeting. The second problem arose when each active state chapter received a designated organizing area, and Texas got Louisiana and Alabama instead of the Midwest, which Gutiérrez wanted and most likely deserved.[9] The Midwest had thousands of potential recruits, but the South had few Chicanos.

Gutiérrez helped polarize the meeting by bringing his own proposals, which called for the chairman to be the sole officer in the Congreso and the only authorized spokesman. He refused to listen to the majority's wish for a slate of officers and so was defeated in the vote taken.[10] In the debate over the issue Gutiérrez remarked that he would ignore the new officers. Later, in a letter to the Congreso delegates, he accused the members of five states of conducting "private elections."[11] Confusion over what happened at the meeting seemed to have settled in quickly afterward. In an article written for *El Gallo*, the Crusade for Justice's newspaper, Tito Lucero of California stated that Gutiérrez had walked out, taking with him a number of other delegates, but a quorum remained and conducted an election for new officers. He added that Gutiérrez simply asked to be told of the elections because he had to leave for pressing business in Texas.[12] Peña remembered it differently years later. Gutiérrez, according to Peña, stayed through the election and left only after the disagreement on the organizing areas. With him went the quorum. Still another version came from Gutiérrez, who said he left because of an impending storm that would have prevented his return to Texas. He claimed to have adjourned the meeting, however.[13]

The move to give the Texas chapter the organizing rights to states outside the Southwest and Midwest was a blatant attempt by the Colorado delegation to eliminate the Gutierrista influence in the national party. Although a majority of the national La Raza Unida Party membership seemed to support Gutiérrez and his vision of the party, the more active ideologues tended to back Gonzales. Many in these groups had become radicalized during the Chicano student movement of the late 1960s and had begun making the transition from nationalism to internationalism and socialism. Gutiérrez saw this trend as ludicrous because it tended to defuse the struggle in the barrio. In a letter that appeared in the November–December 1973 issue of *La Gente*, he wrote:

In the last few months we have seen declarations from California and Colorado that defend the struggle for a free Puerto Rico, in support of Lucio Cabañas, Angela Davis, Cuba, Africa, etc. . . . It would be better to defend one's own first. The reality is that our people comprehend very little and care even less about Cuba, Cabañas, Africa or Puerto Rico. Our people want relief here and now. Capitalism begins its dehumanizing process here with us. When we struggle here, we help the movements in other countries. In becoming strong here, we weaken the enemy over there.

The rhetoric of Marxism [and] socialism may serve to stimulate some, but the greater numbers will be attracted to our struggle by actions and not words. Everyone can be a spit revolutionary but few are fighters for the Raza day-after-day.

My words are useless to those states [California and Colorado]. But then, if they want a revolutionary party let them form it. If they want a socialist party let them join with others that now exist. If they want an international movement let them continue to meddle in other parts of the world. For my part, I have no need to concern myself with them.[14]

The Colorado RUP quickly responded, accusing Gutiérrez of using the "party's strength and reputation to promote counter-revolutionary thought, to promote under-the-table politics for monetary gain and to literally bargain with the respect and dignity of our people."[15]

Gutiérrez called another meeting of the Congreso in September 1973. This time, though, he informed only the delegates from the Midwest, a decision that angered the state chapters of California, Colorado, and New Mexico, which found out about it from *compañeros* in the Midwest. Gutiérrez later claimed that it was a regional meeting, but the excluded activists did not believe him. They arrived at the caucus, where another major verbal fight ensued, and the meeting adjourned after the Illinois delegation introduced a proposal to do away with the position of national Congreso chairman. Following that fiasco the Colorado party called a Congreso de Aztlán conference, where it refused to recognize Gutiérrez's role in the national party. Gonzales accused the Texas chapter of taking money from the Republicans and called for its ouster from the national structure. After that conference the Colorado party members did not attend any more Congreso meetings. The last one was held in 1979, although by 1975 the Congreso was an entity in name only.[16]

Because of the factionalism, plans to raise money and locate space for the national office never materialized, even though Gutiérrez did open a bank account in the Westside Bank of San Antonio. Also, Colorado and some chapters in California never accepted Gutiérrez as head of the party. They claimed that his election as chairman of the Congreso did not make him head of the party, but simply made him a member of the organization that would help develop the structure and philosophy of the national party.[17] Gutiérrez disagreed and in time began to call himself the national president of El Partido de la Raza Unida.

While most of the state chapters jockeyed for position on one side or the other, the New Mexico RUP managed to stay in the middle, if not totally neutral. There were two factions in New Mexico, as in almost every other state, but Peña managed to keep them in line and involved in local issues. As a whole, the state party shared most of Gonzales's political and philosophical views and was one of the first chapters to proclaim itself socialist. But in approach and organizational technique, the New Mexican party members were closer to the *Tejanos* than those of any other state chapter, perhaps because of their proximity to the Lone Star State and because Peña leaned toward Gutiérrez's camp. Besides Texas, the party in New Mexico was the most active of all the state chapters in terms of electoral efforts. It also founded local grassroots organizations in the manner of Ciudadanos Unidos and Familias Unidas, although never with the same degree of success.

Party activity came to the state in the summer of 1972 when Gutiérrez visited New Mexico Highlands University at the invitation of Pedro Rodríguez, a professor who had been active in the Texas party before coming to Las Vegas, New Mexico. Rodríguez became the first county chairman for the RUP in San Miguel County, and Peña became vice-chairman. Manuel Archuleta, who was to play a major role in the state organization was also one of the founders.

The state of New Mexico had three major population regions: south, central, and north. The southern Mexican Americans were recent arrivals from Mexico, or first- and second-generation Americans, and they proved to be rather passive politically. The central area's population was a mixed group and more middle class, thus not as ready to get involved in third-party activities. In the northern part of the state generations-old families predominated. There were few Anglos in this part of New Mexico. This was also an area where Tijerina's alliance was the strongest, especially among the rural people. But Mexican Americans in this part of the "Land of Enchantment" had a history of registering to vote and most had rigid partisan preferences, thus depriving the party of a large reservoir of potential voters. Because of their active participation in politics, New Mexicans had elected many Mexican Americans to local and statewide offices.[18] This fact diminished the attraction of an all-Chicano party, which in itself had been a successful recruiting tool in other states. Particularly in the north, but also true almost everywhere else, Chicano Democrats were in charge. Some were liberal, though few if any played more than a caretaker's role in government. Others developed small dynasties reminiscent of rural Mexico and South Texas. The concept of a third party was also not new in the state. In 1890 El Partido del Pueblo Unido (The United People's Party) began a short but extremely successful existence during which it elected most of its candidates in San Miguel County.[19] In 1968 New Mexicans again witnessed a third party, this one founded by Tijerina's Alianza Federal de Pueblos Libres. The Partido Constitucional del Pueblo (The People's Constitutional Party, or PCP) ran candidates for statewide office in 1968 and 1970 but failed to have any major impact on the elections, although it did help liberalize the state's campaign laws.[20]

The RUP began its electoral campaign in 1972 by running candidates for San Miguel County offices. It also ran candidates for the East Las Vegas school board. In both races the party avoided running against Chicanos in order not to be seen as trying to split the ethnic vote. None of the RUP candidates came close to winning, though they did receive nearly 25 percent of the vote. The next significant race came in the Las Vegas 1974 municipal elections, in which Peña ran for mayor and five other party members for four council seats and the police magistrate's office. Instead of running as Raza Unida members, they ran under the name of the Pueblo Unido (United People). Two other slates ran for office: the Greater Las Vegas Ticket, composed of moderate Chicanos, and the United Citizens, a coalition of conservative Chicanos and Anglos. Peña received 8 percent of the vote and none of the candidates in his slate did any better, but their presence brought about the election of two Anglo candidates over the moderate Chicanos by fewer than fifty votes.[21]

It became obvious from the start that the New Mexico Raza Unida Party would have to convert many Democrats in order to win. And the conversion would have to be ideological and not based necessarily on ethnicity or culture, although that strategy did work with some of the youthful activists in the state. Party ideology, then, became the major concern for the party leaders. Charged with that responsibility were Peña and Archuleta, who, though friends, tended to lean in slightly different directions. Archuleta became a sectarian socialist and eventually joined the Socialist Workers Party, while Peña, by his own admission, was a nationalist with Christian Socialist ideas. They also split in their allegiance in the Gonzales versus Gutiérrez struggle. For the first few years, however, they united to lead an active and ideologically-focused party. That ideology resembled Gonzales's revolutionary nationalism but with a greater commitment to electoral organizing and more emphasis on coalition building.

Peña was a soft-spoken intellectual without much of Gonzales's inciting rhetoric or Gutiérrez's suave charisma. His humble demeanor hid the fact that he was a decorated infantry soldier in Vietnam and a prolific writer of political and philosophical position papers. He debated anyone anywhere and rarely resorted to scathing language to win an argument. These characteristics made him a valuable mediator in the Congreso but never accorded him a major status outside New Mexico in a movement dominated by vociferous, domineering men. At home he served as the intellectual and administrative head of the party, but at times he found it difficult to restrain the more militant of its members, who often sought confrontations with the authorities. When Rodríguez became ill and left his position as head of ethnic studies at New Mexico Highlands, Peña replaced him and found the economic stability to continue his activism. Unfortunately, the obstacles to the party's growth were larger than its resources and capabilities, and the New Mexico chapter's role was relegated to that of a pressure group. The party's message never penetrated the political tradition of many New Mexicans who, even while they were supportive of the party's causes, continued to cast their votes for the Democrats.

La Raza Unida in California faced even greater problems, and by the spring of 1974 the party had declined to the point where it was no longer seen as an electoral threat except in a few rural communities in Southern California. The party's efforts to get on the state ballot were a failure. By January 1974, almost three years after the drive for registering members began, the party still fell nearly forty-six thousand voters short of the required sixty-six thousand.[22] The year before, on October 1973, the party's first central committee had held its inaugural meeting and had come away still split on the degree of centralization for the state's chapters. Few localities seemed anxious to give away their autonomy.

The major reason for the lack of unity had not changed from the one debated before the national convention. The chapters were still divided among Gutierristas and Corkistas, and also a variety of Marxist strains, and the tolerance they had for each other was dissipating rapidly. The Labor Committee of Los Angeles, which had been organized to develop a unionist wing in the party, was an avowed Marxist chapter and, along with the Lincoln-Boyle Heights chapter, purposely dragged its feet on the registration drive and kept arguing at the state conferences that elections were reformist."[23] Several northern chapters shared this view and also spent little energy in getting voters registered. When the number of registered Raza Unida Party members was announced in January 1974 as part of a lawsuit the party was filing against the state of California, many of the organizers were disappointed and discouraged with the low figures, and within the year several of the chapters ceased to exist.[24]

Besides ideology, the composition of the membership created

problems for the party. Students and university employees made up a majority of the core membership, and nearly all the leadership positions were filled by them. At the founding of the party this proved an asset because students had more time, were harder to intimidate, possessed more skills, and their mobility could get them to all the meetings. Many of the students also had working-class origins, which helped them identify with those in the barrio. At the same time, the large number of students presented numerous challenges that, when unmet, and most were not, thwarted the party's efforts to recruit more members and to become more efficient. In most chapters the number of students ranged from 30 to 80 percent of the membership, with the most active local parties being the ones most predominantly student-oriented.[25] The major problems with the students were three-fold: they lacked experience in dealing with the system they were trying to change; they lacked maturity in completing assignments and dealing with people in the barrio; and they were easily discouraged and could be depended on only as long as they were in school.

Most of the students were not familiar with the political process and often spent more energy arguing the unfairness of the electoral system than trying to get the necessary voters registered. They were naive about how to attract people to a political party, and consequently they debated more than persuaded. Few of them understood that for many Chicanos the joining of a political party or changing from one to another was not a decision to be taken lightly. Jobs, careers, political offices, and friendships were things to be considered before a change could be made. For some students it was as easy as saying "You are either with us or against us," and they became frustrated when the people did not understand the theories or were not impressed with the rhetoric. Their reactions caused many people to feel that the students were condescending and immature. Because most of the students were from out of town, the local residents also considered them unreliable and transient. A good number of the students did not stay in the party once they graduated or left the university to look for jobs. Another large group of them dropped out of the party's activities when they did not see any victories on the horizon. The few who stayed created problems because they were not interested in doing the day-to-day, unglamorous busy work needed to keep the party functioning. They wanted protests, boycotts, marches, political

*Raul Ruiz kneels beside a man shot during the
police riot that followed the 1970 Chicano
Moratorium march in Los Angeles. Photo courtesy
of* La Raza Magazine.

During a lull the three major figures at the national La Raza Unida Party convention discuss strategy. Reies López Tijerina, second from left; Rodolfo "Corky" Gonzales, to Tijerina's left; and José

Angel Gutiérrez leaning across the table at right. At left is Juan José Peña, leader of the New Mexico delegation. The man with the sunglasses accompanied Gonzales. Photo courtesy of El Paso Herald.

José Angel Gutiérrez and Rodolfo "Corky" Gonzales shortly after RUP delegates elected the Texas leader national party chairman.

Young man holds up a Raza Unida Party flag during a march and rally in Los Angeles. Photo courtesy of La Raza Magazine.

*Rodolfo "Corky" Gonzales (R.) and César Chávez
during a rally in support of the farm workers's union
organizing activities (date unknown). Photo courtesy
of* La Raza Magazine.

*José Angel Gutiérrez (L.), Reies López Tijerina (C.)
and Rodolfo "Corky" Gonzales in a show of unity
during the Raza Unida Party national convention.
Photo courtesy of Juan R. García.*

José Angel Gutiérrez (L.) stands next to a party poster during a Ciudadanos Unidos fund raiser.

A meeting of the Familias Unidas organization in Robstown, Texas. Photo by Stephen Casanova.

*José Angel Gutiérrez and Luz during the height of
La Raza Unida's power in Crystal City.*

A group of students from Cotulla show support for boycotting students in Crystal City.

Crystal City RUP members march to commemorate the 10th anniversary of the school walkout that led to the party's founding.

Members of Ciudadanos Unidos march in 1979 in celebration of the 10th anniversary of the organization's founding in Crystal City.

Ramsy Muñiz campaigns under a bridge near Uvalde, Texas during 1972 gubernatorial campaign.

CARACOL

octubre
25¢

CAMPAÑA
DEL
'74: POR
CARLOS
RENE
GUERRA

Carlos Rene Guerra, Muñiz's 1974 campaign manager, on the cover of Caracol *magazine. Photo courtesy of* Caracol *magazine.*

A march by the United Farm Workers Organizing Committee in the Rio Grande Valley. Antonio Orendain, middle of the photo in black outfit, later formed the

Texas Farm Workers Union with help from Raza Unida members in Muleshoe, Texas. Photo by Alan Pogue.

Ramsey Muñiz arrives at Nueces County jail after being arrested by Mexican police for jumping bail in Corpus Christi. Photo courtesy of Corpus Christi Caller-Times.

A Raza Unida Party delegation meets with Palestine Liberation Organization leader Yasser Arafat in Beirut, Lebanon. From left: Larry Hill, N.M.; Frank Schafer-Corona, Washington, D.C.; Juan José Peña, *N.M.; Danny Osuna, Calif.; Yasser Arafat; Rebecca Hill, N.M.; Tony González, Calif.; Miguel Pérez, Calif.; Eddie Canales, Tex.; and Fred St. John, N.M.*

Immigration conference workshop discussion. From left: Mario Compean, Texas RUP; Antonio Rodríguez, CASA-HGT; Jorge Bustamante, Mexican immigration scholar; and Pedro Camejo, Socialist Workers Party. Photo by Stephen Casanova.

Mario Compean with his father and family during a campaign fund raiser at Rodríguez Park in San Antonio in the summer of 1978.

Mario Compean (C.) conducts a meeting in Mexico City with El Partido Socialista de los Trabajadores (PST) in 1978. Other RUP leaders attending are Miguel Pérez (behind Compean); José Calderón, Colorado, to Pérez's right; and María Elena Martínez, Texas, far right.

debates, and confrontations, and these activities formed only a small part of the party's daily affairs.

Students nevertheless played an important role in the early years of the party, particularly in the electoral campaigns of Raúl Ruiz, which turned out to be the most significant ones the party conducted in California. Ruiz first ran in 1971 for the 48th State Assembly District, which included a large part of Echo Park in the Los Angeles area. The district had eighty-thousand registered voters, fifty thousand of whom were Democrats and 18 percent Spanish-surnamed. The election was to fill the vacancy left when the incumbent, David Roberti, was elected to the California state senate. In a four-person runoff Ruiz received 2,778 votes, or 7 percent, compared to the Democrat's 42 percent and the Republican's 46 percent. The Peace and Freedom candidate received 3 percent. The Republican victory was a major upset because the Democrat, Richard Alatorre, was expected to win handily. The party quickly took credit for the defeat of Alatorre, claiming that the Mexican American community had split its vote between the Democrat and Ruiz.[26]

The second Ruiz campaign took place the following year when he ran for the 40th State Assembly District, which lay just outside East Los Angeles, against incumbent Alex García. He received 13 percent of the vote, which disappointed many campaign workers, who expected more support from an area of town that seemed so in need of an independent voice. Writing in the February 1973 issue of *La Raza Magazine*, which he had founded, Ruiz stated:

> No matter how we rationalized, it was a disappointment not to receive more votes—especially from the Chicano community. There was not a single precinct that actually came close to giving us a majority. This ... was ... true in the Chicano community.
>
> García certainly was not a strong incumbent. . . . He was probably the weakest ... García does not speak good Spanish and says little or nothing substantial in English. . . . Then why did he win and why did he win so big, especially in the barrios? Another question we have to ask ourselves is "If we did not win, did we actually succeed in politicizing or educating the community of their socio-political condition?"
>
> It means ... that we have a difficult road ahead. We cannot

expect to do away with a political party that has been using and confusing our people for many years ... with a few months of campaign activity. I think it presumptuous, and, as a matter of fact, insulting that we should consider our people's beliefs so lightly.

The people might be wrong in their assessment of the Democratic Party but they nevertheless believe in it and support it with their votes. Our people have formed a traditional voting pattern as strong as their religious pattern. One could say that a Mexican is born a Catholic and a Democrat, neither of those institutions really serve him but he strongly defends and supports them ... The fact of the matter is that we not only lost but we failed to politicize the people to any meaningful depth ... We failed to recognize that new registrants, whether young or old do not necessarily create a dependable bloc of ... votes. ... Many will register because it's different, others because of emotionalism, others because you happen to ask them, and others because they were confused. A very small fraction registered into the party because of a definite political consciousness to create social change.

Our *partido* is not as our name states but rather, it is a goal that all of us should strive to attain.

La Raza Unida is still a dream.[27]

Ruiz's almost brutal honesty offended some. Ideology served few purposes for him, nor did he see it as his mission to "educate the people" or engage in revolutionary debates. "I'm not going to bull-shit people about Plan de Aztlán and crap like that," he told *La Voz del Pueblo*. "People don't understand what the hell you're talking about. When people say, *No tenemos trabajo, hombre* (We don't have a job). *No tenemos educación* (We are not educated). *Me maltrataron a mis hijos* (They mistreated my children), that's real."[28]

From outside California and from the perspective of a national party, Ruiz had seemed the natural statewide leader, but he never became more than a local leader with a movement-wide reputation. His aggressive approach, his criticism of works such as the Plan de Aztlán, the Chicano Manifesto, and his tendency to dismiss sectarian ideological debates made him enemies in almost every camp. Aside from Ruiz, only Bert Corona and Hernán Baca commanded enough respect to have become statewide leaders, but Corona became inactive quite early and Baca was identified too closely with Gutiérrez in a state where Gonzales was the preferred leader. Without a dominant leadership, as there was in Texas, Colorado, and New Mexico, the California Raza Unida Party splintered into small, ideologically diverse groups with little popular support. The Los Angeles Labor Committee went one step further, uniting with a dissident group from New Mexico to form the August Twenty-ninth Movement (ATM), which called for the reconquest of Aztlán through any means possible, including armed struggle. For several years the group spent a great deal of energy attacking the "reformist tendencies" of the La Raza Unida Party mainstream, as they considered themselves the vanguard of the party and the movement.[29]

In one year the national La Raza Unida Party nearly succumbed to internal strife, and of its major supporting chapters, three were either alienated, splintered, or unable to provide assistance and the fourth was willing to let it die a quiet death.[30] Baldenegro, of Arizona, years later blamed the leaders' dissimilarity and regionalism for the breakup of the national party. "They were all very intelligent batos [men] . . . but none of them liked to be told what to do in their areas. They were all very independent and that kept them apart."[31]

The real culprits, though, were Gutiérrez and Gonzales, who were unwilling to compromise on their concepts of El Partido de la Raza Unida, a party both claimed to have founded. Each presented a world view counter to the other's, and both sought the mantel of leadership with a passion. In the end they distrusted each other more than the Anglo power structure they fought. The bitterness with which they attacked each other defeated any move toward unity and provided political ammunition to critics eager to assault the party and the movement from the outside. Federal informers and agents found the atmosphere conducive to fomenting disunity and distrust. Misinformation circulated by these agents as well as by hostile mainstream newspapers was often accepted as truth by rival Chicano groups. Federal surveillance was not unique to the Chicano Movement, as even moderate Mexican American groups had been the target of J. Edgar Hoover's prying, but the spying had evolved from simply monitoring dissidents to disrupting activities.[32]

Such government interference caused some of the more emotionally and philosophically unstable members and organizers, especially in California and Colorado, to become proponents of violence and race hate. In 1973 two Anglo organizers from the

Socialist Workers Party were severely beaten by members of Gonzales's Crusade for Justice when they attempted to make contact. The SWP leadership called on other movement organizations to criticize the action. Many did, including the New Mexico RUP, and this reaction caused Gonzales to isolate himself even more from the other Chicano groups.[33] In the meantime, Gutiérrez and most of the other Texas leaders had become less enthusiastic about national politics. The upcoming 1974 campaign and the early electoral victories in rural Texas attracted most of the party's time and energy. Not until Peña took over the party chairmanship in 1976 did the national party again assume an active role in the Chicano social struggle, a role much reduced from what had been envisioned at the national conference.

Today Aztlán
Tomorrow the world

—Roberto Muñiz

THE PARTY CONSOLIDATES
IN RURAL TEXAS

Both urban and rural communities were supposed to be targets for Texas Raza Unida organizers, but only the rural towns really fit into the immediate future of the party. The Crystal City experience in political organizing proved to be of little help in the urban areas. Races there required large amounts of money, mainstream political endorsements, and large-scale electoral machines, none of which the Raza candidates could claim to possess. In most of the cities they did not have any of the three. The thousands of votes Muñiz received in the urban areas were a potential base for the future, but for the present the identities of the majority of those who had cast them were unknown. In contrast to the metropolitan areas, most rural towns seemed ripe for an electoral revolution. There was organizing activity of some kind in nearly every county in South Texas and in parts of West Texas.

There were two reasons for this compatibility of the party with rural areas. First, it was easier to gain political control in small towns with few voters and a predominantly Mexican American population. Here the limited geography meant that candidates and their supporters could canvass all the precincts personally, and a truck with a loud-speaker would do as well as or better than radio or television spots. The issues were simpler to define and easier to articulate. Also, family networks could be effectively used to get out the vote or to work the polling places. Second, the most experienced organizers were from the rural areas, where they had been recruited in the South Texas colleges and universities during MAYO's most active years. Although the party had no ongoing training program for organizers, MAYO had had one in the past. Many of these organizers were already veterans of school boycotts, picket lines, demonstrations, and litigation. Consequently, these activists had significant contacts with the people in the barrios and were popular in certain sectors of their neighborhoods. They were also likely to be a part of the family networks already in place in the rural areas.

The rural strategy came straight from the Crystal City model: use nationalism as a unifying theme, polarize the town, discredit the vendidos, register voters, and get them out on election day. Along with Crystal City, Cotulla in La Salle County had been one of the earliest areas to embrace the Raza Unida philosophy. Of all the other South Texas towns, none appeared as similar politically and socially to Crystal City as did Cotulla, a town of nearly four thousand, of which three thousand two hundred were Mexican American and of those nearly two thousand were migrant, seasonal farm workers. Cotulla's only claim to fame was that Lyndon Johnson had taught elementary school there in 1928. Seventy miles south of San Antonio and about the same distance from Zavala County, it was even further away from sharing the nation's prosperity of the 1960s and early 1970s.[1] Mexican Americans there were powerless politically, segregation of public schools remained the standard, poverty was rampant, and racial polarization was obvious even to the uncritical eye. One activist described the people's lives this way:

> The discrimination ... has continued. They [Mexican Americans] have been given separate "Hoteles del Gobierno" [housing projects], separate schools, separate health care, separate beatings by Texas Rangers and Border Patrolmen, separate restaurants, in short, separate everything.
>
> Their treatment has been separate but not equal. They have paid the price by having only a 49-year life span.[2]

Cotulla's barrios and their one- and two-room houses were a decrepit island in a sea of beautiful farmland that produced vegetables and profits for its Anglo owners throughout the year. Mexican Americans there were less sophisticated and had no history of politically challenging the Anglo as Chicanos in Crystal City had done in the mid-1960s. Yet the possibilities of a political revolt caught the townspeople's imagination.

Taking advantage of this yearning were several young men: Raúl Martínez; Leodoro Martínez, his brother; Alfredo Zamora, a schoolteacher; and Roel Rodríguez. They began organizing through a voter-registration drive while they were affiliated with MAYO. Later they got involved in self-help neighborhood projects that included picking up trash in the barrio and lobbying for more recreational facilities. These efforts were an attempt to win the confidence of the Mexican American citizens. Once the activists were able to get a following, they formed a loose coalition named Barrios Unidos to serve as a base to register voters and to launch an electoral challenge against the Anglo ranchers and long-time resident families, both Anglo and Mexican American, that supported them.[3]

Voter-registration drives were not new or original in South Texas. Periodically, local individuals, Democratic committees, LULAC, and other groups conducted them to benefit from the Mexican American vote. However, these drives were done on behalf of national and state candidacies and the effort that went into them had had little effect in places like Cotulla; consequently, few of the voters reregistered. Most Anglo politicians had stopped taking the drives seriously—if they ever did—and so they were unprepared for an electoral challenge. After all, few Mexican Americans had ever been elected to office in Cotulla.

While the attention focused on Crystal City and Carrizo Springs, Zamora, who had returned to Cotulla from the Midwest only a year earlier, and the other organizers prepared for the elections by setting up voters' schools, where they taught Mexican Americans, many illiterate, how to vote. Zamora, who ran for mayor, told a reporter:

> We . . . had a little song, a chant telling them who to vote for. We divided the candidates into groups of three and then made a chant according to the position of the La Raza Unida candidate. If there were five groups it went "At the top, at the top, at the top, in the middle, at the top." But if they couldn't see groups—you know some people can't see groups—we would just teach them numbers and those who couldn't read, could read Chicano names okay anyhow.[4]

Finding candidates in the spring of 1970 to run proved as hard as teaching illiterate voters to use the ballot. Many were afraid of jeopardizing their jobs in a town where employment was the first concern. Aside from positions in the handful of service stations and grocery stores, there were few jobs other than those of the farm workers'. Most of the jobs that did exist were with Anglo bosses who did not appreciate their workers' involvement with a party such as La Raza Unida.[5]

The two candidates besides Zamora who did announce were owners of small businesses. They were described by Zamora as "conservatives," though they did stay with the party for at least one more election. They were George Carpenter and Enrique Jiménez. The three pulled an amazing upset in spite of the fact that Anglo precinct judges invalidated one hundred ballots likely to go to them. The Raza Unida organizers expected to duplicate the feat in the November 1970 county elections, but the party was ruled off the ballot and only Roel Rodríguez was elected, as county commissioner, through a write-in campaign.[6]

When the Raza Unida candidates took office, they found the city and county governments in disarray. Rodríguez discovered that he had a budget of $1.13 and that the three other members of the commissioner's court were not interested in his proposals for a more effective food-stamp program, a health insurance plan, or adequate housing for the poor. County roads were in poor condition, and there were no real services for people who lived outside the city limits. The city was in no better shape, as Zamora quickly found out. The fire department was segregated and its equipment antiquated, streets were rutted or unpaved, parks were not maintained, and the city well's water level often fell so low in the summer that some homes had to do without water.[7]

The scarcity of money in the city treasury forced Zamora to look elsewhere for funds. Mirroring the Crystal City approach, he went after federal funds, but he soon found there was more to it than just asking. Unlike Gutiérrez, who had been a successful grant writer even before he came back to the Winter Garden Area, Zamora learned by trial and error. He applied to the Economic Development Administration for funds to dig a new water well, but the proposal was rejected. In the application he wrote that the water well would be used for the citizens. He had to rewrite it to show that it would be used for employment and industry.

Zamora traveled to Washington, D.C., and began making the rounds to learn the process of getting the available monies. His search was facilitated by the fact that Cotulla met just about every one of the criteria of a depressed area eligible for federal funds.[8] In a period of two years the Raza Unida officials were able to get enough local and federal funds to conduct a $15,000 street pavement operation, buy a new fire engine, and begin construction of a new, $175,000 water well. They also installed street lights in the barrio, desegregated the fire department, and refurbished a park on the "Mexican" side of town.[9]

Changes at the school district were less tangible, since Anglos still held numerical control of the board. Two Raza Unida members sat on the board and they were outvoted constantly when they made proposals to reform the district's status quo in the same manner that Gutiérrez had done in Crystal City. Ironically, the biggest change came outside the board's meeting room, and it was initiated by Zamora and several other activists. During the district's fall registration they stood outside the doors of Welhausen Elementary School and encouraged parents to take their children to Amanda Burkes Elementary School, where all the Anglo children attended. Welhausen was where former President Johnson first started teaching and it had not changed much since then. It was a school 100 percent Mexican American in composition, poorly equipped, run-down, and had toilet facilities in an annex room separated from the main building. Both schools housed first through fourth grades. Older children were integrated with Anglos at Amanda Burkes and in junior high and the high school, but even there Mexican American students were segregated by means of a "tracking system" that placed them in classes for slow learners.

School officials defended the school's population composition by claiming that the district had allowed a freedom of choice for more than ten years. Superintendent C. R. Landrum told parents that Welhausen was segregated because it served as "a community school in a Mexican American community."[10] The freedom-of-choice concept was one used by numerous southern and southwestern school districts as a way to get around the 1954 U.S. Supreme Court decision banning segregated facilities for people of different races or nationalities. By the 1970s the federal courts and the federal government were claiming that free-choice desegregation plans were not fulfilling the spirit or letter of the law.

This type of maneuvering had helped school administrators weather a public protest by Cotulla parents in the late 1940s over de facto segregation in the public schools. Several residents ostensibly organized as the Club Latino Americano, brought in well-known

San Antonio attorney Gus García to argue their case before a state education commission. The commission ruled in favor of the parents, but little changed because school officials made no effort to facilitate the transfer of students.[11]

Zamora and ten other Mexican American activists were able to convince almost two hundred parents to register their children at Amanda Burkes through the freedom-of-choice policy. They even offered rides to those parents unable to walk the one-mile distance between the schools. Anglo administrators bound by their own policies accepted the new students, though they murmured about not having enough room in the school for all the transfer students.

A few days later two hundred parents attended a school board meeting with a list of reforms which included demands for bilingual education, an expanded lunch program, more Mexican American teachers and counselors, Mexican history courses, and bus transportation for elementary school children. The besieged non-Raza Unida majority on the board listened attentively and then promised to implement a bilingual education program immediately at the kindergarten level and to consider all other demands at subsequent meetings. Then, with the assistance of the parents and the party leaders, they developed a "total integration" plan. In this plan both Mexican American and Anglo students attending first and second grade would meet at Welhausen Elementary School and those in the third and fourth grade would enroll at Amanda Burkes School.[12]

The meeting proved to be a major victory for the Mexican American community in Cotulla and served to enhance the party's stature in the county. On April 1, 1972, the party again swept to victory at the polls, though it did not increase its majority. This time the slate was headed by twenty-four-year-old Arseno García, director of the Cotulla Neighborhood Center, who was elected mayor.

Zamora decided not to run for reelection because of economic hardships, even though he would have won easily. Shortly after his election in 1970, the school district refused to hire him as a teacher even though he had a college degree and several other teachers did not. He remained unemployed or underemployed until he was hired to teach math at the Crystal City junior high school, but that proved to be a burden because he had to travel ninety miles roundtrip every day. With a wife and four children and a salary of only seven dollars per meeting from the city,

Zamora was forced to leave office and seek employment in the Midwest. He left behind what seemed to be a well-entrenched party.[13] Zamora's exodus marked the beginning of a much larger one throughout Texas by Raza Unida activists. They were forced out of their communities by economic hardships brought about by employers who did not approve of their politics. When people joined the Raza Unida Party, they jeopardized their jobs, financial security, and at times even their reputations.

Nearly two hundred fifty miles to the southeast, Guadalupe Youngblood organized a La Raza Unida Party chapter in Robstown, a cotton-growing community twenty-nine miles west of Corpus Christi. Youngblood had stayed close to his hometown by attending Texas A&I University, twenty-seven miles west of "Robe," as Robstown came to be known. There he became involved with MAYO, first as a participant and later as one of the organizers who traveled around the state founding chapters. A quiet, unassuming individual, Youngblood proved to be the kind of activist MAYO leaders wanted. Though articulate, well educated and a tenacious workaholic, Youngblood never abandoned the Robstown barrio for the city. He did not adopt the militant garb worn by other activists, and he did not expound leftist slogans, which seemed irrelevant to many in the Mexican American community. He was a cultural nationalist of the purest kind. Mexican traditions were important to him, and he spoke mostly Spanish or *calo*.[14]

Robstown's Raza Unida activism, like that of Crystal City, began with a school boycott, but unlike the case in Crystal City, it had reached the walkout stage by the time MAYO organizers entered the scene. Youngblood later recalled: "We called people from San Antonio and Crystal City and we told them: Something happened here and we did not plan it. It was spontaneous! We need support! Help us in any way you can!"[15]

The problems at the high school began in May 1969, when a group of students presented the school board with a list of changes it wanted to see implemented. The demands were similar to those raised by MAYO activists throughout the state. Nothing came of the student rumblings, and by the following year an organization known as Movimiento Chicano de Robe was founded. It consisted of students, parents, and a few civic leaders. Unfortunately, many of the participants were migrant workers, and when they left town to work, the organization folded. In 1971 the students were able to get the school to let them celebrate Cinco de Mayo on the school grounds. One year later, on Wednesday April 5, 1972, the students finally walked out of school over the grievances.

School officials acted promptly to defuse the problem by promising to look into the demands and taking action on the ones they could. A meeting of the board was scheduled for the following Monday on the condition that the students return to school for the remainder of the week. In the meantime, though, the students held several rallies at La Lomita, a neighborhood park, to explain the issues to the parents and to invite them to pack the Monday school board meeting. When the meeting convened, several hundred people were in attendance, causing the board members to feel besieged. The president quickly warned the audience that the meeting would be adjourned if any "disruptions occurred."[16]

The students presented their list of grievances and the reasons for the changes. Most of the demands were greeted by comments of support or criticism by the highly polarized audience, which divided itself along racial lines. The members of the board were not willing to make any commitments and replied with the same answer to all the demands. They promised to investigate each one of them but added that it would take as long as six weeks to gather the information required to make a decision. In six weeks the school year would be over and the protest would face a similar death to the one in 1969, which had been defused by the summer vacation.

In a dramatic move one of the students rose to the microphone and said, "You people don't understand. We want action on these things now. All you want is for us to forget what has been happening. Now what we want to know is, are you going to take action on these demands or not?" A shocked board president replied that the board had voted unanimously to investigate the demands. The student repeated the question and added, "If you're not, I think we are only wasting time here and we are prepared to walk out tomorrow with a lot more support than before." Again the board president restated the board's decision. The student shrugged his shoulders and said into the microphone, "Walkout tomorrow." Most of the Mexican American parents and students then got up and left the high school gym.[17]

At this point the MAYO, now Raza Unida, activists became involved. They quickly moved to organize the school boycotters into a disciplined group with a small newspaper, a place to meet, and parental support. The initial walkout had taken nearly five hundred students out of school. Some of the parents were unsure about the walkout because it came so close to graduation time and the seniors might have to repeat the year. Youngblood, Armando Cavada, and several other activists developed small student teams that went to the Robstown barrios to talk to parents about the reasons for the student protest. In a short time the adult support for the school strike rose significantly.[18]

During the boycott La Lomita became the gathering place for all the students and many of their parents. Rather than allow the young people to stay at home, the student leaders and their Raza Unida advisers kept the students together at the park, days and evenings. Mexican American volunteer teachers from Corpus Christi, Laredo, Kingsville, San Antonio, and Crystal City conducted classes out in the open. Most of the teachers were Raza Unida members or sympathizers and used the open-air classrooms to teach Chicano history, culture, and politics. This curriculum proved new to most of the students, and many of them liked it and actually found learning enjoyable for the first time. One senior student told the group that in his twelve years of school he had never heard anything as interesting as what he learned at La Lomita.

The parents were also kept busy. They were organized into small discussion groups to talk about their own school experiences and other topics that added to their discontent. They were encouraged to be at the nightly rallies where they heard party speakers lambast the Anglo "power structure." Also on the nightly agenda were student musical groups and poets from the locality or around the state. Bumper stickers and T-shirts were sold, dances were held, and barbecued beef was served. A fiesta atmosphere prevailed, and it kept the students and parents together and talking about the problems of the Robstown barrios.

When the crowd grew to several hundred people, the authorities responded by bringing sheriffs, deputies, highway patrolmen, and other law enforcement agents to stand guard at the park. In a short time the accumulation of the officers created a siege mentality among the protesters. One incident almost led to a shoot-out between the crowd and the policemen. It began when liquor-control agents arrested Cavada for not having a license to sell beer. When the crowd protested, the law enforcement officers attempted to intimidate it by cocking their guns. The protesters ran, many searching for their guns in their cars. In Robstown many carried guns, and the Raza Unida activists realized that a bloody confrontation was likely. It took all their efforts, especially those of "Guero" Villarreal, Youngblood, and Muñiz, who at the time was campaigning in Robstown, to calm the aroused, gun-toting protesters. Cavada and Youngblood were arrested but released shortly afterward.[19]

After nearly three weeks the boycotters received a major boost of support. On Saturday, April 30, several busloads of students, parents, school administrators, and city officials from Crystal City arrived to join a four-mile march through the streets of the town. The buses entered the park escorted by Crystal City policemen armed with shotguns. Chicanos at the park were impressed by what the Raza Unida Party could do. For the first time in their lives the "law" and government officials were on their side. The Crystal City support lifted the morale of weary parents and students who were wavering in their commitment to the walkout.

In another week the boycott ended in a stalemate, with students and school officials agreeing to continue the discussion. With less than a month before the end of the school year, the student leaders and their advisers decided to project an image of strong negotiators, rather than letting the boycott end with nothing accomplished.

Although not initiated by La Raza Unida, the student protest nonetheless served the party's purpose. After almost four years of activity Chicano activists finally had an issue controversial enough around which to organize the citizenry. Party members established Familias Unidas, a group based on the concept of the family, with roles for women, men, and children. Interestingly, the women took most of the leadership positions because they had more time and few of them held jobs from which they could be fired. Only families could join, and everyone in the organization had a vote. Business was handled democratically, and initially none of the activists was allowed to hold an office within the entity. Youngblood later said:

> We ... had developed a ... glue ... that emphasized the culture. Without the family it was impossible. We created the ideal family—the model family. ... From there we applied it to the organization. We behaved like a family. There [is] discipline; you pick each other up. We saw each other daily. The meeting was once a week but we kept seeing each other daily. We began to know each other and know what was troubling us.[20]

Within a year of its formation, Familias Unidas won a seat in the city council, but more important, it became a model for other South Texas towns as Crystal City had in the Winter Garden Area. Robstown lay in a strategic area at the edge of the port city of Corpus Christi and on the road that led to the heart of South Texas. At nearby Texas A&I University in Kingsville, students could be recruited from a strong Raza Unida Club that had begun to take control of student politics and the student governing board, which had a budget of forty thousand dollars.

Solidly in control of the party's activities in Kingsville were Raul Villarreal and Abel Cavada, the former a college dropout who managed a bar and the latter a student. Villarreal, like Youngblood, espoused a fervent Chicano nationalism, while Cavada tempered his views with socialist thought. They were close friends and admirers of the Robstown leadership. The two party chapters became the proponents of a cultural isolationism that later ran counter to the politics of the urban Raza Unida chapters, which sought coalitions with Anglo leftist groups and black militants.

Kingsville did not fit the mold of most of the other targeted communities because only 50 percent of the town's population was Mexican American. Adjacent to the town stood the famous King Ranch, which had been built, according to Chicano old-timers, on "Mexican land" and had been the site of the last battle between federal troops and a group of *Tejano* separatists. Numerous Chicanos and Mexican nationals lived on the property, where their children attended a ranch elementary school, and it was not uncommon to find families whose history could not be traced before the ranch's founding.[21]

For Chicano activists the King Ranch represented Anglo oppression and Mexican American subservience. A "takeover" of Kingsville, they believed, would shake the foundations of Anglo control in all of South Texas and ignite electoral revolts in the numerous rural towns that spotted the short stretch to the border one hundred and forty miles to the south. Control of these little towns meant taking over the reigns of the taxing authorities and law enforcement agencies, two powers that could change the political and social equilibrium of the area.

A win in Kingsville, however, required almost the complete backing of the Mexican American community, including the middle class which had designs of its own of taking control. Since the barrios there were not as destitute as the one in other targeted areas, the party used the issues of discrimination and cultural genocide as the main organizing themes. At a time of heightened preoccupation with cultural identification, even better-off Chicanos could be attracted, if not recruited, to the movement. Especially susceptible to the pressures were those Mexican Americans who worked at the university. They were either forced to be role models for the students or were castigated for being *agringados* or Anglocized. Many, trying to avoid conflict with the students and also with the university administration, became silent partners, providing information and some monetary support in private.

At the same time they were receiving quiet support, the Raza Unida activists were visibly taking control of student government budgets and committees. With the student population nearly 54 percent Chicano, it became feasible with some planning. The Raza Unida Club members controlled a Chicano student party named PEP and ran student sympathizers and party members for student government positions, student president, and membership on the Student Governing Board, which regulated facilities and money for events such as dances, concerts, and lectures. Students who ran under the PEP banner who were not Raza Unida members usually ended up being supportive of radical platforms as a result of conversion, coercion, or intimidation.[22]

By controlling money for student activities, RUP activists were able to hire bands for Chicano dances and speakers for militant lectures and to open the university's facilities to Mexican American groups that rarely had access to the campus. State-supported classrooms became Raza Unida Party gathering places.

From an old, graying, white house across the street from the university, Villarreal and his fellow activists made most of the decisions. A former MAYO organizer from Premont, a tiny rural town just south of Kingsville, Villarreal demanded and received unwavering loyalty from student party members, who carried out his instructions. The party had no presence outside the university until the Raza Unida Club organized a countywide workers' association. The university's maintenance workers became the core of the membership.[23] These workers gave the activists legitimacy in the eyes of those in the barrio. No longer were they "just students," but unionists and grassroots organizers. Through the families of these workers, the Raza Unida cadre became involved in the school board meetings and in the governing board of the Texas Rural Legal

Aid, a public agency responsible for providing free or low-cost legal advice and representation to indigent clients. The agency's by-laws required it to have an executive board elected by the people it served, and the Raza Unida members were able to elect Jorge Guerra as the president. Guerra had moved into the "headquarters" and replaced Cavada, who left to go to law school.

Guerra and Villarreal were able to influence the legal agency into filing class-action discrimination suits against the city, the university, and a major chemical plant within the county limits on behalf of Mexican American workers. With all this activity and with one of the better-written and more consistent newspapers in the party, *El Chile*, the Kingsville chapter became more influential than its real political muscle warranted. At that stage it jumped into the electoral activities of the city by running Villarreal for city council in a nonpartisan election that drew an "Anglo slate," a "Mexican American slate," and a Raza Unida candidate. Running for reelection were Gilbert Acuña, a pharmacist who had been the city's first Mexican American mayor, and two other Mexican Americans, who had been part of a "Mexican takeover" of Kingsville only four years earlier. They were later joined by a liberal Anglo woman. Running on the Anglo ticket was another Mexican American who had been elected with Acuña but had split with the mayor and the other two councilmen.

The party decided to run an issue-oriented, nonconfrontational campaign to avoid battling Acuña's slate. Acuña, who had once been a popular mayor, was in trouble because the Anglos seemed solidly behind an Anglo doctor running for mayor. Acuña also had the predominantly Mexican American firefighters' union campaigning against him because of a dispute over collective bargaining rights, which Acuña had helped to defeat in a referendum. The union was supporting Villarreal, the only strong advocate of collective bargaining.

The Raza Unida Party canvassed every house in the barrio in a concerted leaflet campaign. Villarreal vowed to talk to every Chicano in Kingsville and he practically did. With a budget of only seven hundred dollars, the party's intensive walking effort with only a few volunteers gained momentum as the campaign came to a close. In contrast, the Mexican American slate had hundreds of volunteers, an adequate budget, and large rallies but at the last days felt nervous about the outcome. They were shocked at Villarreal's stamina and at the way the Chicano voters seemed to be responding to his low-budget politics. For some of the middle-class candidates and their supporters, it was hard to imagine that a short, overweight, sloppily dressed, unemployed bartender had a legitimate chance for a seat on the city council. They realized only a few days before the election that numerous university professors, staff members, and students were working feverishly on Villarreal's behalf. He had the most educated and best-organized campaign committee in the race. The political flyers were written well, the posters were impressive, and the block walking had been more sophisticated than anyone else's.

Three days before the election the Mexican American slate endorsed Villarreal at a rally and told its campaigners to work for him. They were hoping for a reciprocal endorsement but Villarreal never offered one publicly, although on the afternoon of election day he did walk the streets for the slate. But he did it only after explaining to the firefighters' union that this kind of coalition would make a victory possible.

Election day proved to be a disaster for the Mexican American community as every one of their candidates, except the one on the Anglo ticket, lost. Even Acuña was solidly beaten by the Anglo candidate, who spent election day in bed because of a heart attack days before the voting. Only Villarreal's race remained in doubt until the final count. He lost the city council race by just five votes.

Anywhere else the outcome would have been taken as a triumph, but not in Kingsville. The party leadership there did not believe in political martyrdom or symbolic victories. They felt they had had a magnificent chance for a victory that would have established them as the Mexican American powerbrokers in Kingsville. It would also have proved José Angel Gutiérrez wrong. Gutiérrez had once declared that the Anglos would never allow Chicanos to take over "King Ranch city" and advised Chicanos there to help the surrounding communities and to be content with being political gadflies.[24]

Several party members wanted a recount, but a bitterly disappointed Villarreal was too depressed and financially broke to think about it for the first few days after the election. Only after talking to some of the middle-class slate workers, who offered to pay for the recount, did he decide to go to court and demand it. Within three weeks Villarreal was declared the winner by five votes, and Kingsville had its first Raza Unida official. The party had its foot in the door and quickly began preparing to continue the challenge with a full slate the next time around.

Two other communities proved to be important to the Texas Raza Unida rural strategy. Pearsall, thirty miles south of San Antonio, and San Juan, in the heart of the Rio Grande Valley, became crucial to the net the party sought to cast over the twenty-six counties in the South Texas and Rio Grande Valley area.

Pearsall, like Kingsville, presented a different challenge to the party's strategy because in the spring of 1972 a loosely knit group of families had elected four Mexican Americans to office, two on the city council and two on the school board. Since Mexican Americans were already on both governing boards, many Anglos soon saw it as a "Chicano takeover," even though the candidates were moderates with no official ties to the Raza Unida Party. But within the groups of supporters existed a small core of militants who had kept an eye on Crystal City and were anxious to adopt the same reforms. One of the leaders among this group was Modesto Rodríguez, a melon farmer in his early thirties with strong "anti-Anglo" sentiments. He was deeply involved in the social life of this town of 11,159 as chairman of the Diez y Seis celebration and as vice-president of a community health organization.[25]

Attempts by Rodríguez to get the group, which came to be known as Ciudadanos Unidos Mexicanos, into Raza Unida were futile until after the 1973 city and school board elections. Just before that, the Anglos decided to form the Better Government League (BGL) and combat the "Raza-types." Groups of Anglo citizens went to the meetings of the council and school board to act as watchdogs and challenge the newly elected officials on practically all the decisions they made. Anglo bureaucrats in the city and in the schools dragged their feet in complying with new policies and even physically challenged the new officeholders on matters unrelated to the job at hand. One fight took place between one of the city councilmen and the husband of a city clerk who claimed the councilman called her a "Mexican hater."

Anglo citizens accused the new "Mexican majority" of being belligerent, unsophisticated, and racist. It is probable that some of the Mexican American officials saw this as a good time to get back at Anglos for years of injustice, but for the most part they were not ideologically anti-Anglo. Most of these middle-class Mexican Americans felt that they could work with the "good Anglos" in town. A rude awakening came when they found few if any Anglos willing to join them in a political partnership. In the city elections of 1973 the Ciudadanos were solidly defeated by the BGL. This left them bitter and in disarray, and it opened the door for Rodríguez to push for a strong pro-Chicano stance. He urged them to stop seeking only equal representation and to take control of the city and then the county. With the effects of the defeat still lingering, a small majority of the Ciudadanos group decided to invite Gutiérrez and other party leaders to come establish a Raza Unida chapter in Pearsall.

Rodríguez had pulled off a major feat considering that many in the Ciudadanos organization were middle-class businessmen and a good number were veterans of the armed forces, the same kinds of individuals who had avoided the party in places like San Antonio and Robstown. There was no major exodus from the group by the moderates, but a significant number did begin to miss the meetings The organizational meeting of the Raza Unida chapter had one of the smallest attendances of the year. Still, Ciudadanos had two people on the school board and two on the city council and what seemed a solid five hundred to seven hundred votes. The Raza Unida in Pearsall had been born among the Mexican American middle class by passing up much, though not all, of the grassroots organizing that had made the Crystal City victory possible.

In San Juan, Raza Unida found fertile ground among a group of twenty young people, most of them in college, who created Citizens for a Better San Juan. Leader of this group was Jesús Ramírez, already a veteran of party national politics while a student at Pan American University and editor of *El Portavoz*, the group's newspaper. He projected the image of a strong leader. Juan Maldonado served as his first lieutenant.[26]

On April 3, 1971, Maldonado, Antonio García, and Lalo Arcaute were swept into office under the banner of the Citizens for a Better San Juan. Arcaute was elected mayor and García and Maldonado, city commissioners. It was a surprising victory in an area where Anglos made the decisions, which were carried out by vicious Mexican American law enforcement agents. Only two months before, in the neighboring town of Pharr, a police-brutality protest march had turned into a riot, leaving Alfonso "Poncho" Flores, an innocent bystander, dead from a policeman's slug.[27]

Hidalgo County, where both Pharr and San Juan were located, had the reputation of being the home of more migrants than any other county in the country. More than thirty thousand Mexican Americans left the county each year to work in the fields up north, even though the county's fertile lands were some of the biggest citrus producers in the state. Most of the land was owned by Anglo farmers and ranchers. Amid the bountiful citrus crop of *El Valle de Lágrimas* (the Valley of Tears), the average life expectancy was forty-nine years. High rates of polio, tuberculosis, and malnutrition were the norm. With a dropout rate of more than 50 percent, the cycle of poverty and ill health was perpetuated generation after generation.

Most of the organizing activity among San Juan's five thousand or more Mexican Americans first began in the late 1960s with the United Farm Workers Union. There were marches, strikes, and boycotts in support of the unionization of migrant workers, although this never led to any form of organized politics. Nevertheless, the union activity had prepared the people for Chicano politics. Ramírez and others began planning an electoral revolt in December 1970, and four months later, with a 60 percent turnout at the polls, they had a majority in the city government. The party activists moved quickly to consolidate after what seemed an easy victory. They had done it without a real grassroots organization, and they wanted to go back to Gutiérrez's strategy, which they had seen firsthand in Crystal City. Said Ramírez:

> Some of us would like to see a mass Chicano group that would guarantee Chicanos control of the city council and the school board. We have to organize truckers ... farm workers ... a city employees union, we have to get people to go to school and we have to educate people on the war. We have to make people aware of not only local politics, but also of state, national and international politics.[28]

By 1973 the San Juan chapter had not been able to capitalize on its gains or develop the kind of organization the party had in Crystal City, Cotulla, or Robstown, and it lost control of the city council that spring in nonpartisan elections. But the party did win control of the Pharr-San Juan-Alamo school board. By this time most of the Anglo politicians were out of the picture and the Chicano Democrats were providing the opposition. Although they had been unwilling or unable to strongly challenge Anglo rule, these "new Democrats" saw a great opportunity to run for office against a party that had made ethnic voting a way of life in South

Texas. The Democrats were to have a lot of successes, but between 1971 and 1974, Raza Unida candidates were triumphant in numerous nonpartisan elections.

In the spring of 1973 the party put together a string of impressive nonpartisan victories throughout South Texas and the Winter Garden Area. In Crystal City it retained control of the city and increased its membership on the school board from five to six. It won control of both the city and the school board in Edcouch-Elsa, two city council seats in Kyle, another one in Lockhart, one school board seat in Hebbronville, one in Robstown, and two in Beeville. In Carrizo Springs the party regained a seat in the city council, and in Asherton it won back control of the city council and the mayor's office.[29]

The party made inroads into a new area when it secured control of the Marathon city council, and it maintained a majority presence in Anthony, a little town just west of El Paso. It also won two school board seats, to increase its number to five. In La Joya it picked up three more seats in the schools. In Eagle Pass and in San Marcos, candidates backed by the party won.[30] In a mere three years the party's rural strategy had been extremely successful in the context of a statewide effort. The Aztec warrior symbol appeared to be everywhere in the state. For the Democrats it seemed that a series of political brushfires was threatening to become a full-fledged electoral inferno. Gutiérrez's one-region-at-a-time approach now seemed silly even to his closest advisers, and the party's rank and file began talking of mass takeovers around the state.

We have climbed
the mountain
now the air is thin
and from here on out
we intend to win

—Ramsey Muñiz 1974

PEOPLE TOGETHER: THE 1974 CAMPAIGN

Nineteen seventy-three had been a good year for the party in Texas, and 1974 had the potential to be even better. La Raza Unida Party could now claim a state organization with county chairmen, precinct workers, and legitimate candidates, although the party's real strength still lay in South Texas. Every reported political rebellion in the rural towns caused a rumbling in the state's urban barrios. There were also small groups of Raza Unida supporters in most of the metropolitan areas, particularly in those cities with universities with a Chicano student population.

Social agencies in the barrios were breeding grounds for activists and served as valuable vehicles for organizing individuals, especially young people susceptible to the nationalist ideology of the party. Through these agencies as well as front social-political organizations,[1] Raza Unida activists attracted working-class youth, *batos locos*,[2] ex-*pachucos*, and former barrio politicos who had never been mainstreamed. These were the stormtroopers, the chanters, and the sign carriers needed for the party's supplementary activities such as marches, school walkouts, and picketings. These new members were easy to attract and, at first, easy to control. Most did not follow the formal procedures of the party or participate in the ideological debates in the meetings and conferences. Some, however, did develop the skills to become leaders within the local chapters. The underlying and at times overwhelming reason for their membership in the party was their distrust of the "gringo system" and their attraction to Chicanismo's symbolism.

This animosity toward Anglos among the youth had a long history and stemmed from what many of them considered an unfair administration of law enforcement tactics against them. Chicano youths, particularly those in the cities, had a violence-prone relationship with the police; most of the violence, though, was committed against them. As early as the 1940s, law enforcement agents had a policy of "rounding up" Chicano youths, mistreating them, and letting them sit in jail for a day or two.[3] It did not matter that some of those jailed were exemplary students. In fact, the Brown Berets were founded by a high-achieving Chicano student on the Los Angeles Mayor's Youth Advisory Board, David Sánchez, who had an altercation with the police.

Aside from feeling mistreated, many of the youths felt frustrated because upward mobility proved fleeting in the economically depressed barrios. Donald J. Bogue, in *The Population of the United States* (1959), wrote: "The Mexican Americans constitute the only ethnic group for which a comparison of the characteristics of the first and second generation fails to show a substantial intergenerational rise in socio-economic status."[4]

Urban Chicano youths in the late 1960s and early 1970s seemed a flock without a shepherd. Elizabeth Martínez and Enriqueta Longeaux y Vásquez wrote in their book *Viva La Raza!*:

> The city is one big conspiracy to destroy the creativity of Raza and breed defeatism, to take away our sense of dignity and encourage self-hatred. . . . The older children stay out late at night with friends whom the parents don't know. . . . They seek protection and status within a circle of barrio friends, often getting involved with drugs or petty stealing. . . . The younger children seem to have trouble in school . . . and usually there is one member of the family with a serious health problem that drains the family budget. . . . As this urban life pattern unfolds, it tends to make the family disintegrate more and more. . . . This is the destiny of Raza in the city again and again."[5]

The rhetoric of La Raza Unida offered a way to combat the bleak life of unimportance, poverty, and violence. It gave young Chicanos a cause in which they could play a major role and where they were considered equal participants even though they lacked

money, titles, degrees, or family influence. Movimiento, not necessarily party, politics became all-encompassing to a number of them,
and in 1974 many were ready to work for the Muñiz campaign.

On January 16, at three o'clock P.M. in Corpus Christi, Muñiz
announced that he would again seek his party's nomination for
governor. As he talked about his candidacy, it became obvious that
this was a different Muñiz.

> I've talked with thousands of people, plain ordinary people,
> *of all races*, beliefs and opinions . . . and I've found that they
> are concerned about the same basic things. . . . I am a Chicano.
> . . . But I will not be dealing . . . exclusively [with] Chicano
> issues. I hope that a majority of people will vote for me in
> November because I will have offered the best programs and
> alternatives and not because of my *ancestry*. [author's italics][6]

Nowhere in his five-page announcement did he mention an issue
that could be considered strictly Chicano. In its major points
Muñiz's announcement would have been appropriate for Frances
Farenthold, who was again seeking the Democratic Party's nomination. He continued:

> The Texas of today is vastly different from the Texas of 20
> years ago. Over half of the citizens now live in the four largest
> cities in the state. Today we need a state government that can
> actively deal with these facts. City dwellers need special atten-
> tion to their situation and rural Texans need more than county
> agents and game wardens. New modes of transportation,
> proper financing of our children's education, and new styles
> of medical care are all issues of great importance. We will
> speak firmly and decisively to these issues with creative and
> original solutions.[7]

In one swift utterance Muñiz also changed the name of the party:
"We are a party of people—people together, or as we say in
Spanish, *Raza Unida*."[8] "People together" was not the party leaders'
definition or translation of Raza Unida. When pressed for a translation, Gutiérrez and Compean had used "united people," and the
media had translated the name literally to "united race." Both of
those terms came closer to the political meaning of Raza Unida
than Muñiz's version because they inferred a stronger bond.

Muñiz was indicating either subliminally or consciously that
he wanted a coalition that would put him in office, not necessarily

one that would stay together to transform Texas society into Aztlán. He saw a need to bring different groups into his campaign in order to improve his vote total and possibly to give him a stronger base with which to resist any move by Raza Unida leaders to bring his campaign under stricter party control. The new name struck many of the militant party members as an extension of the 1972 election's liberal recruiting, and they immediately reacted against it in private meetings. Compean, in particular, disagreed with the new translation. By this time, he was having second thoughts about a Muñiz candidacy, and the announcement only confirmed his feelings that the gubernatorial candidate lacked ideological consistency. Once Gutiérrez accepted the translation publicly, however, Compean and others toned down their criticism and waited until the state convention in Houston in September.[9]

Masterminding the 1974 campaign was Carlos Rene Guerra, who, like Muñiz, became one of the most controversial figures in the party. Guerra came to the party from MAYO, where he had served as the first and only national president. A native of Robstown, he had attended Texas A&I and had become friends with Gutiérrez, who later recruited him to MAYO. Raza Unida leaders recognized Guerra's quick mind and sharp tongue, but many condered him too idiosyncratic and pompous. When Compean stepped down as chairman of MAYO, Gutiérrez pushed Guerra for the position but he lost to Alberto Luera, a much more popular activist in the organization. Immediately after Guerra's defeat, Gutiérrez proposed that a national structure for MAYO be established, and when it was agreed to, he nominated Guerra, who was then elected, to head the new entity. Yet MAYO never really did have enough chapters outside of Texas to be considered a national organization.[10]

In the 1972 campaign Guerra did not play a significant role, but he did come to the attention of Muñiz while serving as director of the Texas Institute for Educational Development (TIED). After the election Muñiz's future trips to San Antonio began or ended at TIED headquarters, where he planned his race for 1974, a race that seemed more significant this time around for both the candidate and the party. The 1972 campaign goal had simply been to be on the statewide ballot, but after the enthusiasm generated by Muñiz, some in the party felt that Raza Unida could be influential and even win major races in Texas. These new loyalists were also inclined to believe that Mexican American voters would not support a candidate perceived to be too extreme in his politics or unorthodox in his campaign style. Muñiz's close circle of supporters also viewed the middle-class Mexican American voter as the key to the campaign's success.

Some who were aware of Guerra's militancy might have been surprised by the slick approach of the new campaign, but those who knew him well or had taken time to listen to his rhetoric would have understood. Back in 1970, in a speech at Texas A&I University, he had expounded the concept of "cultural pluralism," or the coexistence of two distinct cultures without the absorbing of one by the other. This was not a new idea or even a radical one, as many ethnic groups, particularly European Americans, had been unofficially practicing it for generations. Nor was it foreign to the Mexican American community. Intellectuals such as George Sánchez, Carlos Castañeda, Arthur Campa, and others had supported that social pattern in their writings in the 1950s. Mexican American politicians, as well as leaders of organizations like LULAC and the G.I. Forum, became proponents of the concept when they realized that their attempts at assimilation had negligible effects on the social and economic status of both the immigrant and the native-born Mexican American.[11]

Politically, cultural pluralism implied coalitions with white liberals and trade unionists under the Democratic Party or, rarely, with the Republican Party. This coalescing infrequently meant the election of a Mexican American. Usually, it meant the election of a liberal and the possible appointment of Mexican Americans to government positions at the state and national level. This approach reflected a slight increase in militance from a community that had developed a small, elite group of leaders from the trade unions, the legal profession, the universities, and the public school system. These leaders sought to turn their community's patriotic service in World War II into a ticket to mainstream society, ever conscious that they could do it successfully only by getting an education and voting for the "right" group.

By the mid-1960s, this strategy had been only a little more successful than assimilation, and the new Chicano leaders quickly questioned not only its logic but its social and moral implications. Cultural pluralism became one of the first discards of the Chicano student movement, and those who expounded the concept were discredited. Activists no longer wanted to share the power, they wanted Chicano empowerment and complete control over their destinies and the community institutions that influenced them.

At Texas A&I Guerra had spoken to a not-yet-radicalized group of students in a conservative environment, and in choosing his words he had been inconsistent with the rhetoric and the organizing strategy of MAYO. Guerra may have used the greater part of valor with this approach, but he gave his enemies within the party ammunition to decry his lack of "real" revolutionary gumption. His eloquence impressed students untrained in the intricacies of movimiento politics but did little to endear him to those whose brand of nationalism demanded scathing condemnations of the system and advocacy of cultural separatism.

Compean disliked Guerra. This antipathy would have meant the end of Guerra's Raza Unida career if he had not had a close relationship with Gutiérrez and Muñiz. With such allies, he moved in party circles with a self-assurance typical of his style, and with the same confidence he took over the Muñiz campaign and charted a course that freed the organization from party control. The top priority became the development of an image of a campaign that bordered the mainstream while it performed before the television cameras but that could still be viewed by most Chicanos as "our party." Muñiz continued his city-hopping, as in 1972, but more effort went into the political rallies and press conferences than before. Endorsements were sought from mainstream Mexican Americans, and media contacts were nurtured more carefully, particularly by Guerra, a master press-release writer and a sophisticated speaker.

The 1974 campaign bothered those who had sought to use a variation of the Crystal City model in the urban centers. The new campaign approach did not necessarily indicate a break with the Raza Unida philosophy or the party, but rather signaled a difference in style and perception. Muñiz felt that the Mexican American electorate wanted an alternative, but one that appeared legitimate enough to vote for, and to their unradicalized minds this meant a candidate who was articulate and had a practical platform, a sophisticated organization, and important endorsements. For Muñiz, who had lived in cities with large percentages of Mexican Americans, there seemed to be enough brown voters to put him in office. This was a mistaken perception prevalent among some party leaders who should have known better. Some claimed that Mexican Americans constituted nearly 33 percent of the voting public in Texas, but that was never so.[12] At the time, Spanish-surnamed individuals made up only about 19 percent of the total population in the state. A history of low registration rates brought the actual voting strength to less than 15 percent.[13]

Nonetheless, in the fall of 1973 the party activists had decided to launch a coordinated effort to get 20 percent of the 1974 gubernatorial vote, because the legislature had revised the election code and now required that a political party receive 20 percent of the vote for governor in order to acquire full legal status. The party would still be recognized if it received more than 2 percent but would not receive funds for its subsequent primaries. Since the vote percentage was tallied from the governor's race, the party had decided to establish a separate committee to focus on that race. A campaign fund of one hundred thousand dollars was the goal.[14] Muñiz also set up a campaign network that in part circumvented the party's county-by-county structure. Local campaign managers were appointed to coordinate the election activities. In a campaign letter he told them "you will be charged with recruiting help, distributing material, promoting advertisement and raising funds. In addition . . . you will be responsible for organizing and arranging my visits . . . should you think that there are private meetings that would benefit our campaign . . . I hope you will arrange them." Nowhere in the letterhead was there a designation of Muñiz's party, and that was also true of his bumper stickers and the brochures that came directly from the state campaign organization. In the letter appointing campaign managers he stressed: "I want you to understand that I am working at winning this election and I cannot afford to alienate anybody or any groups without a good reason. It is better to have people not voting for me than to have them actively working to defeat our campaign."[15]

For some party activists, this policy smacked of Nixon's Committee to Re-elect the President (CREEP). They also did not support the idea of using the primaries to select candidates for the statewide elections. The party had a choice between primary elections and state and local nominating conventions. Those opposed to primaries argued that this method would involve filing fees and would limit the number of candidates willing to run. Another argument against the electoral runoffs was that some areas had enough active supporters for a convention but not enough sympathetic voters for a primary. It would also mean that Mexican Americans who would normally split their votes between Chicano Democrats and Raza Unida candidates would be faced with a choice of casting all their votes for only one party. Since the Democratic Party had the more interesting electoral battles and the greater number of candidates, it was assumed that most Mexican Americans would vote in Democratic primaries.

Compean led the fight for the primaries, pointing out that they were necessary to convince many that the party was a viable electoral alternative. It also signaled the first step toward confronting the Mexican American Democrats head on. For Compean, a swell of support was not possible until these Democrats were "pushed by the wayside." He felt that now, even more than in 1972, they were using militant rhetoric couched in the respectability of a mainstream party and thus offering the best of both worlds to Mexican Americans seeking political change.[16] Albert Peña III, Muñiz's law partner in Corpus Christi, agreed: "They [Democrats] know that as Mexicanos we are very nationalistic. So they send someone who talks the language, can use the phrases. ... But it's still a white man sending a brown man to tell another brown man how good the white man is."[17]

Compean, who had become an expert strategist within the party's hierarchy, won the battle when the executive committee agreed to take the primary route. One reason for the decision was money. The state legislature had recently decided to fund the primary expenses of any party on the ballot. This financial resource was seen as a way to finance party activities, even when they were not directly related to the electoral process. In this debate Compean and Muñiz were on the same side. They both saw the necessity of developing the party structure and strengthening it to be the umbrella for all organizing activities. This approach differed from Gutiérrez's emphasis on local grassroots groups as the core of the movement. Unfortunately for the party, Compean and Muñiz never agreed again on anything significant, and they continued to oppose each other up to the election of a new state chairman.

The state convention was held in Houston, an indication that the urban chapters were now becoming influential and a sign that Muñiz's supporters wanted a bigger media market for their campaigning. But before the delegates arrived, a conflict ensued over the choice of facilities, with one group wanting to use a high school in a barrio where Muñiz had come close to winning in 1972 and another group arguing for the Whitehall, a plush convention and conference hotel.

This dispute had its roots in a bigger one that involved a struggle for the leadership of the Houston RUP chapter. One faction, which claimed to be community based, was led by Daniel Bustamante, a service-union organizer, and the other followed Tatcho Mindiola, who had recently returned from the East Coast to take a faculty position at the University of Houston. Bustamante, a former MAYO activist, sought to move the party away from the university and into the northern barrios of Houston. Despite not holding a position in the party structure, he made many of the day-to-day decisions for the chapter. Mindiola, on the other hand, quickly moved to organize the university students and then became involved in the state party's activities. He renewed his acquaintance with Gutiérrez and made important contacts even within Bustamante's group. When he chose to run for the county chairmanship, he was immediately challenged by Bustamante, and the bitter intraparty fight that ensued led to a permanent split in the chapter. Amid mutual charges of fraud, Mindiola defeated Bustamante by two votes. The conflict carried over to the choosing of a convention facility. Eduardo Canales, chairman of the county organizing committee and a friend of Bustamante's, wanted the convention to be held at Jeff Davis High School in northern Houston. He felt that Muñiz and the other leaders could canvass the two adjacent precincts, visit the barrio stores, knock on doors, and have rallies between sessions and that such a presence might be enough to win there in the November election. To Canales, it was the appropriate place for a working-class party to launch the last half of its campaign.[18]

Mindiola fought for the Whitehall and later claimed that Muñiz had instructed him to do so in order to project an image that would help expand the campaign's base. Muñiz wanted to place more emphasis on attracting the media and felt a hotel would be more suitable. Mindiola saw logistical problems with the school because there were no hotels or restaurants nearby. With the help of the Muñiz supporters, he outvoted Canales, who responded by boycotting the convention's social activities.[19]

This outcome was a victory for Muñiz and he quickly sought to enhance it by eliminating his major nemesis in the party. He called Mindiola and asked him to run for state chairman against

Compean, who was going through a painful divorce at the time and seemed unsure about running for reelection. Muñiz was not the only one thinking of a change. Gutiérrez also contacted Mindiola about making a run for the party's top spot. Mindiola, however, had no interest in going through another electoral fight so soon and he knew that Guadalupe Youngblood had already passed the word that he was considering running for chairman if Compean did not seek reelection. Mindiola said no, and Muñiz quickly shifted his support to Youngblood, who happened to be a friend of Guerra.[20]

The 1972 state convention had been a stage for the party's founders, but in 1974 the focus had narrowed to the gubernatorial candidate and the goal of 20 percent of the vote. Party leaders had hoped to follow the electoral victories of 1973 with more gains and to consolidate power in several other communities but had not been successful, despite the launching of dozens of candidacies in places such as Robstown, Carrizo Springs, Laredo, Corpus Christi, Eagle Pass, Uvalde, La Pryor, Harlingen, Brownsville, Seguin, Raymondville, Deller, Lubbock, Waco, Kingsville, and Hebbronville. Only in Robstown did the party win a seat, on the city water board.[21] In Pearsall the Mexican American converts to the party had split and lost all seven races to the coalition of middle-class Mexican Americans and Anglos of the Better Government League.[22] The party swept Crystal City and Cotulla, but even in those towns there were signs of problems threatening the growth of the La Raza Unida movement.

In Cotulla the young mayor Arseno García, was reelected, but he had to run with two new companions, as his former running mates had left the party after numerous squabbles about the direction of city government and the politics of the state party. The two ex-Raza Unida members were swept from office, but their change in allegiance was an indication that the Cotulla activists had not consolidated their ideological thinking. By June, García had been removed from office by the courts for not living within the city limits. The voting in Cotulla, four years after the takeover, remained a contest between Mexican Americans and Anglos, not between philosophies.

Cristal (Crystal City) was where the philosophical battles were being fought, not between the Chicano third party and the Democrats, but between two Raza Unida factions. A group calling itself Raza Libre (Free People) had formed a slate to oppose the Ciudadanos Unidos candidates. Claiming to be the real Raza Unida, the candidates under the new banner accused the elected officials of working to win their own war on poverty while forgetting the rest of the people. They also described the party's county leadership as dictatorial and always ready to stifle discussion that was critical of the Raza Unida administration. Said Dora Graza, a Raza Libre candidate:

> All my life things were bad under the gringos, but not as bad as they are now. It seems to me that all those people want is power. They get rid of everybody who doesn't agree with them. *Angel* ... was quoted as saying how he had worked in the fields and he understood the problems of the migrants. Huh. I was [sic] to school with Angel. He was a rich boy. He was the middle-class Mexican, not us. We were the ones who really went to work in the fields every summer. ... We were the ones who worked our way up, got some education by fighting and scratching for it. Now he tells us that we're not really for the people because we're too middle class. Because we worked and got some education, suddenly that means we're not really with our people.[23]

Gutiérrez dismissed Raza Libre as "the same tired old group of ... Chicano vendidos who have opposed Raza Unida from the beginning." And they seemed only that when they were soundly defeated in races for two positions on the city council and two on the school board by margins of two to one. Unfortunately for Gutiérrez, the disenchanted losers became permanent enemies susceptible to the Anglo community's advances. They were the first signs of the political storm on the horizon.[24]

Despite these setbacks, however, the convention in Houston opened on a positive note with more than two hundred delegates representing about twenty-five counties. A sizable majority came from the urban areas and provided a new breed of activism, which tended to be slightly more liberal-left and more oriented toward the electoral process than the traditional RUP approach. Rubbing elbows with old, hardline nationalists were young Chicanos and Chicanas brought into the party by Muñiz's campaign. Some of them knew little of the party and even less of the time-tested organizing techniques that had been crucial to the party's founding. South Texas's main organizers were there, but they shared the convention space with campaign professionals led by Guerra who were concerned with media exposure, important endorsements, and the fact that "Sissy" Farenthold had refused to throw her support behind the only "liberal" left in the race. This time the main event was, without doubt, Muñiz. Gutiérrez, by now certain that his regional strategy was the right one, did not play as prominent a role in setting the direction of the convention. He told those who whispered that Muñiz was going astray that he was too preoccupied with Zavala County to worry about the other regions. What he did not tell them was that he could already see that the state elections were taking too much attention and energy away from the organizing activities. Of the twenty-five or so delegations attending, few of them had a solid base, a strong grassroots structure, or a treasury in the black back home.[25]

Gutiérrez lamented the fact that no "real" administrator was available to assume the party chairmanship. Compean had been fiercely loyal to him and a strong motivator of the troops, but he had not proven to be meticulous with details, nor was his nationalistic fervor helpful in attracting more established figures into the party. Compean had also been too strong an opponent in the battles over statewide versus regional politics, and that had hurt the party. Youngblood, a former MAYO activist with a strong grassroots base, a good relationship with Muñiz, and a firm belief in the regional approach, did not alleviate Gutiérrez's concerns. Youngblood was too isolated in Robstown, and his protocol was unrefined. He was also not a party builder, opting more toward community organizing and MAYO confrontational tactics. Gutiérrez believed, and he was partially right, that Youngblood wanted to keep the party leadership among the old activists and away from the urbanites but was not interested in the day-to-day activities. Unfortunately for Gutiérrez, no other strong candidate appeared to challenge Youngblood or Compean, who was still vacillating on whether to run or not. Coming into the state convention the old guard leadership seemed slightly undecided.

Such was not the case with the "new guard" of the Muñiz campaign. They came confident that they had tremendous support at the convention because of the large number of urban delegates and because one of their people, María Jiménez, was chairing the gathering. There were reporters from all the major newspapers and the convention was receiving prime-time coverage, much of it focused on Muñiz.

Muñiz, aware of his strength, nevertheless sought support

from those who questioned his style of politics. He knew they wanted to qualify his nationalism, so he gave the convention a stinging denunciation of the two parties: "Democratic Party, keep your flunkies and hacks. . . . we will not go back to your crooked poker-game party in order to defeat you. We are dedicated to bringing down the kind of politics that the old parties represent."[26] Muñiz also went after the liberals, conscious that the Texas press had added to the discontent in the party by commenting that he was interested in converting the Raza Unida into a populist party to broaden its appeal. "We are the terror of the liberals who have used our people for their own ends. . . . Raza Unida is showing liberals that we will never be used again and we are showing them that we can speak for ourselves. If liberals are so concerned about us, then let them follow our leadership."[27]

In part, Muñiz's rhetorical attack on the liberals revealed a hidden frustration over his inability to attract significant liberal endorsements or money. Even *The Texas Observer*, which had been generous in its praise of Muñiz in 1972, had begun to publish letters and commentaries hostile to the party. That June the magazine published an article entitled "After the Revolution in Cristal," which, though sympathetic, had highlighted what it called Raza Unida failures. It depicted some of the party's technocrats as Cadillac-driving, white-shoes-wearing, nepotistic but efficient fat cats. The law enforcement officers and court officials on the other hand, were described as thugs who owed their jobs to the party, not experience or expertise. This kind of liberal reaction had not been the aim of the "People Together" campaign, and the party rank and file wanted some blood, though Muñiz, even at this stage, left the door open for the liberals.

Another door that opened was the one toward the political left. A featured speaker at the meeting was Imamu Amiri Baraka, secretary-general of the National Black Political Assembly and the chairman of the Congress of African People (CAP). As a black socialist he came to warn the party of some of the pitfalls of nationalism: "We must realize that even though our struggles are at the stage of national liberation movements, that ultimately those struggles will never be resolved until our struggles seek to eliminate the system of private profit. We must find ever-increasing ways of fighting against capitalism and racism together." Baraka told them about Newark, where we have a black mayor and a black police chief with an Afro six inches high who wears a dashiki ... but go to where the masses of black people live and you find that we still have the highest infant mortality rate in the United States ... the highest tuberculosis rate ... [and] our people still live packed up in projects nineteen stories high where the rats and the roaches live like millionaires.[28]

The Houston chapter of CAP had endorsed Muñiz, and its members were out campaigning for him in the black neighborhoods. But they were not the only leftists making overtures to the party. The Socialist Workers Party's gubernatorial candidate, Sherry Smith, sent the convention a letter wishing Muñiz well and commending the party for its "living example for black people and trade unionists of the road of political action independent of the twin parties of war, racism and sexism."[29] At this point only the Texas and New Mexico chapters were still friendly to the SWP, which was barred from party meetings in California and Colorado. Its leaders, especially the Camejo brothers, Pedro and Antonio, had a good relationship with Gutiérrez, though not with Compean or with rural chapter leaders, some of whom had threatened SWP organizers with physical violence if they recruited in their areas. The SWP, which had been thrown out of most of the Chicano Movement's organizations by now, nurtured its relationship with a few leaders in the party and remained supportive of La Raza Unida at a time when the nationalists were under attack by the Anglo and Chicano left.

As had been the case with urban Raza Unida delegates in California, the Texas city delegates, in large part, were concerned with ideology. So were the rural delegates, but the two groups differed in orientation. The urban delegates, with no definable leader—Compean was a nationalist—sought to be an independent part of a larger international movement with a defined ideology such as that of Marxism. Many of them claimed to be socialists and tended to work with other leftist groups on different issues. While they vowed allegiance to Chicano culture, most spoke more English than Spanish and led lifestyles more appropriate to the college environment than to the barrio. A sizable number of the most influential members of this group were either students or faculty and staff of a university or college; others worked in social agencies or the public schools.

The issues important to them revolved around civil rights, Third World liberation movements, and university politics. They were supportive, even extremely supportive, of the party's rural strategy, but they felt isolated from it. They also found it hard to organize urban barrios under the concept of Chicano empowerment because the demographics worked against Chicano political control. Many of them did not live in the traditional barrios, either because they were not from the cities originally or because their education or profession broke many of the bonds they had with their communities. Seeking to organize people with whom they did not always identify was difficult. Not all urban activists had this problem, and some were more successful than others. The effective ones related to the people, organized small groups, and became a force in urban politics, but they were still hampered by the lack of numbers. Those who believed in the adaptation of the Crystal City model for urban Texas were by now in the minority.

Rural delegates, in contrast, came to the conference confident of their possibilities and with a record of accomplishments. At least fifteen county delegations could claim an electoral victory within the last four years or at least a significant amount of support that ranged from 30 to 40 percent of the vote. A good number of these delegates had some semblance of a local grassroots organization based on the Ciudadanos Unidos model. They had definable leaders with ties to the communities they represented and a core group of activists. Rural delegates did not feel dependent on the state party for success or for an ideology. For the most part, they were nationalist, though the zeal for this philosophy varied in intensity and in definition, depending on the locale. Their nationalism was, for some, a matter of replacing Anglos with Chicanos, for others a way of substituting middle-class Chicanos with people from the barrio, and for still others a vehicle for separatism, with the most extreme wing of this element favoring a nationalist liberation posture. Primarily, though, their nationalistic impulses were localized and in accord with their constituents' demands.

Culture was of ultimate importance, and was the activists' most successful organizing technique. Spanish was prerequisite, and for the serious organizer legitimacy in the eyes of *la comunidad* was crucial. Except for some of the returned college students and extreme radical nationalists, the organizers tried to participate in the main institutional activities of their communities, such as those of the church, the school, and the few self-help agencies available. This kind of background distinguished them from their urban counterparts, and by 1974 rural leaders viewed the "other" Raza Unida delegates with suspicion.

Youngblood's decision to seek the chairmanship was prompted by his concern that MAYO principles had ceased to play a part in the party's organizing activities. He saw little movement by the leaders to train the large influx of new members who came to the party with a great deal of energy but little direction. It bothered him to see Raza Unida "spokesmen" proclaiming political doctrines that were inconsistent with the party's ideology. In Robstown the eleventh political commandment, which he originated, read "Thou shalt not be a hero," and he saw many little caudillos in the party, especially in South Texas, who were too preoccupied with turf battles to concentrate on organizing. In running for the chairmanship, he hoped to return to the MAYO tactics of indoctrination and organization and to require discipline.[30] His candidacy was one of rejuvenation, and its popularity among the convention delegates made Youngblood the favorite for the party's top spot.

Compean, distraught over his divorce, withdrew his name from the race after he was nominated. Mindiola did the same. Youngblood quickly became the compromise candidate for both the Compean and the Muñiz delegates, although María Elena Martínez, of Austin, another former MAYO member, was nominated to run against him. She was in essence the urban candidate and, ironically, also Gutiérrez's choice. He saw her as more of a party administrator who would not be overwhelmed or bored by the paperwork involved in partisan politics and someone who did not have a hidden agenda or an interest in acquiring power. She had proved to be a loyal party worker with inexhaustible energy and a quick mind. Those who met her, even some of the rural members who lumped all Raza Unida women into the category of "groupies," were won over by her tenacity and her dedication to the party.[31] Along with other women such as Alma Canales, Marta Cotera, Evey Chapa, Rosie Castro, and Virginia Múzquiz, she had already played a significant role in extending the party to Chicanas. Youngblood, however, proved too popular to defeat.

Compean's absence from the party leadership proved a greater loss than was first thought. Few if any of the Raza Unida leaders could match his zeal for the party and its platform. If Gutiérrez was the mind behind the party, Compean was the heart, the tireless advocate, and the unrelenting noncompromiser who believed with a certainty that Chicanos wanted a third political party. He was

also Gutiérrez's most loyal follower, notwithstanding their differences over the state-versus-regional approach to organizing. But
the divorce from the woman who had worked alongside him in the
movement drained him, and he was burned out. Compean also
wanted to avoid a public fight with the Muñiz forces, who were
fuming because Compean had traveled the state criticizing in private the campaign's direction. He had even attacked Muñiz in his
former home base of Waco, an unforgivable act.

The animosity between Compean and Muñiz had reached an
explosive level by the time both arrived in Houston. Aside from
personal dislike, each saw the other as an obstacle to his direction
for the party. Gutiérrez attempted to mediate between them and
brought them together to discuss the strategy for the convention
at a nearby restaurant. But the conference quickly turned into a
shouting match, and in a violent burst of anger Muñiz took a swing
at Compean across the table. Gutiérrez's quick intervention saved
the party from an embarrassing public spectacle and Compean
from a serious injury at the hands of the much stronger Muñiz.[32]
After this episode, Compean decided that a reelection effort would
divide the convention into two camps. Most likely he realized that
a victory was not certain, although he later stated that he was confident of winning regardless of the opposition.[33]

The decision not to run diminished Compean's influence in
the party, and he went back to San Antonio to fight political obliv-
ion for a time. No one took notice, but Compean's absence also
ended the direct influence of the five original MAYO and Raza
Unida founders. Velásquez had not made the transition to RUP; Patlán by now was concerned only with MAUC; Nacho Pérez never
got involved in the party hierarchy; and Gutiérrez's attention focused almost exclusively on Cristal and the Winter Garden Area.
The chemistry that had created the spirit of La Raza Unida gave
way to the political maneuvering of the Muñiz campaign and the
narrow nationalism of Youngblood and his supporters. The direct
leadership of the five activists who had met at the Fountain Bar in
San Antonio disappeared. Only Compean tried a comeback. Gutiérrez seems to have decided to influence the party from the periph-
ery and not through a position on the executive board. There was
never a doubt who held the real mantle of leadership in the party,
but his isolation from the day-to-day decision-making process reduced Gutiérrez's influence on the direction of the party.

On the surface the convention ran smoothly, and those not
privy to the unseen turmoil went home enthused and ready to

campaign hard the last month of the election. Youngblood and his
supporters returned to South Texas strongly believing that they
had kept the party from going astray, and Gutiérrez went back to
campaigning for the Zavala County judge's seat. Muñiz returned to
the campaign trail with an even greater tenacity, hammering away
at the issues of "quality education," "tax reform," "insurance reform," and "revitalization of rural Texas." His radio advertising continually emphasized his populist theme of the big interests versus
the little man. It also pointed out the insensitivity of the state's
funding priorities: "In 1973 $2 million were spent on bilingual edu-
cation in 254 counties. That same year more was spent in five counties to kill flies. That is the record of the present governor. For me,
education is more important than killing flies; for that reason I am
a candidate for governor."[34]

As the campaign wound to a close, Muñiz challenged liberals
to look at their system and reject it for a new start, to search deeply
within themselves to see if they really wanted a continuation of
the same politics, except now for four instead of two years. "There
is no system more corrupt than a system that represents itself as
the example of freedom," he told them. To Chicanos, particularly
those who were apathetic or who were leaning toward the safe
Democrats, he issued a challenge: "If the most you can do as a man
is crawl like a worm, you forfeit the right to protest when you get
stepped on."[35] Muñiz even resorted to writing scathing poems
about Briscoe:

> Briscoe, Briscoe
> you old buzzard
> This is the Raza man
> and there are a few
> things you must understand
> The Chicano Vote
> has taken a new twist
> and will put an end
> to your midst
> The lies you have
> levied are now at an end
> . . . we have climbed
> the mountain
> now the air is thin
> and from here on out
> we intend to win.[36]

On election eve it became evident early that Guerra's "new look" had not worked. Muñiz's percentage did not rise at all and his overall vote, as well as that of the other party candidates, fell below the 1972 level. His vote total declined from 214,000 to 190,000, and he proved to be no factor at all in the race for governor. Part of the reason was the weak Republican candidate, Jim Granberry, who had quickly been given up for dead by his own party. Briscoe had united the conservative Democrats behind him and had proved to be palatable enough for those Republicans who did not like Granberry. More importantly, Briscoe recaptured some of the Mexican American Democratic votes he had lost to Muñiz in 1972. The liberals had simply held their noses and voted Democrat or stayed home. Muñiz attempted to downplay his low vote by pointing out that the total vote was significantly less than in 1972, but this fact did little to ameliorate the disappointment of his supporters and of the party leaders.

The only bright note of the 1974 election again turned out to be in Zavala County, where Gutiérrez defeated an Anglo Democrat in a close race for the county judgeship, the most powerful administrative position at the local level.[37] The Raza Unida also won a majority of the commissioners' races as well as the offices of county clerk, district clerk, and county treasurer. With these victories the party consolidated its control of Crystal City and the surrounding county. It was an impressive result for Ciudadanos Unidos, which had mobilized the voters throughout the county and taken them to the polls. It was also a personal triumph for Gutiérrez, who had remained committed to Cristal while others concentrated on the state elections. Winning elections represented real power, and Gutiérrez did not have to be accountable to anyone, especially the Anglos. He now had two things he hoped would finally break the Anglos' power in the county: the county courts and the taxing authority.

With that authority Gutiérrez wanted to increase several-fold the taxes paid to the county by the ranchers and the Del Monte cannery. This, he reasoned, would force some of the ranchers either to sell or lease the land to the county, which could then use it to cultivate crops and keep the migrants home. "There's no reason why we have to go 2,000 miles to pick beets in Oregon, potatoes in Idaho, or fruit in California. We can do that right here," he told a reporter from the socialist newspaper, *The Militant*.[38] The land the party sought was either not in use or being worked by machines and thus not providing jobs. Beyond taxing, Gutiérrez also saw the use of eminent domain as a tool to gain ten to twenty thousand acres the first year in office: "Twenty-six gringos own 87 percent of the land in this county. We think this is against the public welfare. Using arguments couched in the language of eminent domain, we can take some of that land away for public welfare."[39]

Keeping the migrants home and providing them with jobs would reinforce the Raza Unida voter rolls. More important, offers of jobs and land would placate the few voices of dissent within the lower classes of Cristal, which had provided the party its main support. The loyalists in the middle class already had been rewarded with teaching positions and jobs in the city government and the school districts. Also, numerous "outsiders" had been recruited to perform functions that were beyond the capacity or training of most local residents. This fact had begun to cause some resentment among those whose overall condition had not changed. They were suspicious of men who made salaries in the twenty-thousand-dollar range, drove new cars, and had working wives. They, on the other hand, had dead-end jobs or none at all and were going to stay in Crystal City even after the federal grants ran out. Landownership was the principal reason revolutions were fought in Latin America, and Gutiérrez knew Chicanos had an affinity for land. The concept of a communal farm also formed the first strategy of a Chicano collectivism that Gutiérrez envisioned as he moved toward socialism.

This mass of supporters was volatile, and Gutiérrez knew he had to prove to them that La Raza Unida did mean a change. Rhetoric and pride would only go so far, especially when a small vocal opposition was accusing the party of being worse than the Anglos. Another important reason for keeping the migrants home and happy was that it would guarantee that their children would stay in school, where they could be indoctrinated into the party philosophy. Gutiérrez saw the Crystal City youth as the future vanguard of La Raza Unida, one trained in party principles and organizing techniques and not susceptible to threats or buy-offs. Already they had proven to be his strongest supporters, and with over 80 percent of those graduating from high school going to college, he knew they were going to be a highly skilled group.[40]

The victory in Cristal revived Gutiérrez's optimism that South Texas could be organized into the Raza Unida camp. The novelty of a few more brown faces in the Democratic Party would pale in comparison to the bold and innovative reforms that the party would implement in Zavala County. Yet, despite his great expectations for the surrounding area, Gutiérrez had no such hope for the state party. The low vote and the fact that gubernatorial elections would now be every four years left the state party without a strategy, especially for the urban centers, where political takeovers were not possible. Gutiérrez realized that a third Muñiz campaign in four years would not have the impact of the first or even the second one, and the possibility remained that the soft support for the party would melt away by 1978, the next time a gubernatorial election would be held.

As was his custom, Gutiérrez called for a discussion of the future role of the state party. He sent a letter to several party leaders outlining the options available. Among them were leaving the political arena completely and concentrating on organizing activist groups, joining the Democratic Party and developing a radical wing, disbanding altogether, or returning to the regional strategy first proposed by Gutiérrez in 1970.[41] A series of meetings then took place, most of them organized by María Elena Martínez, who played a prominent role. Others deeply involved were Mindiola, Bustamante, Armando Gutiérrez, and a small core of party members who had felt left out of the Muñiz campaign. Compean, still shaken by his divorce, attended one or two meetings but did not figure prominently in the discussions. Also missing from most of them was Youngblood, the state chairman, who by then was very active in Robstown politics, one of the few bright spots in the Raza Unida rural strategy. Conspicuous by his absence was Muñiz. A few of his supporters came to the first meetings but soon stopped attending. Most had actually believed that he could win or at least have a major impact on the governor's race. When his showing was less significant in 1974, than in 1972, they were disillusioned, and many of them started moving back toward the Democratic Party.

A few members of the core group still supported Muñiz, but even they could not see a major role for him in future party politics. With state political campaigns out of the picture for at least four years and with most of the core members anxious to do more organizing than campaigning, Muñiz's status as a party leader quickly faded. Some party activists, most notably Compean, were prepared to challenge Muñiz in the Raza Unida nominating convention if he chose to run a third time.[42] Muñiz probably sensed this opposition and decided to take time away from state politics in order to evaluate his own future and to revive a law practice that had been dormant for more than a year.

The extensive discussions soon narrowed down the options to Gutiérrez's original approach of taking one rural region at a time. Gutiérrez told the activists that the statewide electoral campaigns had not worked and that there seemed little hope that things would be different in the near future. He again urged the urban chapters to serve as resource centers for the local grassroots organizations that had a chance of achieving political takeovers, rather than wasting their time on expensive campaigns with no hope of succeeding. This time Gutiérrez did not have an articulate opponent, but in any case the circumstances did not allow for a complete change of strategy. A statewide structure existed that could not simply be ignored, and there were urban chapters that needed to fit into some kind of organizational system. Still, the party activists did give in by pledging more support for the rural chapters and a greater dedication to the arduous task of recruiting new members and developing vanguard units in their locales.[43]

Not all of the chapters felt optimistic about the prospect of better days ahead, however. Particularly pessimistic were the chapters from Cotulla and the Rio Grande Valley, which had been closely associated with the Muñiz campaign. The Cotulla group did not have any real political strategist or ideologue who could guide the chapter. In Compean's view Cotulla was like Mexico—too far from God and too close to the colossus of the north. In this case the "colossus" was Gutiérrez's Crystal City chapter. Consequently, the Cotulla group never fully implemented a local Raza Unida strategy based on a specific ideological view of its political and social circumstances. The activists there remained political reformers who by the middle of 1975 were not attending many of the party's reevaluation meetings.[44]

By contrast, the Valley chapters, headed by Jesús "Chuy" Ramírez, did have a political agenda. And they used the Muñiz campaign to build their network among the Mexican American Democrats who were supportive of the third-party alternative in the governor's race. Extremely astute politicians, they quickly saw the impending demise of the party and the need to build links to the political mainstream. Like the Cotulla group, the Valley activists soon eased themselves out of statewide activities and began to plan their next move before the 1976 electoral campaigns.

Two key individuals also taking time to reevaluate their circumstances were Alberto Luera in Laredo, and Youngblood in Robstown. Luera was director of the Centro Cultural Aztlán, one of several social-service and cultural enhancement agencies founded by party activists to provide a gathering place for supporters and potential recruits. Youngblood continued as head of Familias Unidas. Unlike the activists in Cotulla and the Valley, these two did not seek a link to any other group; instead, they were concerned with their own communities and unsure whether an affiliation with a state Raza Unida Party was an asset.[45] Both seemed ready to revert to a provincialism common in the days before the movement, when mobility was limited for Chicanos. Luera wanted to continue building his center's credibility in Laredo, and that meant toning down his rhetoric. Youngblood had dissenters in Familias Unidas who were not happy with the Raza Unida affiliation, and he had to placate them in order to win the elections of 1975 and 1976 and take political control of Robstown.

In one year the situation had become complicated for La Raza Unida, and a good deal of the enthusiasm had waned. Party activists were burned out, and middle-class Chicanos had gone out to shop for new candidates and a new party. The failure of Muñiz's effort, coupled with the party's inability to establish an urban strategy, left only a few rural areas with any prospect of further victories.

People in La Raza Unida were
naive to think we could use the system
and not have the system come down
on us as hard as it did.

—María Elena Martínez, 1980

THE PARTY IS OVER
FOR RUP

The years 1975 through 1977 were disastrous for La Raza Unida Party. Notwithstanding the pledges of commitment to the rural strategy and to the development of ideology, the party failed to make any significant advances in political victories or in new conversions. The party began to decline rapidly after 1975, even though a few Raza Unida chapters did consolidate power and made some organizing progress. The problems began abruptly in 1975, when Flores Anaya, former senatorial candidate of the party, was indicted for possession of heroin. Anaya denied his guilt and charged that the accusation came about because he accidently discovered the identity of an undercover agent. He was nevertheless convicted and jailed.[1] Although most Raza Unida leaders believed he had been framed, they nonetheless had expected some kind of drug-related action against members of the party because a sizable minority of them was involved in the casual use of drugs. This was especially true in the university-based chapters and among the urban members who believed in the legalization of marijuana. This position drew adamant opposition from rural activists, and it became a matter of contention at the state conventions.[2]

Anaya had not been a prominent member of the party, and his conviction was quickly overshadowed by one more important and more injurious to the Raza Unida. On July 31, 1976, the *Corpus Christi Caller* carried a wide banner headline declaring, "Ramsey

197

Muñiz sought for drug trafficking." The article described an eleven-count indictment, the result of an eighteen-month investigation into the activities of Muñiz and Fred Brulloths, Jr., a convicted drug trafficker already serving time in prison. The indictment charged Muñiz and his brother Roberto, as well as Brulloths, with a conspiracy to possess marijuana with intent to distribute, and the use of the telephone in conspiring to commit a felony. The illegal activities had begun June 1975 and included smuggling marijuana from Mexico by airplane and transporting it to Alabama to be sold.[3] Two Raza Unida members who worked for Muñiz were also indicted.

Raúl Villarreal, of Kingsville, who had a habit of rising early to buy the newspaper, was one of the first Raza Unida members to see the headline. He showed it to Abel Cavada and muttered several times angrily, *"Que pendejo!"* (What a fool!).[4] Villarreal's reaction proved to be consistent with that of most of the South Texas activists, who felt betrayed by Muñiz. The response was harsh partly because he had been so popular in the region and partly because he had committed an unforgivable political blunder.

Shortly after the 1974 election Muñiz had opened a law office in Robstown and had become deeply involved with Familias Unidas, which was readying itself to launch an all-out bid to take over the political control of the city and the school board. He attracted media attention, which assisted in the organizing efforts, and on more than one occasion he subsidized events out of his own pocket. He had been able to penetrate the rural distrust with his charisma and his support of the local chapters. His decision to come to Robstown to help Youngblood with Familias Unidas represented, to rural activists at least, a real commitment to the cause. Muñiz had backed up his rhetoric of Chicano self-determination with a move that threatened to limit his career and his political rise for the sake of his people.[5]

Rural activists could have forgiven Muñiz for any of a large number of judicial difficulties but drug trafficking was not one of them. It went completely against their social values and presented a difficult obstacle to organizing a community that tended to be socially conservative. For local leaders such as Villarreal and Youngblood, as well as Luera, the indictments compromised their credibility and provided ammunition for their Democratic opponents. It seemed to confirm the charge that Raza Unida members were pot-smoking, long-haired *sin verguenzas* (shameless ones) who were constantly in trouble with law enforcement agencies. Muñiz

had seemed different, so respectful and law-biding. Yet there were
those who knew that he was keeping the wrong company and was
receiving large amounts of money that could not be coming from
a chaotic law practice. Others had seen Muñiz attending dances
while high on marijuana.[6] Court testimony later revealed that he
continually got into debt, and bounced checks and yet carried large
amounts of cash with which he paid his employees instead of pay-
roll checks.[7]

Throughout the state, activists scrambled to explain to their
constituents either that Muñiz had been framed for political purposes or that he did not represent the party. The urban chapters
declared the former, and the rural chapters professed the latter.[8]
Both groups believed Muñiz had been singled out because of his
party activities, but although some in the urban chapters wanted
to make him a martyr for the cause, the rural organizers wanted to
avoid any fallout if he proved to be guilty. Few in the party hierarchy ever believed that he had been framed. Most had been privy to
rumors that Muñiz had become involved in drug trafficking. It was
the kind of information that could not be kept out of the networks
of traveling activists who roamed the state spreading gossip and
pieces of news that did not reach the media. The party leaders had
simply ignored the rumors in the hope that Muñiz would not get
caught.[9]

Muñiz's crimes and the indiscretions of others posed a major
dilemma for the party because no provisions had ever been instituted to deal with such problems. Not since the twelve rules of
MAYO had any principles been developed to regulate the conduct
of party members. Problems were usually solved at the local level,
where certain unwritten norms prevailed, such as in Kingsville,
where activists were expected never to be drunk or to use obscen-
ity in a public gathering. In Robstown conduct that reflected negatively on Familias Unidas was dealt with swiftly in one of the
weekly meetings, in which culprits were verbally attacked and
warned of physical retribution if they did not reform their conduct.
Muñiz went through one of those sessions when he first came to
Robstown. He had assumed the role of spokesman of the organization without consulting the membership and was immediately
challenged. In one of the meetings he was seated in front of the
members and told that in Robstown everything was done in a collective manner and only after it was agreed upon democratically.
Then a couple of the more forceful members told him to conform

or face the possibility of being literally "kicked out of town."[10] But this kind of regulation was not common in all chapters and was absent at the state level. A significant number of urban activists and a sizable minority in the rural areas did not like to be told how to run their private affairs.

María Elena Martínez was one who felt that a code of conduct was needed, but neither she or nor any other leader of the party brought it up in the form of a motion at the state conventions. Party members' passions and indiscretions were allowed full freedom at a time when their behavior provided ammunition for attacks from the middle class and the Democrats. The state hierarchy had no real power over the local chapters. Other than threatening not to seat them at the state conventions—a sanction that was never carried out—no provisions were instituted to deal with wayward chapters or members beyond those required by the Texas Election Code. The Muñiz crisis revealed an ideological weakness, an Achilles' heel within the party that prompted critics to say that Raza Unida had no real philosophy by which its members could not only politick but live.

On November 15 things got worse when Muñiz was handed another indictment, this one with four counts, by a San Antonio grand jury for activities similar to those charged in the earlier indictment. The following week he failed to appear at a Corpus Christi federal courthouse, and the headlines read, "Muñiz jumps bond, may be in Mexico."[11] This time it was Compean's turn to say *Pendejo otra vez* (fool, again!), and for the party activists to go through another political convulsion, prompting some of them to demand a resolution of the Muñiz problem altogether. Others hoped that the former candidate would simply disappear into Mexico, never to be heard from again. But drug enforcement agents had mapped out Muñiz well, and they tipped off the Mexican police on his whereabouts. He was captured in Reynosa, Tamaulipas, just across the Rio Grande. By Christmas Eve he was in Nuevo Laredo, and on Christmas Day U.S. law enforcement officers met their Mexican counterparts at the middle of the international bridge and took custody of Muñiz.[12]

It was an unshaved, tired, and battered Muñiz who arrived in the San Antonio jail, where he was visited by Gutiérrez, Compean, and several other members of the party's hierarchy for a few awkward moments. No one asked him about the drug trafficking charge, and he did not volunteer any information. Gutiérrez later claimed that Muñiz told him in a subsequent meeting that he had been "suckered" into drug dealing when he began counseling drug traffickers about their legal rights.[13] After the visit to the jail, some plans were discussed about a defense committee, but it became obvious that Muñiz had only weak support. Abbie, his wife and chief fundraiser for the committee, found some of his former middle-class supporters alienated, unwilling to be associated with a man accused of peddling drugs. Those party members who chose to get involved in the defense found an equal alienation in the core group of members, particularly those who had not yet forgotten or forgiven Muñiz's "People Together" campaign. A number of the activists gave lip service to the Ramsey Muñiz Defense Committee but did little else. Gutiérrez became involved, but even he was ineffective in raising funds.[14]

Some of the party leaders attempted to salvage a political victory by contacting Michael Kennedy, well-known defense attorney who specialized in defending political activists, but his fee of sixteen thousand dollars was too steep for the party coffers. Muñiz did not make things any easier by behaving detached and giving conflicting messages as to whether he wanted help or not.[15] On February 2, 1977, he shocked his supporters again by pleading guilty to one of the four counts in the San Antonio indictments, even as his supporters were combing the state for funds. With his conviction—he was sentenced to fifteen years in jail for both indictments—Muñiz closed the party's door to the middle class and, in essence, to the media, which had been quite friendly to him.[16]

Shortly before Muñiz's indictment Martínez had taken over as party chairperson at the Seguin conference held in the summer of 1976. By her own account, she inherited a party in financial chaos, suffering from a steady desertion of activists and low morale. There were few mid-level organizers or activists left who seemed willing or financially and emotionally able to carry on the struggle. Aside from Crystal City, Robstown, Cotulla, Kingsville, San Antonio, Austin, and some areas in West Texas, Raza Unida activism seemed at a standstill.[17] No training was taking place, and most campus activism was wavering, except that with a Marxist bent to it. The most active members of the party were those who had joined in 1974 and assumed leadership roles in the vacuum that had been created since then. Such was the case with Armando Gutiérrez, an assistant professor of political science at the University of Texas at Austin. He represented the new Raza Unida spokesman: articulate, well educated, university-based, and with little or no experience organizing people in the barrio.[18] These members attracted students and some in the radical chic but did little to excite the masses or the hardcore barrio activists, who were suspicious of the slick-talking intellectuals.

This constituency soon found another base in the Mexican American Democrats (MAD), a conglomeration of numerous activists, trade unionists, bureaucrats, young professionals, and old liberals who sought to take over the "progressive wing" of the Democratic Party. Founded in December 1976, it quickly absorbed many Raza Unida refugees. Among the first converts to MAD were the party leaders from the Rio Grande Valley, led by Jesús "Chuy" Ramírez and Juan Maldonado. Willie Velásquez, the ex-MAYO leader, had arranged a meeting in El Paso between the Raza Unida members and the leaders of MAD. There, Velásquez joked later, "The BAD (born again Democrats) joined the MADs."[19] The desertion of those Raza Unida activists left the party without a capable leader or an effective organization in the Rio Grande Valley. Because of his quick mind and sharp communication skills, Ramírez had been perceived by many RUP leaders as the heir apparent to Gutiérrez. His change of heart was a bitter and personal blow to Gutiérrez, a good friend, who continued to praise Ramírez's militancy even after his switching of political affiliations.[20] The decision to change parties came after intense political pressure. Democrats in control of the county, in alliance with state officials, had found ways of shutting off state and federal funds, and the San Juan activists felt their community being slowly strangled financially.

The Mexican American Democrats' founding was far from auspicious. Almost instantly it could count on a number of elected officials, a strong base of support in South Texas, and a good mixture of young militants and established old militants such as Albert Peña, Jr., and Joe Bernal. Quick to offer a welcoming hand were the Anglo liberals and even some conservatives anxious to see a new organization in direct battle with La Raza Unida Party for the Mexican American vote. By 1977 the new political wing had gained another important following. The Raza Unida chapter from Cotulla changed its affiliation to that of independent and then to Mexican American Democrat, stealing the second most electorally successful structure in the party.[21]

Another group that moved away from the party, if not the party philosophy, was Familias Unidas of Robstown. By the end of his tenure as state chairman in 1976, Youngblood did not believe he could still work with the urban chapters, even though he got along with most of their leaders and served technically as their boss. He nicknamed the urban activists the "Down with the Shah crowd" and used the old Gutiérrez argument that the people of the barrio were not interested in overthrowing the rulers in Iran or in any other Third World country, but were more concerned with the daily issues of jobs, education, and discrimination. Youngblood also questioned the commitment of the urban members to the maintenance of Chicano culture and Chicano traditions and criticized their lack of command of Spanish and, in some cases, their Anglo girlfriends. A sizable number of the members of Familias Unidas concurred with him, as did their neighbors to the west in Kingsville and to the south in Laredo.[22]

By early 1976 Familias Unidas had begun moving away from the party affiliation and toward an independent course that sought to ride out the current urban-dominated party composition. Part of the alienation was prompted by hotly contested races in the city and school elections. Familias Unidas had enough members both in the city council and on the school board to create stalemates in the functions of both entities, and a victory in the spring guaranteed a complete shift of power toward the Chicano community. Robstown promised to be as big a prize as Crystal City, and to achieve it Familias Unidas had to stay together and avoid any political mistakes before the election.[23]

Youngblood and his supporters were well organized and were confident that a strong turnout would mean a victory. Activists in Kingsville saw the significance of a Robstown win, and they were out in the streets supporting the Familias Unidas efforts, hoping that their turn would come in 1977. On election day the town seemed overrun by Familias Unidas supporters driving to and from the voting places. The organization's posters, bumper stickers, and leaflets were everywhere, and vehicles with loudspeakers kept up a continuous broadcast, urging Mexican Americans to go to the polls to defeat the coalition of gringos and "vendidos" who formed the Concerned Citizens of Robstown. But although the opposition was less obvious, it got its supporters to the polls and made sure that the absentee voting went its way. It did at a rate of thirty to one, giving Concerned Citizens enough of an edge to sweep most of the positions up for election.[24]

Familias Unidas members were devastated. There just did not

seem to them to be enough people against them to lose. They quickly challenged the absentee vote, taking the list of voters and tracking down the people who had sent in their ballots. They found numerous empty lots, as well as people who had not voted, but the majority of names were those of people in nursing homes. Those voters, a good number senile, had been herded down to the polling places and told how to vote and had actually been helped to punch out the ballots. Also found was evidence that a large percentage of the ballots had been signed by the same polling judge. Unfortunately for Familias Unidas, a judge ruled that the voting irregularities were not intentional, and the election stood. Without money to appeal, the election challenge simply died, and with it went the morale and zeal of the organization. The Muñiz conviction that summer put the last few nails in The Familias Unidas political coffin and though the organization did exist for at least another year, it did not have much of an impact on the next municipal elections. In the end, the few elected officials remaining in Familias Unidas resigned their posts to close the Chicano activist chapter in Robstown.[25]

As the party collapsed around him, Gutiérrez remained un-scathed. Except for some indirect criticism levied at him by a few in the party—particularly Albert Peña III—he continued to enjoy the support of the other party leaders and most of the member-ship.[26] But things began to change in 1976, and by 1977 he was barely holding on to power in Zavala County and had lost control of the city government to another Raza Unida faction.

Gutiérrez's problems began shortly after he returned from a trip to Cuba, where he and eighteen other activists from across the country had been invited to tour the country by Fidel Castro. As would be expected from a Chicano militant with separatist and socialist tendencies, he was impressed by what he saw, and as was his custom, he told everyone, including the media, that there were things to learn from Cuba.[27] Especially impressive to him was the high level of party organization and discipline. He told a reporter, "We want to emulate their discipline and intensity so we can lift ourselves out of poverty." Shortly after returning, he announced the formation of a *Comité de Nueve* (Committee of Nine), which would make decisions on hirings and firings in the city and schools and would be the top policy maker in the party. This group or a similar one had already been meeting informally for nearly two years, but Gutiérrez wanted to strengthen its powers. Ciudadanos

Unidos already had a twenty-seven-member committee of city and county department heads and elected officials which did much of that work but was accountable to the four-hundred-family membership. It was also more cumbersome, though: too many people participated, and the meetings went on endlessly. When Gutiérrez pressed his idea to streamline the hierarchy, those who were uneasy about his trip and his praising of Cuba's communism quickly moved to stack the committee with their own people, thus dampening Gutiérrez's enthusiasm for using it.[28]

The internal victory by Gutiérrez's opponents ushered in a new era in Crystal City Raza Unida politics. A number of his closest followers began challenging Gutiérrez's decisions and were able to influence enough members of the party to outvote him on issues dealing with hirings and firings. By 1976 the division between the Gutierristas and those politically tied to the Barrio Club, a twenty-five-member social club whose leaders spearheaded the opposition, became so profound that Ciudadanos Unidos split into two organizations, each claiming to be the real Ciudadanos Unidos. There were even two versions of *La Verdad*, the Raza Unida Party newspaper. The parting of the ways left the Barrio Club followers in control of the school board, while the county remained in Gutierrista hands. The reigns of city government shifted back and forth. The dividing of the spoils meant that political persecution of rival followers intensified, causing a shifting of jobs. The pro-Gutiérrez faction resigned en masse from the school district and caused the district to be put on probation by the Texas Education Agency because of a lack of certified administrators. Numerous lawsuits were filed by both parties alleging everything from nepotism to libel and slander. Families were split, and the hostilities became pronounced.

When the media found out about the conflict they highlighted it in features and articles, thinly veiling a condescending and stereotypic view that insinuated that *envidia* (envy, jealousy) was the motivating factor behind the dispute. *Texas Monthly* magazine's Tom Curtis began his "exposé" on Crystal City by retelling Gutiérrez's version of the "crab story": An Anglo fisherman on a coastal jetty has caught a bunch of crabs and has put them in a shallow bucket near him. When he turns his back on the bucket to return to crabbing, the people next to him cry that the catch will escape. "It's OK," he reassures them. "They are *Mexican* crabs—they'll pull each other back down." Curtis first denied that this was the case in

Crystal City but contradicted himself in the conclusion by stating
that the party's failure there was a "testimony to the enduring
power of . . . ambition, vanity, *greed* and *envy*" (author's italics).[29]

This kind of explanation was an oversimplification promoted
by the media and even by many within the party. It fully ignored
the passion and idealism of those involved in the internal struggles.
There were a number of opportunists on both sides and probably
some provocateurs in alliance with the Anglo ranchers, but the
majority of active combatants were convinced that the other side
was wrong and, if allowed to, would cause disaster for Crystal City.
From the time of the school board victory in 1970, there had been
several currents of thought among the members of Ciudadanos
Unidos. There were the spit-revolutionaries interested in slogans
and buttons; the Mexican supernationalists, who wanted to do
away with the English language; and the war veterans, who disliked
the Anglo but not his policies. Gutiérrez had maintained power
because he was successful in creating and sustaining coalitions
among the varied constituencies. He stood out among them because of his education, his organizing abilities, and his economic
stability, which allowed him flexibility and independence. He was
a world traveler in a rural pond where mobility beyond the migrant
stream was almost nonexistent.

Gutiérrez's influence could be felt everywhere, and in time
that bothered those who remembered the modest young activist
who had refused the spotlight during the school walkout and the
subsequent elections. Some of those who became his most determined enemies had been his strongest early supporters. One candidate who shared the Raza Unida school board ticket with Gutiérrez
turned against him by 1974. In an affidavit to the Federal Bureau of
Investigation he stated: "It didn't take long for this organization
[Ciudadanos Unidos] to have control over anything that was happening in Raza Unida Party."[30] He went on to detail meetings in
which Gutiérrez conspired to have people fired and to have truck-
ers given traffic violations because they were transporting scabs to
the ranches of Anglos resisting unionization. He also charged that
the party had city and urban-renewal employees working the
streets for the party on election day. He went on to say: "On election day they have a special table next to the entrance to the polling place, to make sure you are a faithful 'Raza Unida.' You have to
sign your name with them on that special table, and especially if
you work for a federal program."[31]

Particularly indignant about Gutiérrez's prominence and power were some of the young turks who felt ready to take positions of leadership. Few had any desire to challenge him directly, but they were not hesitant about defying those he appointed to positions in the city, county, or school district. A good number of those appointees were outsiders who failed to integrate into the Crystal City community. Interestingly, some of them were not strong members of the party but were simply loyal to Gutiérrez. Like Muñiz, Gutiérrez attracted a number of well-educated, middle-class followers who seemed to bypass the party hierarchy in their access to the real power.[32]

At the same time, in Crystal City his strongest supporters continued to be the less-educated, poorer, and more traditional families within Ciudadanos Unidos. They were the people for whom the revolution was meant, and he communicated easily with them. Those residents of Crystal City—in fact, most of Crystal City—were isolated from the chaotic state party politics and consequently were less affected by the ideological battles. Unfortunately for Gutiérrez, those who did develop politically began to question his almost absolute power. He aggravated their concerns by saying on more than one occasion that he was the smartest one of them and needed to be the one making all the decisions. "I do think that I'm smarter than anybody else here. . . . I know more, I have better contacts—that's why they followed me for seven years. Now they think they're grown up and can run things; they can't. We still need to have one leader."[33] He also accused his opponents of being political "tortillas"—opportunists who switched sides every time the political grill got too hot.

The conflict in Crystal City affected the party even nationally, as groups debated the causes of the internal problems and took sides. Theories abounded about the struggle. One theory that surfaced in California placed the blame on a group of Brown Berets in Crystal City who became part of the Barrio Club. By this time the Berets were believed to have been infiltrated by federal agents, and so Gutiérrez's opposition was labeled as a band of provocateurs. No evidence was ever uncovered, however, even from documents Gutiérrez later obtained under the Freedom of Information Act, that the federal government was directly involved, though the possibility continues to be credible among some.[34]

Father Sherill Smith, a Catholic priest active in the civil rights movement and an early supporter of Gutiérrez, was one of those

disenchanted with the party leader's "total Machiavellian" approach
to playing politics and his unwillingness to share power. "If you're
going to elevate people, you're going to have to deal with them
once they're elevated," Smith told a reporter in 1977. The response
from the Gutierristas was swift, ruthless as well as sententious, and
depicted the priest as both a liar and a coward. The meaness of the
rhetoric only served to further alienate the priest and a group of
families outraged at what they perceived to be malicious attacks
on the Church.[35] Ciudadanos Unidos members were not beyond
threatening and using physical violence. Before the Barrio Club
split from the Gutiérrez faction, its members had served as goons,
since many of them were rough characters with police records and
a history of involvement in vice, particularly the transporting of
drugs. When the Barrio Club repudiated Gutiérrez, it turned its
intimidation tactics against party members.

The anti-Gutierristas did not hesitate to fire their opponents
from their jobs, nor were they shy about using city and school
funds to increase their strength and diminish Gutiérrez's. As soon
as they gained control of the schools, they began to make changes,
such as toning down the rhetoric and the political indoctrination
and erasing the Raza murals on the walls.[36] By 1976 they were
secretly dealing with the Anglo Democrats to oust Gutiérrez from
office through the ballot box or the courts. They acquiesced when
the Texas Rangers opened an office in Crystal City to "investigate
the county." And they were not necessarily displeased when the
state attorney general opened a branch office in the city, the only
such office in rural Texas, to investigate county government. No
convictions, however, came from any of the investigations. In fact,
no Raza Unida officeholder anywhere in the state was ever convicted of a crime while in office.

In 1976 Gutiérrez suffered his first major electoral defeat
when the anti-Gutierrista candidates swept to victory in the April
school board races by margins of nearly three hundred votes. A
week later the opposition repeated its success, this time in the city
council races, with a margin of two hundred votes. In the space of
a week Gutiérrez's hold on power slipped substantially. The Barrio
Club members had learned Gutiérrez's organizing techniques well.
They came into the party not as one entity but rather as members
of the different organized sectors within Ciudadanos Unidos. The
Ciudadanos Unidos organization attempted to represent all the different groups in the county: labor, government, teachers, women,

students, and so on. By having its members spread throughout the sectors but voting and working together, the club was able to get its members to be selected as candidates without being accused of monopolizing power. Since the Barrio Club had no real ideology, it could form coalitions with any group that would help it to gain power. Gutiérrez's opponents felt confident, and next they challenged him in the county races. Three different groups took part. The Anglos ran a Mexican American Democrat for sheriff, and with quiet help from Gutiérrez's rivals he easily defeated the Raza Unida candidate by a vote of 2,081 to 1,431. The anti-Gutierristas, unwilling to run as Democrats, ran a write-in candidate for county commissioner in a district considered a strong Gutiérrez stronghold and came within nineteen votes of achieving an upset. The people of Crystal City had learned the write-in method well from Gutiérrez and were now ready to use it against him. But they also claimed that Gutiérrez had learned well from the Anglos, and they accused him of using technicalities to turn back the challenge. They charged that his supporters, serving as election judges, had thrown out enough flawed votes whose intent was clear to preserve a RUP victory. One reporter captured the irony of the situation by reminding his readers that Gutiérrez's organizing tract, *A Gringo Manual on How to Control Mexicans*, told how Anglos retained power by invoking technicalities against write-in candidates.[37]

Gutiérrez realized that one of the reasons for the party's problems was the fact that the county had no economic base. There were only so many positions of leadership to give out, and the Anglo ranchers still remained a powerful force because they could finance elections and in time would be able to attract some of the opposition, as they did in the sheriff's race. Political patronage, he knew, was important in keeping the loyalty of the people who had no interest in ideological conflicts. Migrant workers had been an unintimidated source of support because they did not depend on the Anglos for their jobs. But Gutiérrez recognized that with the rising opposition within the party he needed to have most of them around all year long. With his opponents controlling the patronage in the school and city, he had to provide another avenue by which he could dispense jobs. Beyond political expediency Gutiérrez also wanted to develop an economic base that would one day challenge that of the ranchers in the area.

From the beginning of his days in MAYO and then in Ciudadanos Unidos, Gutiérrez had been planning and initiating economic development projects to enhance the party's financial structure. From a hog farm to a beer franchise to a record distributorship, the attempts met with no success. There was never enough capital or clients. When "Brown Capitalism" did not work, Gutiérrez decided to seek federal funds to buy one thousand acres on which to establish a collective farm that would be administered by the Zavala County Economic Development Corporation (ZCEDC), an organization of about two hundred families who paid dues of ten dollars a year and elected a board of directors. The corporation, headed by Jesús Salas, envisioned a collective farm with a salary scale above the minimum wage, fringe benefits such as life insurance and hospitalization coverage, and an employer-employee investment plan for either scholarships or low-cost housing. There would be hot meals in the fields and day-care centers for the employees' children who were too young for school.[38]

The plans called for cultivating five hundred acres with vegetable crops for the produce market. Half of those crops would be labor-intensive, such as cherry tomatoes, cucumbers, broccoli, and spinach, and the other half would need less care but could keep the processing plant running to provide jobs. The other five hundred acres were intended for grain crops used for feed. Fifty families were to be hired on a permanent, full-time basis, and two hundred other families would be employed from six to eight months, a time span similar to that of the migrant season. Salas described the operations in a holistic manner:

> We're planning a complete Manpower Development Program within the farm itself, from the actual planting, the hoeing, the thinning, and the utilization of whatever herbicides and insecticides ... necessary ... to deliver our produce to the hospitals or chain stores or wherever we sell it. It's a whole integrated operation and we see establishment of some kind of job program so that there can be mobility so that people are not relegated to working in the fields for the rest of their lives. ... Part of the development of the cooperative farm has to be involved in putting [back] dignity into the work of raising food.[39]

An integral part of the proposal was an export-import branch in which the ZCEDC would serve as a broker for produce coming from Mexico. The farm workers would grade, select, and pack it, and then ship it out under the ZCEDC label. The exporting of goods to Mexico would also be attempted, with the assistance of the Instituto México Comercial Exterior, which at the time had been sponsoring trade fairs in San Antonio.

Through the efforts of a young Mexican scholar, Jorge Bustamante, Gutiérrez had developed a personal relationship with Mexico's left-leaning president, Luis Echeverría Alvarez, who was trying to establish himself as the leader of the Third World and was thus open to dealing with radical groups. Echeverría, whom Gutiérrez later described as the most sensitive Mexican president with respect to Chicanos, became partial toward the Raza Unida Party and its leader. He donated a statue of Benito Juárez to Crystal City and even set up meetings between his advisers and leaders of the party to discuss economic development in the border area. José López Portillo, Echeverría's successor, retained the cordial contacts and implemented a scholarship program entitled "Becas de Aztlán," which provided millions of dollars in scholarships to send Mexican American students to professional schools in Mexico. This type of relationship with the Mexican government gave Gutiérrez confidence in the import-export part of the project.[40]

ZCEDC submitted a $1.5 million grant proposal to the Community Services Administration (CSA), which at first seemed to favor the idea and provided nearly $200,000 in seed money to help develop the project. The Ford administration, like the Nixon administration before it, seemed inclined to provide most of the federal funds requested by Crystal City. This irked the Democrats, especially Briscoe, who still resented the close race forced on him by the Muñiz campaign. He also did not like the idea of collective farming, because he owned nearly twenty-two thousand acres near Zavala County as well as the largest bank in the area. The collective farm was a competitor to both of his economic enterprises.

Briscoe branded the project an effort to promote socialism and used it as an issue against the Ford administration during the presidential campaign of 1976. In stumping for Democrat Jimmy Carter, he told fellow conservatives:

> If you want your tax money used to establish a little Cuba in Texas—to establish a communal farm in Texas—to promote socialism in Texas—If you want federal funds to finance efforts to destroy the free enterprise system, the capitalistic system that has built this state and this nation, then you want a continuation of power of an administration that makes such grants to the Raza Unida Party.[41]

At Briscoe's request, state attorney general John Hill filed suit to stop the $1.5 million, which had tentatively been approved, from being distributed or used. The action was taken to forestall a decision on the grant until a new Democratic administration was in office. The actions by Briscoe and Hill began a frontal political assault on Crystal City which proved effective in swaying some public opinion against the party. The charges of "socialism" and "little Cuba" came at a time when the party was still struggling with the Muñiz indictments. The Democrats could and did charge that Raza Unida was a party of drug pushers and communists.

The governor's attacks, launched at the 1976 Democratic state convention, were partly effective in stalling the grant until Jimmy Carter was sworn in as president. But the principal culprits of the delay were the officials of ZCEDC because they were late in submitting the final proposal. The Community Services Administration under Ford had tentatively approved the grant and likely would have approved the final version before the changing of presidents.

After Carter was elected, Briscoe continued his lobbying, at times in person, against the ZCEDC project. His pressure soon bore fruit, as the Community Services Administration's political appointees began to find fault with a proposal that had already been approved by the regular staff. Gutiérrez accused the CSA of playing politics—"Democrat politics." Graciela Olivárez, Carter's appointee to head the CSA, denied the charge though admitted later in court that the White House had made numerous inquiries on ways to terminate the grant. The agency's objections, she argued, were based on technical problems with the proposal and on the fact that the ZCEDC cooperative did not really promote economic well-being for Chicanos but rather created a "new class of stoop laborers." On these grounds the CSA suspended the grant money.[42]

The ZCEDC board of directors quickly filed suit to lift the suspension of funds. U.S. District Judge Gerhard Gesell advised the two sides to avoid a trial and settle out of court. The CSA then made a proposal that called for the removal of the ZCEDC board of directors from a direct role in running the cooperative. The collective's attorneys were in the process of advising the organization to accept the proposal when the CSA lawyers withdrew their offer the following day because of pressure from President Carter and Attorney General Griffin Bell.[43]

Unable to settle out of court, ZCEDC pursued its suit and spent twenty thousand dollars in legal fees trying to persuade the courts to force the White House to turn over the Carter-Briscoe correspondence, which Gutiérrez believed contained information on political maneuvering that denied Crystal City its funds. Unfortunately for Gutiérrez, the court ruled that no evidence of wrongdoing existed and consequently chose not to overrule the president's claim of executive privilege.[44] Unable to afford an appeal, ZCEDC let the proposal die and with it went Gutiérrez's last major effort to stave off his rivals and gain the upper hand in the 1978 elections.

But even as things soured back home, Gutiérrez involved the party in a major conference on immigration reform. Among government officials as well as Chicano activists, the future of the Mexican undocumented worker in American society was a major point of debate. President Carter had unveiled a legislative package intended to stop what some perceived as an invasion of "brown hordes" from south of the border.[45]

While calling for limited and conditional amnesty, the Carter plan introduced sanctions against employers who hired undocumented workers and provided for more officers in the Border Patrol. Most activists saw the new law as singling out all Latinos as potential "undocumented workers" and causing employers to be leery of hiring them. They also saw the strengthening of the Border Patrol as a militaristic action against Chicanos. Opposition to the bill arose quickly, but it was not a united effort, as several organizations vied for leadership of the opposition. The opponents of the government's position divided along three lines within the Chicano community: Stalinist, Trotskyist, and independent.

The Stalinists were represented by the Center for Autonomous Social Action-Brotherhood of Workers (CASA-HGT), a Chicano (they called themselves Mexican) organization with close ties to the U.S. Communist Party and the Puerto Rican Socialist Party. Founded by Bert Corona, it had shifted to a Marxist-Leninist ideology, considered the Chicano Movement misdirected, and did not recognize Chicanos as a separate national entity from the Mexicans in Mexico. The Trotsky line was promulgated by the Socialist Workers Party, and numerous Chicano organizations comprised the independents.[46]

Gutiérrez sought a forum to bring together the opposition to Carter's plan. He had no intention of presenting a Raza Unida Party alternative. He felt that most of the Mexican American and Latino organizations involved in the issue were in agreement on the basic premises but were just not communicating with each other.[47] Also not part of the communication were the moderate organizations such as LULAC, G.I Forum, MALDEF, and others. These organizations had no cadre of activists and were more inclined to be cautious in their assessments and recommendations. Gutiérrez wanted to get them more involved. Any significant opposition to the Carter plan had to come from an ideologically diverse confederation.[48] One reason for this was that Carter had appointed Leonel Castillo as head of the Immigration and Naturalization Service. Castillo had been a popular city controller in Houston and was seen by many as trying to "sensitize" the *migra*.

From the beginning the effort to call a national conference was plagued with divisive bickering between CASA, and SWP, and the independent groups favoring one or the other. Antonio Rodríguez, the head of CASA, did not trust Gutiérrez or other nationalists as leaders in an issue he considered to belong to his organization. In its propaganda literature CASA declared that the Chicano Movement "brought with it no political strategy or tactics to achieve the goals it set for itself so idealistically in the Spiritual Plan of Aztlán and other plans which grew out of the movement." "In addition," it continued, "we take the position that the goals of the Chicano movement were for the most part defined by elements of the Mexican people with no direct ties or participation in the working force . . . it was students, unemployed youth (often ghettoized and lumpenized) and other popular sectors . . . who shaped and defined the goals and methods of the Chicano movement."[49]

The Socialist Workers Party presented a different problem. It claimed to support the Chicano Movement and its nationalism, but its members tended to take liberties on its behalf. They called unauthorized meetings and used individuals' and organizations' names— without permission—to promote their activities. The SWP also had its members join Chicano groups to acquire voting privileges in them, and this practice angered many Chicano activists.[50]

Bringing the two groups together meant trouble, but no conference could be called legitimate without the participation of at least one of them. Gutiérrez, who sent out the official call for a Chicano-Latino immigration meeting attempted to minimize the potential disruption by pushing for the meeting to be held in San Antonio and by staffing most of the working committees with members of the party. Compean was named chairman of the conference.

Nonetheless, problems arose. Chicano groups in California attempted to oust the SWP from the planning group, and Gutiérrez, who had ousted the SWP from the national La Raza Unida convention in 1972, ended up defending its participation.[51] SWP members did not make it easy for him, however. They continued to be disruptive in the meetings and to make even more enemies.

When the conference convened on October 28, the SWP members were alienated from most of the other organizations. They made things worse when they attempted to open the discussions beyond the issue of immigration. CASA activists, who sought to recruit new members and take the leadership of the immigration protest movement, became obsessed with presenting counter moves to the SWP. The mainstream participants found themselves alienated by both the radicalism of the proposed resolutions—unconditional amnesty and open borders—and the continuous infighting. Gutiérrez further isolated many of them by lashing out at Castillo and the Democratic Party. Vilma Martínez, of MALDEF, was particularly angered, and she ended her organization's active participation early.[52]

In this environment the Raza Unida rank and file felt left outside any meaningful participation and uninformed as to which group or resolution to support. The confusion emanated from a sharp disagreement between Compean and Gutiérrez on who to support, and from the lack of an ideological agenda. Compean vowed before and during the conference that he would never work with the SWP again.[53] Gutiérrez, angered by CASA's attacks on him and by its reluctance to work with the Trotskyites, made it a point to side against CASA.

In the final session, as tempers flared, the meeting turned into a rhetorical fistfight that alienated the independent groups and killed any efforts to develop a united front to battle the Carter plan. The divisiveness spread to the party ranks, and several members privately accused Gutiérrez of negotiating with the SWP to gain its support for an upcoming congressional race.[54] They also blamed him for the party's minuscule impact on the conference and the final resolutions. Some felt that the party had enough activists involved in immigration issues to have constructed its own proposals. They also believed that they could have attracted enough votes of the mainstream participants to have passed party resolutions. The opportunity to regain the leadership of the movement and to gather mainstream support had been lost, some felt, because of Gutiérrez's bartering.[55] This dissatisfaction became reason enough for some to decrease their party activity.

The conference debacle revealed the party's dilemma in dealing with the Chicano left. Texas Raza Unida leaders distrusted socialist groups. They saw them as opportunists who lived in ideological spheres far removed from the Mexican American barrios. Yet by this time a large number of the party activists felt that their nationalist ideology was inadequate when compared to that of the socialists. Even Gonzales's revolutionary nationalism did not provide them with a scientific methodology for classifying and simplifying the issues as concisely as Marxist ideology did for the left. The intellectuals in Raza Unida found themselves outmanned in ideological debates because they had no volumes of theory to fall back on and because most of them had socialist tendencies anyway. The inability to trust the left made coalitions with it difficult. And the perceived ideological inferiority made some party members vulnerable to advances from the Chicano left.[56]

With the immigration conference an ideological failure, the Raza Unida Party found itself sputtering toward the 1978 gubernatorial election without support from the left or the middle class and with its core membership greatly reduced.

La Raza Unida
Jamás Será Vencida

—RUP slogan

LA RAZA UNIDA
IN RETROSPECT

Election day 1978 proved to be devastating for La Raza Unida Party and particularly for Mario Compean, its gubernatorial candidate. By 10 P.M. it had become evident that news commentators would not even bother to announce the party's vote total or to acknowledge the third man in the governor's race. The party, which had garnered 214,000 and 190,000 votes respectively, in 1972 and 1974, received about 15,000 votes in a race won by Republican William Clements.[1]

Compean claimed that his presence in the race was responsible for the Republican victory, but few people took notice. What some did note was the remark by LULAC President Ruben Bonilla that "La Raza Unida Party is in the political cemetery where it belongs."[2] By not receiving at least 2 percent of the vote, the party lost its ballot status and the state funds for its primary. More important, the dismal showing eliminated the party as an alternative to the Republicans and Democrats.

Many of the RUP's former supporters had joined the political bandwagon of John Hill, the state attorney general, who had defeated Briscoe for the Democratic nomination. Running as a moderate, though his record was that of a conservative, Hill gained the endorsement of the Mexican American Democrats (MAD) and of almost every important Mexican American political leader in the state.[3]

A larger number of Mexican Americans than usual went the other way and supported Clements, a millionaire who met with Compean several times during the campaign and even explored the possibility of offering him a role in the administration. Compean considered but then rejected the notion.[4]

The 1978 gubernatorial effort never had the full support of the party cadre, especially those who had become prominent figures by 1977. They were more interested in creating coalitions, working on local issues, or waiting for the RUP to disband legally in order to make the transition to the Democratic Party. A Compean candidacy committed them to engage in a public fight against potential local allies in a fruitless effort.

The new leadership, with the exception of María Elena Martínez, did not see Compean as a good candidate. Even among his close associates, Compean found loyalty and enthusiasm in short supply. Compean's problems in inspiring confidence stemmed from two factors, one personal and the other external. Raza Unida followers, used to the charismatic, good-looking, and physically imposing Muñiz, did not see Compean as a better alternative. He seemed too fragile physically to withstand a vigorous campaign, and his speaking ability paled in comparison to the former candidate's.

Muñiz had catered to the middle class, but he had nonetheless enjoyed, for the most part, a cordial relationship with the Chicano left. Compean had no base or following in either camp. The middle-class Mexican Americans did not like him because he had no "credentials" and because he never showed an interest in wooing them. For some, he was too barrio-ized and lacked the stable family, the significant career, and the "presence" to bring legitimacy to Mexican American issues. Among the left, Compean was regarded as a narrow-minded reactionary nationalist who did not like Anglos, even radical ones, and who had no ideology. Those leftists who disliked Gutiérrez considered Compean his lackey, and those who admired Gutiérrez felt that Compean did not measure up in stature to the Crystal City leader.[5] Those sympathetic to Compean believed that he had simply chosen a bad time to run. Some thought he had been out of the party's top hierarchy too long and that his views were outdated. His closest friends also felt that his body, weakened by a childhood bout with tuberculosis, seemed ready to give out.

The major external problem Compean faced was the burned-out state of the party cadre. Those still active were scrambling to regroup from the political shellacking of the past two years. In a meeting of the remaining leaders of the South Texas Raza Unida chapters, Compean was presented with a bleak picture of the party's status. Party leaders such as Youngblood, Vicente Molina, Luera, Villarreal, Cavada, and others frankly told him that they were not enthused by another gubernatorial race, nor did they have the resources to do more than put up a few signs just before the election. Some even expressed a concern that he was going to stir up the anti-Raza Unida forces. Only the Kleberg County chairman offered assistance, a gesture that led to a split in the Kingsville chapter which eventually ended the party's activities there.[6]

Muñiz had been able to overcome some of the party's financial problems by attracting support, endorsements, and funds from sources outside the party. Compean had few such connections and in fact consciously avoided seeking such support until just before the end of the campaign.[7]

Compean did not set out to be a martyr. He believed that the party members needed another cause to which to rally. His two campaigns for the city council in San Antonio had laid the groundwork for MAYO's electoral phase. Ever the optimist, Compean believed that the troops could be regrouped one more time. More important, a successful race would help topple the Democrats from the governor's mansion and make the Chicano vote critical in future elections. In the end, however, Compean's campaign did not revive the party and played only a minor part in the Democratic Party's defeat.

In many ways Compean was the "first and real" candidate of the La Raza Unida Party. He had been one of the founders of MAYO and an early exponent of the party. He had been the first state chairman and had been involved in developing the RUP platform. After the party idea was announced in 1969, he had been the point man, along with Gutiérrez, in spreading the word throughout Texas. He was also the first to meet with "Corky" Gonzales as an official of the party. In the 1972 convention he had been the delegation whip and the chief lobbyist for Gutiérrez's candidacy for the chairmanship. In his obsession with the party he had sacrificed a wife, two children, and a career.

Ideologically, Compean had been the most consistent. He never believed that the MAYO philosophy or party ideology had to be rethought in order to attract the middle class, endear the Chicano left, or create coalitions. *Mi raza primero* (my people first) seemed to be his personal philosophy. He had been one of the most popular leaders among the rank and file during the party's early period. Unfortunately for Compean, he never sought to find a niche for himself in the party. He acquiesced to Gutiérrez on most ideological and policy matters, except for the debate on state versus regional organizing. Muñiz overshadowed him and rose to higher prominence without the day-to-day effort that drained Compean. When most of the top organizers left the party or decided to pursue issues peripheral to the party's goals, Compean picked up the banner and carried on. In the end, he became the party's political cannon fodder.

By 1978 the national party was a political creature with an active brain but no moving parts. Juan José Peña had taken over as chairman and had initiated numerous activities at the national and international level. An untiring writer of letters and position papers, Peña attempted to keep the party at the forefront of what was then an illusory Chicano Movement. He tried to give the party an international status and develop an ideology that would speak to all issues from the land-grant question to the role of Christianity in Aztlán. His was a nationalist party with leftist tendencies.[8]

Unfortunately for the national party, most of the state chapters were in disarray structurally, had few faithful followers and no money, and were questioning their own ideologies. An analysis of the national La Raza Unida Party reveals, as in the case of Compean's candidacy, a two-fold problem that finally brought about its demise. Although each state had its dynamics and political idiosyncracies, the pressures on each state chapter came from both within and without. The internal problems for the national party began almost immediately after its founding. If California, Colorado, and Texas are taken as case studies, it is easy to identify a chaotic beginning.

In California the party was founded not as a state organization but as a confederation of chapters with fidelity to local leaders and local priorities. The California chapters' only agreement was their willingness to disagree. The closest they came to having a state organization was the development of regional confederations of chapters. Ideologically, the chapters also never found common ground, and thus there was no encompassing platform or political document acceptable to the majority. Except for the Ruiz campaigns, the party did not launch any significant challenges to the established political structures and never gathered enough signatures to be officially on the state ballot.[9]

Colorado, in contrast, had a better focused beginning. Like its counterpart in Texas, the Colorado Raza Unida evolved from a precursor organization, in this case the Crusade for Justice. It had strong statewide leadership in the person of "Corky" Gonzales, and in the Plan Espiritual de Aztlán it had an organizing document that expounded an ideology. Nevertheless, time would show that these individual features were less substantial than they purported to be. The Crusade for Justice began as a local organization and at first provided social services and cultural activities for the Denver community, but it quickly changed its role to that of a vanguard group with national leadership aspirations. Its resources and time never seriously shifted toward political bloc work, voter registration, election strategies, or get-out-the-vote campaigns. Its candidates expounded philosophical "truths" but did little to attract voters. Chicano empowerment was a rhetorical byword of the Plan Espiritual de Aztlán, not a practical strategy. In Gonzales the party had an overpowering and overbearing leader who thwarted the development of leadership beyond the grassroots level. Everyone was a lieutenant or a foot soldier in Colorado. There was only one "jefe."[10]

The Texas Raza Unida seemed more in tune with its political party concepts, but it too had a precarious beginning and established some weak foundations. The party idea began with the founding of MAYO, but the concept did not become implemented until it became evident that Crystal City was adopting the third-party strategy with or without the rest of MAYO. Even at its official announcement in Mission, the party had to share the spotlight with the concept of a Chicano college, and it was not until two years later that the party established a platform that outlined its goals and philosophy. The party in Texas never really had any bylaws except those necessary to qualify as a legally registered party in the state.

The founding of the national party was a case of the parts coming together to make the whole. By the time they did, most of the state chapters had established some basic platforms and were not willing to supplant their political agendas or philosophies with those of the national party. In its few years of existence the national party failed to develop a working platform, raise funds, or attract new chapters. Its leadership, El Congreso de Aztlán, was meant to be a collective type of directorate, but it was internally divided. Consequently, two conflicting ideologies resulted, each with a major proponent. "Corky" Gonzales preached an ideology with a nationalist heart and a socialist mind which sought to develop a revolutionary cadre that would in turn create coalitions with other Third World groups and lead to the building of Aztlán. Because an unspecified social-cultural revolution was the objective, the electoral process was deemphasized. Raza Unida would, in essence, be a vehicle to alert the masses and rally them to the building of a Chicano nation. Gutiérrez's ideology was that of the balance-of-power and its primary emphasis was on action rather than theory. It, too, attached little importance to politics—at the national level—and sought to use the national structure as a forum to attract attention and support for local efforts. The conflict in philosophy led to the quick demise of the national party. But the dispute did not singlehandedly weaken the numerous state parties; instead it undermined the development of a unified direction for the party cadre. Failure to achieve agreement on basic principles resulted in an underdeveloped political agenda and a failure to establish a training process for new members.

Martínez later commented that the party used certain political catchwords that remained purposely vague. "I never really understood what we meant by 'self-determination.' Was it revolution or a nation within a nation?"[11] The concept of nationalism was so encompassing among some that one South Texas organizer once referred to himself as a member of the right wing of the party as he assailed a former friend for being a member of the fringe left wing.[12] In time, some of the candidates' views covered much of the political spectrum. Like their Democratic counterparts, they did not adhere to their party platform. Raúl Ruiz and Ramsey Muñiz were prime examples of candidates who stretched their state party's platform to accommodate their campaigns. The party leaders did not passively accept the distortion of their platform, rather they actively sought to jump on the bandwagon of any candidate who could bring the party some recognition and new adherents.

Political thought varied with the situation. Some communities suffered from almost complete segregation, and Chicanos there saw any kind of change from Anglo dominance to Mexican American representation as a vast improvement. They were pleased with reforms that were totally unsatisfactory to more militant members. These moderates became the first group to leave the party and join the liberals in the Mexican American Democrats, whose own call for change was never extreme.

The more radical members wanted to duplicate the Chicano empowerment concept of Crystal City. They saw in Cristal a wholesale change of attitudes among the people about discrimination, poverty, and political disenfranchisement. The militant members saw coalitions in a positive light only as long as they did not require a sharing of power in a locality where Chicanos were a large majority.

At first the groups had joined together, particularly in the Muñiz and Ruiz campaigns, but eventually disputes among the factions prevented a truly united effort. The discord, the large geographical area, and the lack of resources diluted the efforts to make training an ongoing process. Except for occasional statewide workshops or local training initiatives, no continuous developmental process ever took hold. The most successful Raza Unida organizers and leaders all came, with a few exceptions, from MAYO, the Crusade for Justice, and the UFW organizing battles. There they had developed their ideologies, priorities, and their techniques. When Raza Unida became flooded with new recruits, no process existed to turn them into disciplined, ideologically consistent foot soldiers. Most of the leaders were too busy directing the party's affairs to do any training. Gutiérrez later lamented the large influx of students who joined the party without any kind of organizing skills.

Compounding the problems of ideological splits and few trained organizers were the meager resources available to the party. Most funds came from poor Mexican Americans. There was never enough money to set up a headquarters, maintain a party newspaper, or provide traveling expenses. The lack of funds led to the disintegration of the party from within. Its chief result was the loss of the moral and ideological high ground in the party's politics, as some party leaders chose allies whose ideologies or methods were offensive to the Mexican American community, or they resorted to name-calling among themselves.

By the late 1970s Raza Unida no longer had admirers outside its ranks and most of its political goals were offensive to groups across the political spectrum. Few liberals considered the party an alternative to the still-entrenched conservatives in the state government. Among less militant Mexican American groups the Raza Unida Party had stopped being an advocate for their concerns. Raza Unida leaders were seen not as valiant young men on a moral crusade to free Chicanos of Anglo oppression, but as contentious political fanatics more anxious to create conflict and division than to run qualified candidates and offer solutions. Their inability to temper their partisan fervor made them unwelcome in most coalitions except those of a few leftist groups.

Internal problems alone, however, did not destroy the party. Just as responsible, and perhaps more so, was the pressure from without. The Raza Unida Party was subjected to an incessant political, judicial, ideological, social, and physical pounding almost from the day of its founding. Unlike other Mexican American organizations, the party posed a direct challenge to those in power. A successful Raza Unida meant the removal of Anglo officeholders or the usurpation of the power of the old barrio politicos. It meant changes in how and to whom the wealth was distributed, and it required an allegiance to a culture and a language foreign to the majority of Americans. Not since the armed rebellions of the early 1900s had any movement sought to rally Mexican Americans to an all out confrontation with the status quo as did Raza Unida.[13]

Attempts were made to keep the party off the ballot and to co-opt its members. When those efforts were not enough to destroy the party, a campaign to discredit the membership was launched at different levels. This strategy, helped along by the party's own miscues, proved partially effective. The final attack and eventually the one launched to end the party was the one waged on the judicial and legal front.

Raza Unida members were continually under surveillance.[14] Every major conference and activity was either infiltrated or closely monitored. Muñiz, though admittedly guilty, had been under federal and state scrutiny for more than eighteen months before he was indicted. Crystal City became the target of probe after probe as the attorney general, the Texas Rangers, and the FBI attempted to find evidence of wrongdoing. Except for Muñiz, Flores Anaya, and some anti-Gutierrista party members, few were ever actually convicted. The Raza Unida members proved to be law-abiding.

The judicial and legal maneuverings were not, however, carried out simply to find guilt. They were calculated moves to discredit party members and ensure their electoral defeat. Particularly in smaller communities, Raza Unida members were arrested just before election time, usually on drug charges, and then released without charges after the voting was over. In many other cases law enforcement agencies baited members to cause confrontations. Again, most Raza Unida members proved to be prudent.

The greatest abuse of the judicial system, however, came in the courts' decisions on electoral challenges. Repeatedly, the courts ruled against the party, removing candidates from the ballot, rejecting and reversing vote counts and voiding election results. The party in Crystal City never lost a majority of its races, but in 1978 and 1979 the courts reversed the results. In the 1979 election the party had actually made a resurgence, but the courts ruled that there were irregularities and ordered a re-vote in which only Gutiérrez won.[15] By 1982 Gutiérrez, besieged by a majority of Democrats on the county commissioners' court, resigned and left Crystal City to go to Oregon to teach political science.[16] The final chapter on the activities of El Partido de la Raza Unida ended with Gutiérrez's departure. Ironically, the Mexican American majority on the county commissioners' court replaced Gutiérrez with an Anglo. Only five years earlier he had predicted that no Anglo would ever hold the top office again in Zavala County.[17]

The conditions that had made the rise of La Raza Unida possible no longer existed by the late 1970s. With the party's challenge to the political system had come a wave of new "mainstream" Mexican American politicians. In South Texas, where Anglos had dominated politically, Mexican American Democrats had captured most of the offices by the late 1970s. The Democratic Party, particularly its liberal wing, had heavily recruited Mexican Americans to run for office and to work in the county and precinct structures. Spanish campaign literature and media spots were common, and some of the militant rhetoric became the domain of the Mexican American Democrats. The political leadership vacuum that had existed before MAYO and La Raza Unida had been filled.

The political and social institutions had regained their legitimacy in the minds of some Mexican Americans. The Democratic Party had again become the party of the working people, of the minorities and the liberals. This change in direction came about through the influx of activists who joined or returned to the Democratic fold. At the El Paso meeting the Democratic leadership had agreed with the ex-Raza Unida members that half of the Chicano representatives to the National Democratic Executive Committee would be former Raza Unida members.[18]

Government also regrouped and reclaimed its role in health,

education, and job training through legislation that provided funds for many small communities and for the barrios in the urban centers. Even the conservative Texas state government opened a Governor's Office of Migrant Affairs and revamped its funding formula for school districts to make more money available to poor schools. Organizations such as Communities Organized for Public Service (COPS) and the Southwest Voter Registration and Education Project founded by ex-MAYO members gave legitimacy to working for change "within the system."[19]

While many of the changes did not eliminate the deep-rooted prejudices that Mexican Americans faced, or significantly alter their economic status, there was, nonetheless, a perception among Mexican Americans that things had gotten better. One area where things did get better was in the protection of civil rights. Since the movement had been seen by many as a struggle for Chicano civil rights, the goals were assumed to have been achieved. As explained in the preceding chapters, the leadership that initially gave the party its strength did not remain intact for long. It split along ideological lines, it burned out, it joined other groups, and more important it left no one behind to replace it. When the founders scattered, a cohesive, united leadership became impossible. Other leaders were to rise, but they were limited by geographical boundaries, scarcity of resources, and the burden of their own local organizing efforts. None of them ever aquired the influence of the party's founders.

Gutiérrez was criticized by those who wanted him to come back and resume command of the party. His only response was that Crystal City occupied too much of his time.[20] He later confided that he had decided to let those who opted for a statewide party sink or swim on their own and with *their* party structure. Although his feelings did not become an adamant dislike of the state structure, they did dampen his enthusiasm to help when things were difficult. His detachment became such that Youngblood spoke to him only twice during his own tenure as state party chairman.[21]

It was wishful thinking on the part of a faithful few to assume that Gutiérrez or anyone else could save the party once the period of decline had set in. No one person could have raised adequate funds to run campaigns or register voters; no one person could undo the party's negative public image; and no one could turn back the clock to the mid-sixties, when conditions were conducive to the organizing of a nationalistic, all-Chicano party. Furthermore, the ethnic focus of the party restricted recruitment to a limited pool of people. And this pool was further reduced by ideology, assimilation, and rivalries. Many saw the party doomed to fail because of this focus. Had the party not foundered so quickly, it would have had to deal with this problem sooner or later, especially in the development of a nation-within-a-nation philosophy. One former party activist stated years later that there were too many voting precincts in the Southwest and "not enough Mexicans."[22] The party became another casualty of a political system that had survived numerous other ethnic, populist, regional, and ideological challenges.

Yet the party played a major role in the evolution of a more historically and politically conscious community. The cultural renaissance that came with the Chicano Movement spawned activities, periodicals, music, and literature in a community that had been facing a growing identity crisis. Young Chicanos rediscovered their language and were exposed to their history for the first time. They wrote novels, short stories, poems, and plays about the movimiento, el barrio, and la gente and about the gringo, border patrol, Texas Rangers, and other institutions considered anti-Mexican. Teatro groups appeared in many Chicano communities, and a sizable number of Chicanos and Chicanas went to college to pursue the arts. Chicano scholars challenged social science theories that depicted Mexican Americans as victims of their own cultural and moral dificiencies. They developed research models that presented Chicanos in a more positive light, and destroyed the myth of the "passive" Mexican. Through pressure, Chicano students and faculty forced numerous universities to establish Chicano studies programs. Beyond giving academic credit, the programs served as centers of student activism and cultural rejuvenation. These programs also opened the university to the Mexican American community for the first time.

Mexican American women, in particular, gained ground through the party's efforts. Although the party's male leaders were not avowed feminists, and some were, in fact, anti-feminists, the organizing activities and the electoral campaigns initiated gave women the opportunity to become involved at numerous levels. This was especially true in Texas and to a lesser extent in California and New Mexico. The first Raza Unida county chairperson was Luz Gutiérrez. The last state chairperson and the only one ever reelected was María Elena Martínez. In Crystal City most of the party members who served in office were women. By 1974 nearly all of the Zavala County officeholders were women. They also conducted most of the training for the campaigns and held many of the offices in the Ciudadanos Unidos organization.

Under the party umbrella many Chicana feminists developed and many women had their first opportunity to live a political life. Feeling that the party's platform gave them a role, RUP's Chicanas, led by fiery leaders such as Marta Cotera, Evey Chapa, Virginia Múzquiz, and others, demanded and fought for inclusion in the party hierarchy.[23] Even in rural areas, where no philosophical feminism existed, women played a major role in the political trenches, and they earned their places among the leadership cadre. Always less intimidated than the men and usually the hardest workers, they gave the party a base in many communities, often in spite of male opposition. Virginia Múzquiz was often referred to as Gutiérrez's political mother and mentor. She ran for the state legislature in 1964, and Gutiérrez and Patlán served as campaign managers. Under the Raza Unida banner she was elected county clerk.

Women played dual roles in the party. Some, like Viviana Santiago, Choco Meza, and Martínez, provided leadership and were involved in the party's day-to-day affairs. Others, like Cotera, Irma Mireles, and Chapa, offered themselves as candidates, worked to expand the party's philosophy on the role of women in society, and pressed the male leadership to open the hierarchy to Mexican American women. Most of these women remained committed to the party until the end. Through their efforts and those of other Chicanas in California, two feminist organizations developed within the party: the Federación de Mujeres de la Raza Unida (in California) and the Mujeres Pro-Raza Unida (in Texas).

The party's influence on the Mexican American population proved significant even in areas where it had almost no presence. Changes came about because the Raza Unida was a perceived threat. Those in power believed it was better to recruit Mexican Americans for political office or government appointments and to make some changes in the schools than it was to confront a local chapter of the party. The rhetoric of the party's activists also encouraged more moderate ombudsmen to express their desire for change. The more Raza Unida rocked the political and educational boat, the more space became available for Mexican Americans to climb aboard.

These new entrants into the public life came better prepared through their participation, direct or peripheral, in the party's politics. They also came "culturized" to the barrio's nationalism and they spread it into the mainstream. Public service became an important ingredient and one of the factors on which new Mexican American politicians were judged. The new social awareness nurtured by the party made it more difficult for blatant racism to be executed as public policy.

Willie Velásquez, who became perhaps the most prominent Chicano activist of contemporary times before his untimely death in 1988 at the age of forty-four, credited the party with having

> implemented progressive ideas in a generation of leadership. It made those people [Raza Unida members] the soul of the Chicano Movement when they became involved in national politics. ... Those who have been the sleaziest in the movement were the ones that weren't in La Raza Unida in the beginning. The ones that have been the truest to the movement, that have continued ... that have stayed true to the basic ideals, are the Raza Unida people.[24]

The Raza Unida Party inspired a whole generation of Mexican Americans to participate in the electoral process on a scale never before attempted. It aroused a strong feeling of compassion, and many became involved in service to their barrios and to forgotten segments of the population such as farm workers, school dropouts, welfare families, ex-convicts, and others who desperately needed a helping hand. Not all the party members' actions were positive. There were some bitter feelings and violent acts, and wounds were inflicted that never completely healed, but viewed from a wide perspective, Raza Unida helped to orient a large segment of the Mexican American population, especially the youth, toward the electoral process and its importance. This orientation brought about democratization in many southwestern communities for the first time. The one-person one-vote concept became a reality in places like Cotulla, Pearsall, Crystal City, Greeley, La Puente, Las Vegas, and other small communities. After Gutiérrez resigned, an editorial in the Corpus Christi Caller commented, "The work of La Raza Unida has [not] been in vain. On the contrary, it succeeded in raising the political consciousness of people who had for too long been ignored in the decision-making process. It awakened pride in people who had been scorned by an insensitive ruling clique."[25]

Mexican Americans, in and outside the party, were emboldened to seek public office, oftentimes challenging entrenched politicians who had forgotten the meaning of public service. For those Mexican Americans in office, the Raza Unida helped develop a more active constituency that supported them as they pushed for more concrete legislative and governmental action. It would be an exaggeration to say that the party did all of this single-handedly, for numerous other forces, including many old-line Democrats who were sincere in their efforts to make changes in society, were involved. But the party did play a major role and possibly a unique one.

Although surely not its intent, the Raza Unida Party opened the American political system to Mexican Americans and may have accelerated their physical, if not social, integration into the mainstream.[26] This integration, though, was unlike the assimilation of earlier years, because it represented an entrance into the political activity of a people more aware of their cultural heritage and sensitive to the needs of poorer people of all nationalities. A good number of the party leaders remained active in politics, others committed themselves to the founding of community outreach organizations. Not all remained radical or even liberal, but those who turned away from militant politics rarely left behind their concern for their communities. The legacy of La Raza Unida is likely to live on as long as Chicanos remember how things were before they came together and challenged the institutions and laws that had oppressed their communities for many generations.

Only time will tell if that legacy will prove useful as Chicanos enter the twenty-first century. There are new problems and many of the old ones have been compounded. Voter participation among Mexican Americans seems to have stalled, and few of them have been elected to statewide offices. There is talk, among a few, of another political movement of the third kind. They would greatly benefit by reading this book and learning from history.

NOTES

The Prelude

1. David Montejano, in his outstanding work *Anglos and Mexicans in the Making of Texas, 1836–1986*, pp. 220–234, discusses what he calls the culture of segregation, a pervasive attitude that governed the Anglo view of the Mexican American.

2. Ibid., pp. 275–276.

3. See *Mexican Americans and the Administration of Justice in the Southwest* (A Report of the United States Commission on Civil Rights, March 1970), p. iii.

4. Guadalupe San Miguel, Jr., *Let All of Them Take Heed*, pp. 113–134. In his chapter "Compelled to Litigate," San Miguel outlines the major legal suits brought by Mexican American activists against the Texas public school system.

5. Ibid., pp. 39, 40, 49, 55. Also see Robert A. Carlson, *The Quest for Conformity: Americanization Through Education*.

6. This was the case in many schools in the Southwest. The author experienced such practices when he attended junior high school in San Antonio in 1962–63.

7. Leo Grebler, Joan W. Moore, and Ralph C. Guzmán, *The Mexican American People*, pp. 18–23.

8. Stephen Castro was a student leader at Sidney Lanier High School in San Antonio and a friend of the author. He made those comments during the time the school was threatened with a boycott by students in 1968.

9. Thomas E. Sheridan presents an excellent explanation of these attitudes in "Mexicans and the Tucson Public School System," chapter 13 of his *Los Tucsonenses: The Mexican Community in Tucson, 1854–1941*, pp. 217–233.

10. Grebler, Moore, and Guzmán, *The Mexican American People*, pp. 18–23.

11. James T. Patterson, *America's Struggle Against Poverty, 1900–1985*, p. 115.

12. Ibid., p. 151.

13. Lewis Nordyke, *The Truth About Texas*, p. 50.

14. Sheridan, *Los Tucsonenses*, pp. 111–122.

15. Alberto Juárez, "The Emergence of El Partido de La Raza Unida: California's New Chicano Party," *Aztlán*, 2 (Fall 1972): 177–203.

16. Maurilio Vijil, *Chicano Politics*, p. 221.

17. Montejano's "The Rivalship of Peace," in his *Anglos and Mexicans*, provides a glimpse of voting in Texas, characterized often as the most repressive state for Mexican Americans. See also Arnold De León, *They called them Greasers: Anglo attitudes toward Mexicans in Texas, 1821–1900*.

18. Evan Andres, *Boss Rule in South Texas*, p. xii.

19. Ibid., pp. viii–ix.

20. Montejano, *Anglos and Mexicans*, p. 300. See also Jovita González, "Social Life in Cameron, Starr and Zapata Counties" (master's thesis, 1930).

21. Mario T. García, "In Search of History: Carlos E. Castañeda and the Mexican American Generation," *Renato Rosaldo Lecture Series Monograph*, 4 (Tucson: Mexican American Studies & Research Center, 1988).

22. In *History, Culture and Society: Chicano Studies in the 1980s*, p. 1.

23. J. Montiel Olvera, *Latin American Yearbook*.

24. Rodolfo Alvarez, "The Psycho-Historical Socioeconomic Development of the Chicano Community in the United States," *Social Science Quarterly* 53 (March 1973): 920–42.

25. These two organizations recruited mostly middle-class to lower-middle-class Mexican Americans. Both LULAC and The American G.I. Forum were deeply engaged in the litigation battles of the 1940s and 1950s. For more on the two organizations, see Carl Allsup, "Education Is Our Freedom: The American G.I. Forum and the Mexican American School Segregation in Texas, 1948–1957," *Aztlán* 8:27-50; Edward D. Garza, "LULAC: League of United Latin American Citizens" (master's thesis, 1951).

26. For information on MAPA, see Miguel David Tirado, "Mexican American Community Political Organization," *Aztlán* 1, 1 (1970): 53–78. Information on PASSO can be found in Robert A. Cuellar, "A Social and Political History of the Mexican American Population of Texas, 1929–1963," chaps. 5 and 6 (master's thesis, 1969). See also "The Struggle for P.A.S.O.," in *The Texas Observer* (14 June 1963): 3–6.

27. Tirado, "Mexican American Community Organization," pp. 67–70; Alvarez, "Psycho-Historical and Socioeconomic Development," pp. 44–49.

28. Ibid.

29. Three sources provide excellent information on the Crystal City electoral revolt of 1963: "The Struggle for P.A.S.O."; John Staples Shockley, "A Social and Political History of the Mexican American Population in Texas, 1929–1963," chap. 6, and "The Revolt," chap. 2, in *Chicano Revolt in a Texas Town*.

30. "The Struggle for P.A.S.O.," pp. 5–6.

31. Ibid.

32. *Chicano* was an old term in the barrio used by lower- working-class people and youth gangs. It signified that they were Mexicans born in the United States. Many considered it derogatory until the 1960s, when it came to symbolize a Mexican American proud of his heritage.

33. For a look at the role legitimacy plays in politics, especially in the eyes of youth activists, see David Easton, *A System's Analysis of Political Life*; S. I. Benn

and R. S. Peter, *Social Principles and the Democratic State*; and Frederick Leo Wallace, "Legitimacy and the Youth Movement of the 1960s" (Ph.D. dissertation, 1976).

34. Armando B. Rendón, *Chicano Manifesto: The History and Aspirations of the Second Largest Minority in America*, p. 354.

Los Cinco de MAYO

1. José Angel Gutiérrez, interview with author, Independence, Oregon, 13 September 1985.

2. Ibid. Also subsequent interview with Gutiérrez, Houston, Texas, 24 June 1988.

3. Ibid.

4. Ibid.

5. Mario Compean, interview with author, Tucson, Arizona, 10 September 1985.

6. Ibid.

7. Ibid.

8. For a general overview of these two leaders, see F. Chris García, ed., *La Causa Política: A Chicano Politics Reader*; Stan Steiner, *La Raza, The Mexican Americans*.

9. Compean, interview, 1985.

10. Gutiérrez, interview, 1985.

11. Ibid.

12. Guadalupe Youngblood, interview with author, Robstown, Texas, 16 July 1985. For a more extensive explanation of cultural nationalism, see Richard Santillán, "The Politics of Cultural Nationalism: El Partido de la Raza Unida in Southern California 1969–78" (Ph.D. dissertation, 1978).

13. Compean, interview, 1985.

14. Ibid. For an example of this kind of activism, see Alonso S. Perales, *The Mexican American: Are We Good Neighbors?* Perales was one of the founders of the League of United Latin American Citizens (LULAC), and the one to whom Compean referred.

15. Compean, interview, 1988.

16. Ibid. See also *San Antonio Express and News*, 5 July 1967, p. 1.

17. Compean, interview, 1985. For an analytical work exploring the need of protest groups to attract publicity in the media, see Michael Lipsky, "Protest as a Political Resource," *American Political Science Review* 62, 4 (1968): 1144–58. Also see Armando Navarro, "El Partido de la Raza Unida in Crystal City: A Peaceful Revolution" (Ph.D. dissertation, 1974), pp. 136–137.

18. Gutiérrez, interview, 1985.

19. The United Farm Worker's Union provided the first organizing symbol nationally for Chicano activists. No other organization was more symbolically identified with the Chicano Movement than Cesár Chávez's union.

20. Gutiérrez, interview, 1985. Also interview with Willie Velásquez, San Antonio, Texas, 22 December 1986, conducted by Stephen Casanova.

21. Rendón, *Chicano Manifesto*; pp. 130–131. Also Compean, interview, 1985; and Velásquez, interview, 1986.

22. Mario Compean, interview with author, Boulder, Colorado, 14 April 1988.

Velásquez spoke about the conference in his interview with Stephen Casanova and claimed to have come up with the name. Compean remembers differently, saying that Nacho Pérez came up with the name and that Velásquez was instructed to present it to the El Paso conference.

23. "Bernal Urges Political Involvement To Make Gains, 2,000 May Be at UMA Meet," *San Antonio Express and News*, 4 January 1968. Several more Raza Unida conferences were convened, but most of the middle-class participants slowly left as the conferences became more militant. The organization, Raza Unida, that came from the El Paso Conference did not remain active long, though offshoot groups such as the Ohio Raza Unida and the Michigan Raza Unida survived as social advocate agencies until the late 1970s.

24. Gutiérrez, interview, 1985; Compean, interview, 1985.

25. Gutiérrez, interview, 1985. For more on the MAYO structure and its inner workings, see Navarro, "El Partido de la Raza Unida in Crystal City."

26. Navarro, "El Partido de la Raza Unida," p. 557.

27. Ibid., p. 32.

28. Velásquez, interview, 1986.

29. Compean, interview, 1985.

30. Ibid.

31. Velásquez, interview, 1986.

32. *San Antonio Express and News*, 11 October 1968, 15 April 1969.

33. *San Antonio Express and News*, 23 September 1973, p. 1-C.

34. *Congressional Record* (15 April 1969): 9059 and (16 April 1969): 9309. This information also comes from insterviews with Gutiérrez and Compean and from the author's personal knowledge of MAUC.

35. *San Antonio Express and News*, 18 October 1980.

36. "On the History of LRUP," *Para La Gente* 1, 4 (October 1977): 13. This was the official newspaper of the La Raza Unida Party, though it came late in the party's development and at times was disguised as simply a Chicano statewide newspaper.

37. *Congressional Record* (15 April 1969): 9059. For an example of the contents in a MAYO pamphlet, see an article by Kemper Diehl, "MAYO Leader Warns of Violence, Rioting," *San Antonio Express and News*, reprinted in *Congressional Record* (3 April 1969): 8591.

38. Two of the best sources on MAYO newspapers are Navarro's dissertation, pp. 56–58, and an unpublished paper by Stephen Casanova, "La Raza Unida Press," author's personal collection.

39. *El Deguello* was the bugle call ordered by General Antonio de Santa Anna at the Battle of the Alamo so no prisoners would be taken.

40. Navarro, "El Partido de la Raza Unida," p. 57.

41. Ben H. Proctor, "The Modern Texas Ranger: A Law Enforcement Dilemma in the Rio Grande Valley," in *The Mexican American: An Awakening Minority.* Also *Mexican Americans and the Administration of Justice in the Southwest* (A Report of the United States Commission on Civil Rights, March 1970), p. 16.

42. Julian Samora, Joe Bernal, and Albert Peña, *Gunpowder Justice.* For a mainstream look at the Texas Rangers, see Walter Prescott Webb, *The Texas Rangers: A Century of Frontier Defense.*

43. *San Antonio Express and News*, 8-16 December 1968, and *San Antonio Light*, 8–16 December 1968. Also Gutiérrez, interview, 1985.

44. Gutiérrez, interview, 1985. Also see the booklet by Ruben Salazar, *Strangers in One's Land* (U.S. Commission on Civil Rights, Clearinghouse Publication no. 19, May 1970), pp. 38–45.

45. "MAYO Leaders Merely Confused," *San Antonio Express and News*, 12 April 1969, p. 10-B.

46. "Mexican Americans Stage Protest March in Texas," *San Antonio Express and News*, 31 March 1969.

47. "Fisher Asks House Probe MAYO," *San Antonio Express and News*, 23 April 1969, p. 12-A.

48. "Race Hate," *Congressional Record* (3 April 1969): 8590.

49. "Foundation Responsibility," *Congressional Record* (16 April 1969): 9308–9309.

50. *San Antonio Express and News*, 11 April 1969. Also Appendix 2 in John Staples Shockley, *Chicano Revolt in a Texas Town*, p. 230.

51. *San Antonio Express and News*, 15 April 1969.

52. Navarro, "El Partido de la Raza Unida," p. 33.

53. Particularly involved in education issues were LULAC, the American G.I. Forum, and the Mexican American Legal Defense and Education Fund. See San Miguel, Jr., *Let All of Them Take Heed*.

54. Salazar, *Strangers*, pp. 23–29.

55. Compean, interview, 1985. To base funds on school attendance was a common practice in many states.

56. Little has been written on the MAYO boycotts other than Navarro's excellent section in his dissertation starting on p. 66. Unfortunately, Navarro deals only with the boycotts in Edcouch-Elsa, Kingsville, and Crystal City, and not with the one in Sidney Lanier. Stephen Casanova's unpublished paper, "The Movement for Bilingual/Bicultural Education in Texas: School Boycotts and the Mexican American Youth Organization," gives an overall analysis of the use of the boycott. The paper also sheds some light on the Lanier controversy. Most of the information on that student protest, though, comes from personal experience as the author was a junior at Lanier High School when the protests occurred.

57. Ibid.

58. Ibid.

59. From an unfinished autobiography by the author which deals in depth with Sidney Lanier High School and the west side of San Antonio.

60. Casanova, "The Movement for Bilingual/Bilcultural Education," p. 11.

61. Ibid., p. 10. Also author's personal recollection.

62. Navarro, "El Partido de La Raza Unida," pp. 70–80.

63. Casanova, "The Movement for Bilingual/Bicultural Education."

64. Gutiérrez, interview, 1985.

Crystal City Reignites

1. See Shockley, *Chicano Revolt in a Texas Town*, pp. 24–41. For information on Mathis see "Mexican Americans 'Want To Get on Top,' and They're Gaining," *National Observer* (Monday, 12 April 1965).

2. Gutiérrez, interview, 1988.

3. Ibid.

4. Ibid.

5. Navarro, "El Partido de la Raza Unida," p. 97.

6. Samora, Bernal, and Peña, *Gunpowder Justice*, pp. 112–114.

7. Luz was a native of Falfarrias, Texas. She attended Texas A&I University for a short time, where she met Gutiérrez. A strong-willed woman, she served as Gutiérrez's right hand in organizing the women of Crystal City and became the first party official La Raza Unida ever had when she became county chairperson in Zavala County. Luz and José Angel were later divorced.

8. Gutiérrez, 1988; Navarro, "El Partido de la Raza Unida," pp. 149–151.

9. Navarro, "El Partido de la Raza Unida," p. 213.

10. Gutirrez, interview, 1985.

11. For an overview of Compean's campaign see issues of the *San Antonio Express* and the *San Antonio News*, 1 March–4 April 1969. For a more in-depth but biased view of the election results I used Miguel Berry, Armando Cavada, Richard Sánchez, and Ernesto Flores (all members of MAYO or La Raza Unida Party), "Latent Resentment Against the Political Order: An Interpretation of Chicano Voting Behavior" (research paper, 1971). Personal collection.

12. Ibid.

13. San Antonio newspapers, 1 March–4 April 1969.

14. Navarro, "El Partido de la Raza Unida," pp. 192–194.

15. Ibid., p. 201.

16. Ibid., p. 213.

17. Gutiérrez, interview, 1985; Shockley, *Chicano Revolt in a Texas Town*, p. 120.

18. Shockley, *Chicano Revolt in a Texas Town*, pp. 120–121.

19. Gutiérrez, interview, 1988.

20. Ibid.

21. Shockley, *Chicano Revolt in a Texas Town*, p. 121.

22. Navarro, "El Partido de La Raza Unida," p. 223.

23. Gutiérrez, interview, 1988; Navarro, "El Partido de La Raza Unida," pp. 221–222.

24. Ibid., pp. 219–220.

25. Crystal City Anglos knew about Gutiérrez's tenure at MAYO and some were suspicious, but his low profile kept them from investigating his activities. When the student walkout occurred, he was the first to be blamed.

26. José Angel Gutiérrez, "Aztlán: Chicano Revolt in the Winter Garden," *La Raza Magazine* 1, 4 (1973): 41.

27. Navarro, "El Partido de la Raza Unida," p. 46.

28. Ibid.

29. Shockley, *Chicano Revolt in a Texas Town*, pp. 127–128.

30. Ibid.

31. Gutiérrez, interview, 1988; Shockley, *Chicano Revolt in a Texas Town*, pp. 127–128; Navarro, "El Partido de la Raza Unida," pp. 109–110.

32. Gutiérrez, interview, 1988.

33. Shockley, *Chicano Revolt in a Texas Town*, pp. 129–130.

34. Ibid., p. 130.

35. Gutiérrez, interview, 1988; Navarro, "El Partido de La Raza Unida," pp. 111–112.

36. Navarro, "El Partido de La Raza Unida," pp. 113–115.

37. Gutiérrez, "Aztlán," p. 41.

38. Information on Albert Peña's involvement in the 1963 electoral victory can be found in Samora, Bernal, and Peña, *Gunpowder Justice*, pp. 94–113, and "The Struggle for P.A.S.O.," in the *Texas Observer* (14 June 1963).

39. Shockley, *Chicano Revolt in a Texas Town*, p. 135.

40. Ibid., p. 137.

41. During his involvement with Los Cinco, Gutiérrez had a run-in with the Texas Rangers. Only his mother's intervention, with a shotgun in hand, saved him from a bad beating. Gutiérrez, interview, 1988.

42. Gutiérrez, interview, 1985; Shockley, *Chicano Revolt in a Texas Town*, p. 132.

43. Gutiérrez, "Aztlán," pp. 39–40.

44. Gutiérrez, interview, 1988.

45. Shockley, *Chicano Revolt in a Texas Town*, p. 132–138.

La Raza Unida Becomes a Party

1. "MAYO's Strength Proves Big Surprise," *San Antonio Express*, 10 May 1970.

2. Navarro, "El Partido de La Raza Unida," p. 38.

3. Gutiérrez, interview, 1988.

4. For an explanation of Gonzales's ideology, see Christine Marín, *A Spokesman of the Mexican American Movement: Rodolfo "Corky" Gonzales and the Fight for Chicano Liberation, 1966–1972.*

5. Navarro, "El Partido de La Raza Unida," p. 39; Gutiérrez, interview, 1988.

6. Navarro, "El Partido de La Raza Unida," p. 43.

7. Compean, interview, 1984. For more information on Colegio Jacinto Treviño, see "An Interview with Narciso Alemán," *La Raza*, 1, 11 (1973): 30. Alemán was the director of the Chicano college. For more on the convention, see Navarro, "El Partido de La Raza Unida," pp. 174–178.

8. Navarro, "El Partido de La Raza Unida," pp. 176–177; Compean, interview, 1984.

9. Navarro, "El Partido de La Raza Unida," pp. 250–252.

10. Ibid., p. 250. Gutiérrez disagreed during an interview with Navarro's information. Though he could not recall specifically the details, he claims to have always supported the name Raza Unida.

11. Shockley, *Chicano Revolt in a Texas Town*, pp. 141–142.

12. Ibid.

13. Shockley, *Chicano Revolt in a Texas Town*, pp. 142–143.

14. Ibid.

15. Navarro, "El Partido de La Raza Unida," p. 258. Also see "MAYO Is Accused of Trying to Hide Story," *Corpus Christi Caller*, 3 April 1970. Gutiérrez was quoted as saying God was a pimp. Gutiérrez denied ever saying that.

16. Shockley, *Chicano Revolt in a Texas Town*, p. 147–148.

17. Ibid., pp. 150–154.

18. Gutiérrez, interview, 1985.

19. "MAYO's Third Party Drive Said Creating Racial Blocs," *San Antonio Express*, 29 March 1969.

20. Ibid.

21. Velásquez, interview with Stephen Casanova, San Antonio, Texas, 22 December 1986. In an interview with the author, Velásquez described himself as such.

22. Compean, interview, 1984.

23. Velásquez, interview, 1986.

24. Ibid.

25. See Gutiérrez, "Aztlán" p. 42; Shockley, *Chicano Revolt in a Texas Town*, p. 148; Navarro, "El Partido de La Raza Unida," p. 263.

26. Alfredo Zamora, interview with author, Cotulla, Texas, Summer 1985; Navarro, "El Partido de La Raza Unida," p. 262.

27. "Raza Unida Party Displays Strength," *San Antonio Express*, 6 April 1970. Also "La Raza Has 4 Winners in City Races," *San Antonio News*, 8 April 1970.

28. Shockley, *Chicano Revolt in a Texas Town*, pp. 150–195.

29. Ibid.

30. Ibid.

31. "'Brown Power' Push Is Seen," *Corpus Christi Times*, 6 April 1970.

32. Shockley, *Chicano Revolt in a Texas Town*, p. 157; "La Raza May Sweep Posts," *San Antonio News*, 8 May 1970.

33. "La Raza Unida election plea is rejected by 4th court," *San Antonio News*, 28 September 1970, p. 7-A.

34. Martin made this decision after the Hidalgo County attorney requested information on placing RUP candidate Alejandro Morales on the ballot; See "Martin says La Raza can't get on the ballot," *San Antonio News*, 9 June 1970.

35. "3rd party hearing opens," *San Antonio News*, 9 September 1970, p. 7-C.

36. Ibid.

37. "Raza Unida blocked by Supreme Court," *San Antonio Express*, 30 September 1970.

38. "La Raza Unida election plea," p. 7-A.

39. Ibid.

40. "High Texas Court To Hear Raza Plea," *San Antonio Express*, 29 September 1970.

41. "Raza Unida blocked by Supreme Court."

42. Ibid.

43. Ibid.

44. "U.S. Court Action Set on La Raza," *San Antonio News*, 1 October 1970.

45. "41 Subpoenaed for La Raza Case," *San Antonio Express*, 7 October 1970.

46. "Court Denies La Raza Plea," *San Antonio Express*, 8 October 1970.

47. "Petitioners Have Right to Names of Nominees," *San Antonio Express*, 8 October 1970.

48. Ibid.

49. "Three Judges to Hear Raza Plea," *Corpus Christi Times*, 10 October 1970.

50. "Burnett Illness Forces Withdrawal from Raza Case," *San Antonio Express*, 13 October 1970.

51. "Write-in Ballot Upsets Sought by Raza Unida," *San Antonio News*, 3 November 1970.

52. "How They Stole La Raza Unida's Vote," *The Militant* (20 November 1970): 10; Gutiérrez, interview, 1985.

53. Ibid.

54. Ibid.

55. Ibid.

56. "How They Stole La Raza Unida's vote."

57. Shockley, *Chicano Revolt in a Texas Town*, p. 159.

58. Ibid.

59. "Incumbents Beat Raza Write-ins," *San Antonio Express*, 4 November 1970. See also "Texas Raza Unida Charges Election Fraud," *The Militant* 13 (November 1970). Rodríguez was twenty-four years old at the time of the victory.

60. "Texas Raza Unida Charges Election Fraud," p. 20.

61. Gutiérrez, interview, 1988; Compean, interview, 1986.

62. Gutiérrez, "La Raza and Revolution: The Empirical Conditions for Revolution in Four South Texas Counties" (master's thesis, 1968).

63. Compean, who favored a statewide strategy, told the author that Gutiérrez's initial enthusiasm had spread to many of the organizers, especially those in the urban centers who felt left out of the Crystal City struggles and those of the other rural communities.

64. Compean, interview, 1986; Tatcho Mindiola, interview with author, Salt Lake City, 10 April 1987. Also see "Statewide Status Proposal Approved by Raza Unida," *Corpus Christi Times*, 31 October 1971.

65. "Statewide Status Proposal Approved"; Joe Bernal, interview with Stephen Casanova, San Antonio, Texas, 6 January 1987. Bernal claims that about ten members of the party were in his office trying to convince him to run. He told them the plan was not feasible and that, as the only Mexican American senator in the state, he could not abandon his position.

66. Compean told the author this version during a conversation in December 1986. For Calderon's version, see Tom Smith's interview with Ernesto Calderon, "Oral History Memoir" (Baylor University Program for Oral History, Waco, Texas, 27 March 1973), pp. 102–107.

Ramsey Muñiz and the 1972 Campaign

1. "Ya basta!" *The Texas Observer* (25 August 1972): 1.

2. Gutiérrez, interview, 1988.

3. "Ramsey Muñiz, A Short Biography," RUP campaign literature.

4. Ibid.

5. The party platform was not adopted until June. The party depended on its MAYO networks for a semblance of structure.

6. Alma Canales, questionnaire. Also an informal conversation with Mario Compean, 28 December 1986.

7. Mario Compean, interview, 1986.

8. "Raza Unida releases candidate list," *Corpus Christi Caller*, 10 February 1972.

9. Ibid.

10. Ibid.

11. "Smith blasted by Raza's candidate," *Corpus Christi Caller*, 24 March 1972.

12. "Muñiz raps major parties," *Corpus Christi Caller*, 16 March 1972.

13. María Elena Martínez, interview with Stephen Casanova and author, San Antonio Texas, 27 December 1986.

14. "Signature goal near for Raza Unida," *Corpus Christi Caller-Times*, 28 May 1972.

15. Conversation with Mario Compean, 28 December 1986.

16. "Mrs. Farenthold gets sympathy," *Corpus Christi Caller*, 5 June 1972.

17. Fernando Piñón, *Of Myths and Realities: Dynamics of Ethnic Politics*, p. 76.

18. Ibid., p. 77.

19. Ibid.

20. "Muñiz asks backing of Farenthold camp," *Corpus Christi Caller*, 8 June 1972.

21. *The Texas Observer* (25 August 1972).

22. The one thing people most often mentioned about Muñiz was his ability to overshadow those around him, and his skill at taking charge of a meeting or conversation.

23. Smith, Tom, interview of Ernesto Calderon, "Oral History Memoir," p. 107.

24. Texas Raza Unida Party platform preface (June 1972).

25. Ibid., pp. 4–17.

26. Ibid.

27. Texas Raza Unida Party platform.

28. Conversation with former party leader, December 1986.

29. For a better understanding of the secretary of state, see "No Bull Bullock," *The Texas Observer* (3 March 1972).

30. Gutiérrez, interview, 1988.

31. Joe Bernal, interview with Stephen Casanova, San Antonio, Texas, 6 January 1987.

32. "Muñiz glad Briscoe is his opponent," *Corpus Christi Caller*, 27 June 1972.

33. "Muñiz hopes Wallace runs," *Corpus Christi Caller*, 24 June 1972.

34. Ibid.

35. "Gutiérrez tapped to lead campaign," *Corpus Christi Caller-Times*, 26 August 1972. Also see Tony Castro, *Chicano Power: The Emergence of Mexican America*, p. 174.

36. "Liberals defecting Demos, Says Muñiz," *Corpus Christi Caller*, 1 September 1972. Bobby Smith, an all-state running back and formerly of the Buffalo Bills, was a friend of Muñiz.

37. "Gutiérrez tapped to lead campaign," 26 August 1972.

38. "Muñiz Says GOP Fat Joke," *Corpus Christi Times*, 24 August 1972.

39. "Ya basta!"

Unidos Ganaremos: The Party Goes National

1. By this time the concept of La Raza Unida Party had spread throughout the Southwest and into some other parts of the country.

2. Tijerina was jailed after he was convicted of destroying federal property in a national park during a takeover by the Alianza of an area it claimed belonged to the original land grant-holders.

3. Marín, *A Spokesman of the Mexican American Movement*, pp. 1–3. Also see Steiner, *The Mexican Americans*, pp. 380–385.

4. Marín, *A Spokesman of the Mexican American Movement*, pp. 3–4.

5. Steiner, *Mexican Americans*, pp. 383–384.

6. Rodolfo Gonzales, "Yo Soy Joaquín," *El Gallo* (1967).

7. Marín, *A Spokesman of the Mexican American Movement*, pp. 11–13; Steiner, *Mexican Americans*, pp. 389–392.

8. Ibid.

9. Castro, *Chicano Power*, pp. 130–132. See also Arturo Madrid-Barela, "In Search of the Authentic Pachuco," *Aztlán*, 4, 1 (1974).

10. Ibid.

11. Marín, *A Spokesman of the Mexican American Movement*, pp. 11–13.

12. *Documents of the Chicano Struggle* (New York: Pathfinder Press, Inc., November 1971), pp. 4–6.

13. Ibid., p. 4.

14. Ibid., p. 6.

15. Marín, *A Spokesman of the Mexican American Movement*, pp. 16–17.

16. Ibid., pp. 17–18.

17. "1000 at Convention of Colorado Raza Unida," *The Militant* (24 July 1970): 6.

18. Ibid.

19. "Raza Unida nominee discusses party stands," The Militant (17 July 1970) :9.

20. Marín, *A Spokesman of the Mexican American Movement*, pp. 19–21; also see "Denver Chicano leaders arrested," *The Militant* (11 September 1970): 3; and *Los Angeles Times*, 29–30 August 1972 issues. Another account, more biased against police, was written by Antonio Camejo, "The Los Angeles cops attack Chicano rally of 20,000," *The Militant* (11 September 1972): 3.

21. "Denver Raza Headquarters raided," *The Militant* (13 November 1970): 20. Also see *Denver Post* for more complete election results. It was common for major newspapers to ignore Raza Unida Party vote totals. *The Militant*, of the Socialist Workers Party did a good job, for the most part, in covering these details.

22. Carlos Muñoz, Jr., and Mario Barrera, "La Raza Unida Party and the Chicano Student Movement in California," *Social Science Journal*, 19, 2 (April 1982).

23. *Documents of the Chicano Struggle*, p. 8.

24. Ibid.

25. "La Raza Unida Party," *La Raza Magazine*, 1, 5 (1970): 10–11.

26. "La Raza Unida Party holds convention," *The Militant* (2 March 1971). The information about the use of an independent study course to organize the party was given to me by Dr. Richard Santillán, author of *La Raza Unida*.

27. Carlos Larralde, *Mexican American Movements and Leaders*, pp. 168–183.

28. Bert Corona, "MAPA and La Raza Unida Party, A Program for Chicano Political Action for the 1970s." (Pamphlet found in the Berkeley Chicano Collections, date unknown). This pamphlet was used for recruiting purposes by the San Diego chapter of the party.

29. "Bert Corona Speaks on La Raza Unida Party & The 'Illegal Alien' Scare," (New York: Pathfinder Press, June 1972), pp. 8–9.

30. For more information on CASA-Hermandad General de Trabajadores, see David G. Gutiérrez, "CASA in the Chicano Movement: Ideology and Organizational Politics in the Chicano Community, 1968–1978," Working Paper Series, 5 (Stanford Center for Chicano Research, August 1984).

31. Muñoz, and Barrera, "La Raza Unida Party," p. 114.

32. This vote was taken at a meeting in San José, California, on April 8 and 9, 1972. A resolution was passed that a central statewide committee not be established "at this time." See Richard Santillán, "The Politics of Cultural Nationalism: El Partido de La Raza Unida in Southern California 1969–1978," (Ph.D. dissertation, 1978), pp. 166–168.

33. To the knowledge of this author, Gonzales never publicly outlined a plan for armed revolution, although he encouraged the founding of barrio self-defense committees and his bodyguards carried arms. His Crusade for Justice was accused, even within the movement, of being responsible for acts of violence; however, no evidence exists that its members willfully committed any seditious acts.

34. Marín, *A Spokesman of the Mexican American Movement*, pp. 25–26.

35. "RU Conference Held in Denver," *El Gallo* 4, 5 (June 1972): 1.

36. Santillán, "Politics of Cultural Nationalism," p. 124.

37. Marín, *A Spokesman of the Mexican American Movement*, p. 26.

38. Gutiérrez, interview, 1988.

39. Ibid. Juan José Peña, an admirer of Gonzales but a supporter of Gutiérrez, and Salomón Baldenegro, who supported Gonzales, both confirmed that the Colorado leader was arrogant, demanded complete allegiance, and tended to be impatient. Philosophically, both backed Gonzales but later came to feel that Gutiérrez's approach to the party was probably the most feasible.

40. Nellie Bustillos, interview with author, Tucson, Arizona, 3 September 1987.

41. John L. Espinoza, "Raza Unida Conference: Unidos Ganaremos," *La Luz*, (November 1972): p. 10.

42. "Raza Unida delegate murdered in N.M.," *El Grito del Norte*, 4, 7–8 (October 1972): p. 4.

43. "Chicano activist shot down in New Mexico," *The Militant* (September 1972).

44. Espinoza, "Raza Unida Conference," p. 10.

45. Salomón Baldenegro, interview with author, Tucson, Arizona, 17 September 1987.

46. "On the Status of La Raza Unida Party in Califas, Aztlán: A Position Paper," Unpublished position paper of the Southern California Raza Unida, dated 21 August 1972, p. 2. This paper is part of the CASA Collection at Stanford University.

47. Antonio Camejo, "La Raza Unida parties say no to McGovern and Nixon," *The Militant* (22 September 1972).

48. Gonzales's speech was printed in its entirety in the November 1972 issue of *El Gallo*.

49. Ibid.

50. Ibid.

51. Baldenegro, interview, 1987; Bustillos, interview, 1987.

52. Camejo, "What strategy for Raza Unida Parties?" *The Militant* (13 October 1972).

53. Ibid.

54. Ibid.

55. José Perales, "National Raza Unida Conference: El Paso," *Chicanismo* 4, 1 (Fall 1973).

56. Espinoza, "Raza Unida Conference," p. 11.

57. Tony Castro, "La Raza Convenes," *The Texas Observer* (22 September 1972): 5. Mario Compean pointed out that it was Raúl Sandoval.

58. Ibid.

59. Compean, interview, 1988.

60. Castro, "La Raza Convenes," p. 5. See also Castro's *Chicano Power*, pp. 177–181.

61. Ibid.

62. Castro, *Chicano Power*, pp. 179–180.

63. See Francis L. Swadish, "The Alianza Movement: Catalyst for Social Change in New Mexico," in *Chicano: The Beginning of Bronze Power*, p. 27.

64. See "Raza Unida parties say no to McGovern and Nixon."

65. "Raza Unida Rejects Nixon and McGovern," *El Paso Herald*, 4 September 1972.

66. Ibid.

67. Ibid. California had 65 votes but ended up casting 66. "La Raza Unida Chairman Election," *El Chicano* 6, 7 (13 September 1972): 8.

68. Ibid.

69. Gutiérrez, interview, 1988.

70. Marín, *A Spokesman of the Mexican American Movement*, p. 31; and Espinoza, "Raza Unida Conference," p. 12.

71. "La Raza Unida Chairman Election," p. 8.

72. "Raza Unida Rejects."

73. "Raza Unida parties say no."

74. "La Raza Unida Chairman Election," p. 8.

75. Ibid.

76. "Gutiérrez New Chairman," *El Paso Herald-Post*, 5 September 1972.

77. Baldenegro, interview, 1987. The Arizona delegation's debate was so intense that its leaders decided simply to split their votes evenly.

78. Baldenegro, interview, 1987

79. "La Raza Unida Chairman Election."

80. Ibid.

81. Ibid.

82. Ibid. Baldenegro did not like either style, but he was an ideologue and he cast his vote for Gonzales.

83. Ibid.

84. "Gutiérrez New Chairman."

85. "Texan Heads Raza Unida," *El Paso Herald-Post*, 5 September 1972.

86. "Raza Unida parties say no."

87. Ibid.

The Six Percent Victory

1. Muñiz, La Raza slate endorsed by Bonilla," *Corpus Christi Caller*, 14 July 1972.

2. Ibid.

3. "Muñiz, McGovern Endorsed," *La Otra Voz* 3 (8 September 1972).

4. "Confident Candidate Muñiz names local campaign chief," *Corpus Christi Times*, 8 September 1972.

5. "Confidence marks campaign," *Corpus Christi Times*, 7 October 1972.

6. "School no diploma mill," *Corpus Christi Caller*, 24 February 1974.

7. "Albina Muñiz happy again," *Corpus Christi Times*, 12 April 1982. Also see "Life after Ramsey," *Corpus Christi Caller*, 1 March 1984.

8. "Confidence marks campaign."

9. *Chicano Times*, October 20-November 3 issue.

10. "Raza Unida Candidate in San Antonio gets 35 percent of vote," *The Militant* (1 December 1972): 12.

11. Ibid.

12. *Chicano Times*.

13. "Ya basta!" *The Texas Observer* (25 August 1972): 4.

14. Ibid.

15. Ibid., p. 5.

16. "Smith vs. Gutiérrez," *The Texas Observer* (29 September 1972): 14.

17. "Gabacho racists," *The Texas Observer* (29 September 1972): 24.

18. "A Vote for Muñiz," *The Texas Observer* (22 September 1972): 15.

19. Tank Barrera, "Raza Unida Party Campaigns in Texas," *The Militant* (20 October 1972). Moreno had lost a reelection bid in the primaries and decided to endorse Muñiz when the Raza Unida candidate was in El Paso for the national convention. Leland began a colorful political career as a maverick liberal radical. He was eventually elected to Congress.

20. "Ya basta!" p. 4.

21. "Smith vs. Gutiérrez," p. 14.

22. The memo was written on 14 September 1972 and was one of the documents collected during the Watergate hearings, which led to President Nixon's resignation.

23. Gutiérrez, interview, 1988.

24. Memo dated 9 October 1972, from Armendáriz to Fred Malek. It seems that Armendáriz was at the convention or was privy to inside information.

25. Memo dated 8 September 1972, from Armendáriz to Fred Malek.

26. Gutiérrez, interview, 1988. Gutiérrez denied that he ever took money from the Republicans, saying it was stupid to even consider it. But he did unequivocally state that he negotiated to get his grant proposals funded. He felt he had nothing to lose since the party, both national and state, had already made it clear it would not endorse anyone in the presidential elections.

27. Armendáriz memo, 9 October 1972.

28. Compean admitted this to be true when I asked him about some claims by the Socialist Workers Party that the Texas delegation was leaning toward endorsing McGovern. Compean indicated that Gutiérrez was supportive of the idea, which implies that Gutiérrez was negotiating with the Republicans without the knowledge of Compean, who was party chairman.

29. *La Verdad* 4, 6 (December 1973).

30. Piñon, *Of Myths and Realities*, pp. 11–12.

31. Afternoon fiestas that can include from one or two family picnics to whole neighborhood gatherings. Campaigning at the tardeadas was a way to eliminate the negative image that some had of the Raza Unida candidates.

32. Harry King, "Raza Unida organizes throughout Texas," *The Militant* (10 November 1972): 16.

33. Ibid.

34. "Briscoe Alien use charged," *Corpus Christi Caller*, 6 November 1972. These charges were similar to others made against most ranchers in South Texas. Few ever bothered to deny them because most of the time they were true. Even though native-born farm workers worked for low wages, Anglo ranchers still sought even cheaper labor from Mexico.

35. "Muñiz campaign chairman restates Briscoe charges," *Corpus Christi Caller*, 7 November 1972.

36. This anecdote was told to the author by Emilio Zamora in Kingsville, Texas. Zamora later ran for state representative.

37. For the most thorough analysis available on the La Raza Unida's participation in the 1972 gubernatorial election, see Piñón's *Of Myths and Realities*, chap. 4. Piñón is extremely biased against the Raza Unida Party, but he brings up interesting questions and provides statistics and information not compiled anywhere else.

38. "Briscoe Wins Election," *Corpus Christi Times*, 8 November 1972.

39. Piñón, *Of Myths and Realities*, p. 84.

40. Ibid., p. 81.

41. Ibid., pp. 88–90. Figures used in making these claims are from Douglas S. Harlan, ed., "U.S. Census of Population and Texas State 1972." Because they are only projections, these figures may include black and white liberal voters.

42. Ibid., p. 83.

43. Harvey Katz, *Shadow on the Alamo*, pp. 36–37. The final senate race count was held up as state officials waited for Ballot Box 13 from Alice (Jim Hogg) Texas, which went heavily to Johnson. Years later investigators found that 203 ballots had been added after the polls closed. In Duval County a Mexican American poll judge admitted shortly before his death that he had been told by the Parr family to stuff ballots for Johnson after the polls were closed.

44. Ibid. John Connally, who served as governor until 1970, brought rural conservatives into the twentieth century by adding public-relations people, financial advisers, speech monitors, and pollsters to the big business/landowners rural coalition.

45. Katz, *Shadow on the Alamo*, p. 248–257.

46. "Muñiz wins six percent of Texas vote," *The Militant*, p. 12. In Zavala County the party demanded that the ballots be impounded. Also in Zavala, Gutiérrez's wife, Luz, was physically carried out of a polling place for protesting irregularities.

47. This was such an effective method of controlling the Mexican American vote that Raza Unida and Republican leaders were united in several cities to promote anti-lever campaigns.

48. "Muñiz wins six percent," p. 12.

49. Ibid.

50. "Muñiz showing puts Raza Unida on map," *Corpus Christi Caller*, p. 9.

Unidos Venceremos: The National Party Falters

1. "Congreso for Land and Cultural Reform," *El Grito del Norte*, 5 (November 1972): 8.

2. Ibid.

3. Castro, *Chicano Power*, p. 126.

4. Ibid., pp. 127–128.

5. Ibid., p. 127. At the time, he had resigned as president of the Alianza because at its annual convention it had passed a resolution calling for the turning over of the Southwest to Chicanos.

6. "Congreso," p. 8.

7. Ibid.

8. Castro, *Chicano Power*, p. 128.

9. Juan José Peña, interview with author, Albuquerque, New Mexico, 5 January 1982.

10. Ibid.

11. *El Gallo* 5, 1 (April 1973), reprints a letter dated 24 January 1973 from Gutiérrez to Tito Lucero.

12. "Vote La Raza Unida," *El Gallo* 5, 1 (April 1973).

13. Peña, interview, 1988.

14. Gutiérrez's letter was reprinted in *El Gallo.*

15. Ibid.

16. Most RUP leaders, including Baldenegro of Arizona, Gutiérrez of Texas, and Peña of New Mexico, agree that the national structure raveled after the first meeting in 1973 and that factionalism only became worse in 1973. By the third meeting in 1974, held at Crystal City, most of Gutiérrez's major opponents were absent. See Santillán, "Cultural Nationalism," for more on Colorado's move away from the national party.

17. "Vote La Raza Unida," p. 8.

18. Vigil, *Chicano Politics*, p. 221.

19. Rodolfo Acuña, *Occupied America.*

20. Tijerina was the gubernatorial candidate in 1968 but was removed because of his conviction on felony charges. From its founding, the party faced constant legal challenges to its ballot status. See Vijil, *Chicano Politics*, pp. 210–219.

21. Vijil, *Chicano Politics*, pp. 210–219.

22. Muñoz and Barrera, "La Raza Unida Party," p. 112.

23. Santillán, "Politics of Cultural Nationalism," p. 181.

24. Ibid., pp. 185–186.

25. Muñoz and Barrera, "La Raza Unida Party," pp. 107–110.

26. Santillán, "Politics of Cultural Nationalism," pp. 203–210.

27. "La Raza Unida Party," *La Raza Magazine* (February 1978): 4–5.

28. "The Selling of the Raza Unida Party," *La Voz Del Pueblo* 3 (April 1972): 6–7.

29. This information comes from Juan José Peña, who kept a better chronicle of the Chicano Movement than the other leaders.

30. The three major supporters of the national party were the California, Colorado, and New Mexico chapters. Also supportive, but less able to provide any tangible assistance, were the chapters from Illinois, Nebraska, and Arizona. The Texas chapter's leadership had always been reluctant to play national politics. Though some Texas activists were active supporters of a national structure, Gutiérrez, Compean, and Muñiz were not. In retrospect, they turned out to be right in that the national effort was time-consuming but not fruitful.

31. He said this during a conversation with the author in the summer of 1986.

32. José Angel Gutiérrez, "Chicanos and Mexicans Under Surveillance: 1940 to 1980," *Renato Rosaldo Lecture Series Monograph*, 2 (Tucson: Mexican American Studies & Research Center, 1986): 29–58. In this article Gutiérrez details the federal government's effort to spy on the Mexican American and Mexican communities and to disrupt their activities. Interestingly, he does not deal with the surveillance on La Raza Unida, but in private conversations he did point out numerous instances of it. He also has hundreds of pages of surveillance material on his activities which he obtained through the Freedom of Information Act.

33. Peña, interview, 1988.

The Party Consolidates in Rural Texas

1. See José Angel Gutiérrez, "La Raza and Revolution."

2. "Cotulla Tejas." Mimeographed, unpublished paper by Jorge Anchondo that briefly recounts the Raza Unida's work in Cotulla in the first two years. Author's collection.

3. The organization was so loosely formed that it had no real hierarchy and no developed by-laws. Alfredo Zamora, who served as mayor of Cotulla under Raza Unida, did not even remember the group when he was interviewed in the summer of 1985.

4. "Young Mayor Finds Work with Chicanos Rewarding," *Dallas Times Herald*, 7 October 1970, p. 16-A.

5. "South Texas Latins Learning," *Houston Chronicle*, 23 August 1970.

6. Ibid.

7. See "Cotulla Tejas," p. 45, and "South Texas Latins Learning."

8. Ibid.

9. Ibid.

10. "Cotulla Group to Enroll." Undated newspaper clip with UPI dateline. This clip was taken from the personal file of Alfredo Zamora.

11. This information comes from a letter sent to Alfredo Zamora on August 27 1970, by Antonio M. Rojas, who had served as a minister of the Iglesia Metodista Mexicana of Cotulla from 1944 to 1949. Zamora's personal files.

12. "Total Integration Approved for Two Schools in Cotulla." From Zamora's personal files.

13. "Cotulla Tejas"; also an interview with Zamora conducted in the summer of 1985.

14. *Calo* is sophisticated slang common among Mexican American youth gangs. See "Pachuco: The Birth of a Creole Language," by Rafael Jesús González, in *Perspectives in Mexican American Studies*, 1 (Tucson: Mexican American Studies & Research Center, 1988): 75–87.

15. Youngblood, interview, 1985.

16. "La Lomita de la Libertad," *El Grito del Norte*, 27 June 1972. This article is actually a letter from Robstown High School students explaining the reasons for their walking out of school. Judging from its sophistication, it is probable that some older Raza Unida activist helped in the composition. Unfortunately, little other information was available on the school protest.

17. Ibid.

18. Ibid. Youngblood, interview, 1985.

19. Youngblood, interview, 1985.

20. Ibid.

21. Richard Kleberg . . . Plan de San Diego, 1915. The author spent four years in Kingsville during the height of the party's strength there and in the neighboring communities. He eventually became county party chairman and vice-president of the local organization, Trabajadores Unidos de Kingsville (United Workers of Kingsville).

22. Ibid.

23. Most of these events happened after the 1974 election but had their origin before the second statewide race. This case study, nonetheless, provides a better view of party activities and strategies. It also underscores the diversity of political priorities, approaches, and opportunities.

24. Gutiérrez's comments had come during an informal meeting with Kingsville activists a few years before. Gutiérrez had never attempted to organize in the community while he was a student activist at Texas A&I.

25. Douglas E. Foley, Clarice Mota, Donald E. Post, and Ignacio Lozano, *From Peones to Politicos: Ethnic Relations in a South Texas Town 1900–1977*. This monograph recounts the history of Pearsall, Texas, but does it by changing the name of the town and the people involved. Although not well done, it is one of only two sizable works on the Raza Unida Party's activities. The monograph takes a general approach and does not detail party inner workings. Most of the information on Pearsall comes from an interpretation of this book and from the author's personal knowledge of Rodríguez and his activities.

26. "San Antonio, and San Juan, Texas, follow Crystal City lead," *The Militant* (28 May 1971).

27. M. Fislow, "Poncho Flores Is Dead," *The Texas Observer* (26 February 1971) :1.

28. "San Antonio, and San Juan, Texas."

29. "La Raza Unida Party wins seats in Texas elections," *The Militant* (1 June 1973): 18.

30. Ibid.

People Together: The 1974 Campaign

1. The urban RUP chapters were never able to develop the kinds of grass-roots, family-oriented organizations that were so successful in South Texas. Consequently, the urban leadership organized groups, gave them a name, by-laws, and a symbol; and sent them out to agitate. There were groups in the barrio which were legitimate, but few of them were "taken over" or founded by the party.

2. *Batos locos* are dropouts involved in crime, drugs, street violence, or just heavy drinking. They, along with the others mentioned, were the barrio's *lumpen proletariate* that no one had tried to organize before.

3. The most infamous event of police repression was the "Zoot suit riots" in Los Angeles during the mid-1940s when law enforcement officers allowed sailors and Marines to attack a Chicano barrio, where they beat and stripped youth wearing Zoot suits. In this instance, as was the case in the 1960s and early 1970s, the newspapers fanned the hysteria with headlines blaming the youths for a number of crimes. For accounts of harassment, see Celia S. Heller, *Mexican American Forgotten Youth at the Crossroads*, p. 63. For attitudes on Mexican American

youth and gangs, see E. S. Bogardus, "Mexican American Youth and Gangs," *Sociology and Social Research* 28 (September 1943): 55–66, and Walter M. Miller, "Lower Class Culture as a Generating Milieu of Gang Delinquency," *Journal of Social Issues*, 14 (1958): 5–19.

4. Donald J. Bogue, *The Population of the United States*, p. 59.

5. Elizabeth Sutherland Martínez and Enriqueta Longeaux y Vásquez, *Viva la Raza! The Struggle of the Mexican American People*, pp. 236–237.

6. This excerpt comes from a copy of Ramsey Muñiz's 1974 announcement address. It is a five-page document.

7. Ibid., p. 3.

8. Ibid., p. 2.

9. Gutiérrez nonetheless disapproved of Muñiz's tactics and chose to phase himself out of the election. This he told the author during an interview in April 1988.

10. Carlos René Guerra never enjoyed a favorable reputation within the leadership circle of the party or with the organizers in general. He nevertheless was a friend of Muñiz, Gutiérrez, and Youngblood and that gave him access to power and enabled him to play a role in a number of the party's major events. Compean provided the information on Guerra's election to the national chairmanship.

11. See Santillán's "Politics of Cultural Nationalism," pp. 30-71, for a more thorough explanation of cultural pluralism and its chief proponents. Santillán's dissertation also provides an explanation of other philosophies present in the barrios, such as assimilationism and nationalism. For more on Guerra and his rhetoric see Robert T. Lee, "Rhetoric of La Raza" (Ph.D. dissertation, 1971).

12. Compean cited that figure to a college student while on a campaign tour for his own race for governor. The student had asked him if he really thought he could win. Compean answered that with 34 percent of the vote, which would come from Chicanos, he could win if the Republicans and Democrats split evenly the rest of the 66 percent. The author was present during that conversation.

13. Accurate figures are difficult to obtain, but census records and voter-registration records seem to back up these estimates. See *U.S. Bureau of the Census*, U.S. Census of Population, General, Social and Economic Characteristics, U.S. Department of Commerce PC (1) C45, Texas 1970. Also, "Current Population Report, Population Characteristics of Spanish Speaking Population in United States," U.S. Department of Commerce, March, 1975, pp. 7–9.

14. Texas Raza Unida Plans Big '74 Campaign," *The Militant* (28 December 1973): 19.

15. These quotations are taken from two undated letters found in the Ramsey Muñiz file in the Raza Unida Party collection in the University of Texas archives.

16. "Texas Raza Unida Plans."

17. Ibid.

18. Eduardo Canales, interview with the author, San Antonio, Texas, 28 December 1986.

19. Ibid.

20. Ibid. Also Tatcho Mindiola, interview with the author, Salt Lake City, Utah, 10 April 1987.

21. "New Gains for Raza Unida Party in South Texas," *The Militant* (19 April 1974): 19.

22. Foley, *From Peones to Politicos*, pp. 201–214.

23. "After the Revolution in Cristal," *The Texas Observer* (5 July 1974): 4.

24. Ibid.

25. "Texas Raza Unida gears up for Fall Campaign," *The Militant* (25 October 1974): 17.

26. Ibid.

27. Ibid.

28. Ibid.

29. Ibid., Youngblood, interview, 1985.

30. Ibid.

31. The Raza Unida group in Kingsville was particularly suspicious of Martínez, but on a trip there a few years later, as chairperson, she converted its members to her side. She turned out to be a real "*mujer revolucionaria.*"

32. Compean, interview, 1986.

33. Ibid.

34. A sample radio spot found in the Muñiz files at the University of Texas archives.

35. These are undated notes from speeches found in the Muñiz file.

36. Undated poem in Muñiz file.

37. "Texas Raza Unida Leader Elected as Judge," *The Militant* (29 November 1974): 21.

38. Ibid.

39. Ibid.

40. "After the Revolution in Cristal," p. 5.

41. Mindiola, interview, 1987.

42. Compean revealed this during a conversation about the meetings that followed the 1974 campaign. He felt strongly that by 1975 the core activist group was unwilling to go along with another Muñiz campaign. A challenge to Muñiz in 1978 would have been formidable because most of his strongest supporters had left the party.

43. Mindiola, interview, 1987; also Mario Compean, interview with author, Boulder, Colorado, 14 April 1988.

44. Compean, interview, 1988.

45. Ibid.

The Party is Over for RUP

1. Anaya, interview, 1986.

2. María Elena Martínez, interview with author, December 27, 1986, San Antonio, Texas.

3. "Ramsey Muñiz sought for drug trafficking," Corpus Christi Caller, 31 July 1976.

4. The author was present that morning of July 31, 1975, when Raúl Villarreal showed the newspaper to Cavada and later when other activists started arriving at the headquarters in disbelief. Because it took quick action to explain to the community that Muñiz was not the party and that all of this could have been a political conspiracy, the Kingsville chapter suffered less than most other rural chapters.

5. Muñiz had the ability to win over people. He stood out as a leader anywhere he went, whether in an urban or a rural setting. The fact that he was a lawyer, had

been a star athlete, and was forceful in his manner intimidated many who would have otherwise challenged him.

6. His attendance at the dances while high on marijuana was the topic of much gossip in Robstown activist circles. Interestingly, most of the gossip was spread by some of his strongest supporters.

7. "Smuggling tie denied by Garza," *Corpus Christi Caller,* 17 February 1977. Also see "Politics, Muñiz bookkeeping gets involved in Garza's trial," *Corpus Christi Caller,* 23 February 1977.

8. A sizable number of the urban activists smoked marijuana, and some may have taken other drugs. They were unusually liberal in allowing others their vices. Even those who claimed to be Marxists rarely discussed the issue of self-discipline.

9. Compean, interview, 1988.

10. Youngblood, interview, 1985.

11. *Corpus Christi Caller,* 23 November 1976.

12. "Muñiz held in Laredo," *Corpus Christi Caller,* 26 December 1976. See also "Ex-fugitive Muñiz back in jail here," *Corpus Christi Caller,* 28 December 1976.

13. Gutiérrez, interview, 1988.

14. Compean, interview, 1988. The Muñiz defense committee never really got off the ground. A lot of talk circulated around the state, but too many activists did not show any interest in helping. Most did not have money to offer and did not want to raise funds among their constituents, who barely provided enough financial backing for the local organization. A number of them simply chose to avoid any more bad publicity.

15. Mindiola, interview, 1987.

16. By and large the urban media ignored the local Raza Unida activities, though they gave ample coverage to Muñiz's campaign. Without Muñiz, most of the small party chapters did not get in the newspapers or on the air.

17. Martínez, interview, 1986.

18. "Union support is step forward for Texas Raza Unida Party," *The Militant* (1974).

19. Velásquez, interview, 1986. Velásquez was a major exponent of this new organization. It seemed to go right along with his philosophy of Jeffersonian activism.

20. Compean, interview, 1988. Compean told the author that it was common to hear party members say that Ramírez had all the characteristics to succeed Gutiérrez.

21. This information comes from the author's personal knowledge, as well as from conversations with Alfred Zamora and Leodoro Martínez, both leaders of the Cotulla RUP.

22. Youngblood, interview, 1985.

23. Ibid. There was already some conflict within the organization because of Carlos Guerra's involvement. Guerra seemed to have a penchant for being disliked.

24. Familias Unidas did win one seat on the school board race but still lost the majority on the board. See "Political gulf widens," *Corpus Christi Caller,* 4 May 1976; "Robstown ballots still not canvassed," *Corpus Christi Caller,* 9 April 1976; "Robstown trustees must certify returns," *Corpus Christi Caller,* 19 April 1976.

25. "City elections spur rumors in Robstown," *Corpus Christi Caller*, 21 February 1978.

26. Albert Peña III was one of those whose rhetoric was always more radical than his actual politics. He was a strong supporter of Muñiz but a critic of the party's hierarchy.

27. Gutiérrez's trip to Cuba created a flurry of dissension within and outside party circles. See "Two views on La Raza from Washington," sixth in a series; "New Worlds or Old Words," *Corpus Christi Caller*, 27 June 1975. Also Tom Curtis, "Raza Desunida," *Texas Monthly* (February 1977): 102.

28. Tom Curtis, "Raza Desunida," p. 106.

29. Ibid., p. 107.

30. This statement comes from an affidavit obtained under the Freedom of Information Act in the Gutiérrez file in the University of Texas archives. The name of the candidate is not given.

31. Ibid.

32. Curtis, "Raza Desunida," p. 102.

33. Ibid., p. 132.

34. This theory was told to the author by Leo Salazar, who had been a student in the Chicano Studies Department of the University of California at Northridge, where pro- and anti-Gutiérrez groups continually debated the issue.

35. Curtis, "Raza Desunida," p. 107.

36. Ibid., p. 132.

37. Ibid.

38. "La Raza's Cmmunity Farm Plan," *The Texas Observer* (15 October 1976).

39. Ibid.

40. See article by José Angel Gutiérrez entitled, "The Chicano in Mexicano—Norte Americano Foreign Relations," in *Chicano Mexicano Relations*, Mexican American Studies Monograph No. 4, Tatcho Mindiola and Max Martínez, eds. (Houston: University of Houston, 1986).

41. "La Raza's Community Farm Plan," p. 1.

42. Lisa Spann, "Zavala County Co-op: Waylaid again," *The Texas Observer* (22 September 1978): 10–11.

43. Ibid., p. 11.

44. Ibid., p. 11.

45. For a concise overview of immigration over the last fifteen years, see Christine Marín Sierra, "Latinos and the 'New Immigration': Responses from the Mexican American Community," in *Renato Rosaldo Lecture Series Monographs*, 3 (Tucson: Mexican American Studies & Research Center, 1987), pp. 33–61.

46. Richard A. García does an excellent job describing the structure of both CASA-HGT and SWP and their activities in his article, "The Chicano Movement and the Mexican American Community, 1972–1978: An Interpretive Essay," *Socialist Review* 8, 4–5 (October 1978): 124–127.

47. Gutiérrez, interview, 1988.

48. According to Sierra, in "Latinos and the 'New Immigration,'" the mainstream Chicano organizations had been anti-Mexican in their position toward undocumented immigration in the earlier part of the century, (see pp. 38–39). By the mid-seventies these organizations had changed their view.

49. "C.A.S.A. General Brotherhood of Workers Salutes National Chicano Forum," CASA pamphlet, 1976, p. 3. CASA Collection, Stanford University.

50. "Minutes of the Albuquerque, New Mexico, Meeting, 1977." This is a report of a meeting of the organizing committees of Colorado, California, Arizona, Texas, and Utah, which met to plan the conference and to try to iron out conflicts between participants. CASA Collection, Stanford University.

51. José Angel Gutiérrez letter to Mario Compean, 9 October 1977. CASA Collection, Stanford University.

52. The author attended the conference and witnessed both Gutiérrez's speech and Martínez's reaction.

53. The author was present at a Texas Raza Unida caucus when Compean made this statement.

54. Emilio Zamora, Eduardo Canales, and Tatcho Mindiola expressed such a belief in their interviews with the author. Also see Richard A. García, "The Chicano Movement," p. 128. Juan José Peña agreed with Gutiérrez's denial of such designs.

55. Zamora, Canales, and Tatcho Mindiola interviews. Other RUP members who left the party to join leftist groups also expressed the feeling that RUP had a superficial ideology. Scholars such as Mario Barrera, Carlos Muñoz and Richard Santillán have made the same observation. A Raza Unida analysis of the left is presented in Tatcho Mindiola's "Marxism and the Chicano Movement: Preliminary Remarks," *Perspectives en Chicano Studies* (1979).

La Raza Unida in Retrospect

1. Compean received 15,250 votes. This information was not available from the state election office because of some inaccurate reporting by county recorders. The most accurate account is found in a letter by Richard Winger to José Angel Gutiérrez on January 9, 1979. He found the announced total of 14,207 inaccurate because the Compean vote of 1,043 in El Paso had not been counted. Winger's letter is in the Gutiérrez collection in the University of Texas Latin American collections.

2. Bonilla made those remarks angrily because he, like other Mexican American Democrats, blamed the defeat of Hill and of Bob Krueger, candidate for Congress, on the party.

3. When Hill ran against Briscoe, he did so on the platform of cleaning up the state government. Several indictments had been handed down against the Mexican American administrators of the Governor's Office of Migrant Affairs for misappropriation of funds, and most Mexican American Democrats blamed Briscoe for the embarrassment. There were also some influential members in MAD who were former members of La Raza Unida, and they pushed hard to have the organization oppose the incumbent.

4. In 1978 Compean discussed the offers with the author as they were made.

5. The Socialist Workers Party in particular did not like Compean because of his efforts to defuse its role at the Chicano/Latino Immigration Conference at San Antonio in October 1977.

6. The author was the county chairman and one of those responsible for setting up the meeting with the party leaders.

7. Compean spent his savings and encumbered large debts to run for governor. He had few contributions and the fundraisers were less than successful because those who came had little money to give. Only as the campaign wound down did he make a greater appeal to middle-class Chicanos and even populist liberals.

8. Peña always retained a cordial relationship with the Chicano left as well as with the nationalists. He remained a friend to Gutiérrez, Gonzales, and Tijerina without alienating the others. He was one of the few party leaders to write his positions and disseminate them, and consequently his papers provide a better picture of his state chapter than Gutirrez's of Texas.

9. Barrera and Muñoz, in their article "La Raza Unida Party and the Chicano Student Movement in California," state that by 1975 the party had ceased to be a factor in the state's Chicano politics.

10. By the mid-1970s Gonzales's domineering attitude had alienated him from the Anglo socialists, the Chicano left, and from most of the nationalist groups.

11. Martínez, interview, 1986.

12. Raúl Villarreal made the comment during a conversation with the author in 1975.

13. For a history of Chicano resistance to Anglo policies and Anglo discrimination, see Robert J. Rosenbaum, *Mexicano Resistance in the Southwest*.

14. Gutiérrez has several thousand pages of surveillance documents on the party attained from the federal government through the Freedom of Information Act. There are also some surveillance documents in the Gutiérrez file at the University of Texas.

15. "Judge voids Zavala elections," *Corpus Christi Caller*, 5 February 1979.

16. "Co-opted by System," *Corpus Christi Caller*, 24 February 1981; also see "Neglect of Office Charged," *Corpus Christi Times*, 30 October 1980.

17. Gutiérrez told this to the author in Crystal City in 1979.

18. Velásquez, interview, 1986.

19. Ernie Cortez founded COPS, and Willie Velásquez was the founder of the Southwest Voter Registration and Education Project.

20. Gutiérrez, interview, 1988.

21. Youngblood, interview, 1985.

22. Velásquez, interview, 1986.

23. See Martha Cotera, *Diosa y hembra*, which deals with the role of women in the party in one of her chapters. Also see Cotera's comments in "The Chicano Struggle: a racial or national movement?" *The Freedom Socialist*, 10, 4 (June–August 1988).

24. Velásquez, interview, 1986.

25. *Corpus Christi Caller*, 24 February 1981.

26. By physical integration I mean that legal barriers to running for office, registering to vote, and voting were eliminated. Social integration would mean receiving endorsements and monetary support from the elites within the two mainstream parties. This has happened in a few cases, and will probably become more common. See Steven J. Rosenstone, Roy L. Behr, and Edward H. Lazarus, *Third Parties in America: Citizen Response to Major Party Failure*.

BIBLIOGRAPHY

Books

Abruch Linder, Miguel. *Movimiento Chicano, demandas materiales, nacionalismo y tácticas*. Publisher and date unknown.

Acuña, Rodolfo. *Occupied America*. San Francisco: Canfield Press, 1972.

Alinksy, Saul D. *Reveille for Radicals*. Chicago: University of Chicago Press, 1946.

Andres, Evan. *Boss Rule in South Texas*. Austin: University of Texas Press, 1982.

Apter, David E., ed. *Ideology and Discontent*. New York: Free Press, 1964.

Barrera, Mario. *Race and Class in the Southwest: A Theory of Racial Inequality*. Notre Dame: University of Notre Dame Press, 1979.

Bayes, Jane H. *Minority Politics and Ideologies in the United States*. Novato, California: Chandlerd Sharp Publishers, 1982.

Bell, Daniel. *The End of Ideology*. Glencoe, Illinois: Free Press, 1960.

Benn, S. I., & Peter, R. S. *Social Principles and the Democratic State*. London: George Allen & Unwin, 1959.

Blauner, Robert. *Racial Oppression in America*. New York: Harper & Row, 1972.

Bogue, Donald J. *The Population of the United States*. Glencoe, Illinois: Free Press, 1959.

Camarillo, Albert. *Chicanos in California: A History of Mexican Americans in California*. San Francisco: Boyd & Fraser, 1984.

Carlson, Robert A. *The Quest for Conformity: Americanization Through Education*. New York: John Wiley & Sons, 1975.

Carmichael, Stokely, & Hamilton, Charles V. *Black Power: The Politics of Liberation in America*. New York: Vintage Books, 1967.

Castro, Tony. *Chicano Power: The Emergence of Mexican America*. New York: Saturday Review Press/E. P. Dutton, 1974.

Chávez, John R. *The Lost Land: The Chicano Image of the Southwest*. Albuquerque: University of New Mexico Press, 1984.

Cotera, Martha P. *The Chicana Feminist*. Austin: Information Systems Development, 1977.

———. *Diosa y hembra*. Austin: Information Systems Development, 1976.

de la Garza, Rodolfo O. *Chicanos and Native Americans: The Territorial Minorities*. Englewood Cliffs, NJ: Prentice Hall, 1973.

de la Garza, Rodolfo; Bean, Frank D.; Romo, Ricardo; & Alvarez, Rodolfo, eds. *The Mexican American Experience*. Austin: University of Texas Press, 1985.

de Leon, Arnold. *They Called Them Greasers: Anglo Attitudes toward Mexicans in Texas, 1821–1900*. Austin: University of Texas Press, 1983.

Easton, David. *A Systems Analysis of Political Life*. New York: John Wiley & Sons, 1965.

Flores Macías, Reynaldo, gen. ed. *Perspectivas en Chicano Studies*. Los Angeles: National Association of Chicano Social Sciences, 1975.

Foley, Douglas E.; Mota, Clarice; Post, Donald E.; & Lozano, Ignacio. *From Peones to Politicos: Ethnic Relations in a South Texas Town 1900–1977*. Austin: Center for Mexican American Studies of the University of Texas at Austin, 1977.

Galarza, Ernesto; Gallegos, Herman; & Samora, Julian. *Mexican Americans in the Southwest*. Santa Barbara: McNally & Loftin, 1969.

Garcia, Chris F., ed. *La Causa Política: A Chicano Politics Reader*. Notre Dame: University of Notre Dame Press, 1974.

García, Richard A. Political Ideology: A Comparative Study of Three Chicano Youth Organizations. San Francisco: R & E Research Associates, 1977.

Goodman, Mitchell. *The Movement Toward a New America: The Beginnings of a Long Revolution*. pp. 435–497. New York: Alfred A. Knopf; Philadelphia: Penguin Press, 1971.

Grebler, Leo; Moore, Joan W.; & Guzmán, Ralph C. *The Mexican American People*. New York: Free Press, 1970.

Heller, Celia S. *Mexican American Youth: Forgotten Youth at the Crossroads*. New York: Random House, 1966.

Katz, Harvey. *Shadow on the Alamo*. Garden City, NY: Doubleday, 1972.

Kinch, Sam, Jr., & Procter, Ben. *Texas Under a Cloud*. Austin: Jenkins; New York: Pemberton, 1972.

Kruszewski, Anthony Z.; Haugh, Richard L.; & Ornstein-Galicia, Jacob, eds. *Politics and Society in the Southwest: Ethnicity and Chicano Pluralism*. Boulder: Westview Press, 1982.

Larralde, Carlos. *Mexican American Movements and Leaders*. Los Alamitos, California: Hwong, 1976.

LeVine, Robert A., & Campbell, Donald T. *Ethnocentrism: Theories of Conflict, Ethnic Attitudes and Group Behavior*. New York & London: John Wiley & Sons, 1972.

Marín, Christine. *A Spokesman of the Mexican American Movement: Rodolfo "Corky" Gonzales and the Fight for Chicano Liberation, 1966–1972*. San Francisco: R & E Research Associates, 1977.

Martínez, Elizabeth Sutherland, & Longeaux y Vásquez, Enriqueta. *Viva La Raza! The Struggle of the Mexican American People*. Garden City, New York: Doubleday, 1974.

McAdam, Doug. *Political Process and the Development of Black Insurgency, 1930–1970*. Chicago: University of Chicago Press, 1982.

Mirandé, Alfredo. *Gringo Justice*. Notre Dame: University of Notre Dame Press, 1987.

Moguin, Wayne, & Van Doren, Charles, eds. *A Documentary History of the Mexican Americans*. New York: Praeger, 1972.

Montejano, David. *Anglos and Mexicans in the Making of Texas, 1836–1986*. Austin: University of Texas Press, 1987.

Moore, John W. *Mexican Americans*. Englewood Cliffs, NJ: Prentice-Hall, 1970.

Mora, Magdalena, & Del Castillo, Adelaida, eds. *Mexican Women in the United States: Struggles Past and Present*. 2d ed. Los Angeles: University of California Chicano Studies Research Center, 1982.

Morgan, Gordon D. *America Without Ethnicity*. Port Washington, New York, & London: National University Publication Kennikat Press, 1981.

Morin, Raúl. *Among the Valiant Mexican Americans in World War II and Korea*. Los Angeles: Borden, 1963.

Mosqueda, Lawrence J. *Chicanos, Catholicism, and Political Ideology*. Lanham, Maryland: University Press of America, 1986.

Nordyke, Lewis. *The Truth about Texas*. New York: Thomas Y. Crowell, 1957.

Olvera, Montiel J. *Latin American Yearbook*. San Antonio, 1939.

Ortega y Gasset, José. *The Revolt of the Masses*. Notre Dame: University of Notre Dame Press, 1985.

Patterson, James T. *America's Struggle against Poverty, 1900–1985*. Cambridge: Harvard University Press, 1986.

Perales. Alonso S. *The Mexican American: Are We Good Neighbors?* New York: Arno Press, 1974.

Piñon, Fernando. *Of Myths and Realities: Dynamics of Ethnic Politics*. New York: Vantage Press, 1978.

Rendón, Armando B. *Chicano Manifesto: The History and Aspirations of the Second Largest Minority in America*. New York: Macmillan, 1971.

Rose, Arnold. *The Power Structure*. New York: Oxford University Press, 1969.

Rosen, Gerald Paul. *Political Ideology and the Chicano Movement*. San Francisco: R & E Research Associates, 1975.

Rosenstone, Steven J.; Behr, Roy L.; & Lazarus, Edward H. *Third Parties in America: Citizen Response to Major Party Failure*. Princeton: Princeton University Press, 1984.

Rubel, Arthur J. *Across the Tracks: Mexican Americans in a Texas City*. Austin: University of Texas Press, 1966.

Samora, Julian; Bernal, Joe; and Peña, Albert. *Gunpowder Justice: A Reassessment of the Texas Rangers*. Notre Dame: University of Notre Dame Press, 1979.

San Miguel, Jr., Guadalupe. *Let All of Them Take Heed*. Austin: University of Texas Press, 1987.

Santillán, Richard. *La Raza Unida*. Los Angeles: Tlacuilo Publications, 1973.

Sheridan, Thomas E. *Los Tucsonenses: The Mexican Community in Tucson, 1854–1941*. Tucson: University of Arizona Press, 1986.

Shockley, John Staples. *Chicano Revolt in a Texas Town*. Notre Dame: University of Notre Dame Press, 1974.

Simmons, Ozzie G. *Anglo Americans and Mexican Americans in South Texas.* New York: Arno Press, 1974.

Smith, Anthony D. *An "Ethnic Revival"?* Cambridge: Cambridge University Press, 1981.

Sookup, James R.; McCleskey, Clifton; & Holloway, Harry. *Party and Factional Division in Texas.* Austin: University of Texas Press, 1964.

Vijil, Maurilio. *Chicano Politics.* Washington, D.C.: University of America Press, 1978.

Webb, Walter Prescott. *The Texas Rangers: A Century of Frontier Defense.* New York: Houghton Mifflin, 1965.

Booklets/Pamphlets/Newsletters

Alvarado, Roger; Camejo, Antonio; & Gonzales, Rodolfo "Corky". "LA RAZA! Why a Chicano Party? Why Chicano Studies?" New York: Pathfinder Press, March 1978.

"Bert Corona Speaks on La Raza Unida and the 'Illegal Alien' Scare." New York: Pathfinder Press, 1972.

Compean, Mario, & Gutiérrez, José Angel. "La Raza Unida Party in Texas." New York: Pathfinder Press, 1970.

Corona, Bert. "MAPA and La Raza Unida: A Program for Chicano Political Action for the 1970s." Publisher and date unknown. Berkeley Chicano Collection.

Delgado, Abelardo. "The Chicano Movement." Totinem Publications, July 1971.

"Documents of the Chicano Struggle." New York: Pathfinder Press, November 1971.

Gómez-Quiñones, Juan. "Mexican Students Por La Raza." Austin: Relámpago Books, 1978.

Gutiérrez, José Angel. "El Político: The Mexican American Elected Official." Prospectiva número 2. MICTLA Publications, date unknown.

"La Raza Unida Michigan." Public Relations Department of La Raza Unida Michigan, date unknown.

"A Political Action Program for the '70s." Texas Raza Unida Party booklet on party platform, 1972.

"A Positive Alternative for Travis County." Pamphlet from the 1974 Muñiz campaign, 1974.

Revolutionary Union. "The Chicano Struggle and the Struggle for Socialism." Chicago, June 1975.

Rodríguez, Olga, ed. "The Politics of Chicano Liberation." New York: Pathfinder Press, 1977.

Salazar, Ruben. *Strangers in One's Land.* U.S. Commission on Civil Rights, Clearinghouse Publication no. 19, May 1970.

Yeager, Carlos. "The Crystal City Model in Alternative Chicano Education." *The A.M.A.F. Alternative Education Newsletter,* No. 10, 8 February 1974.

———. "The Ramification of the La Raza Unida Party Success to Alternative Education in California." *The A.M.A.F. Alternative Education Newsletter,* No. 11, 22 February 1974.

———. "The Raza Unida Party Alternative in Education." *The A.M.A.F. Alternative Education Newsletter,* No. 9, 25 January 1974.

Chicano Periodicals

Aragón, Roberto y José. "Needed: A Chicano Voting Rights Act—Now." *Regeneración* 1 (1970).

"Colorado's La Raza Unida Party Position Statement." *El Gallo* 6 (November–December 1973 & January 1974): 5–7.

"Congreso For Land and Cultural Reform." *El Grito del Norte* 5 (November 1972): 8.

"Elecciones." *La Verdad* 1 (April 1970).

"Electoral Closes to Chicano Revolution." *Regeneración* 4 (1970): 12.

"En cuidad Cristal se trasluce la auto-determinación del Chicano." La Raza Unida Magazine 2 (1974).

Garza, Agustín. "The Selling of La Raza Unida Party." *La Voz Del Pueblo* 3 (April 1972): 6–7.

Garza, Manuel. "La Raza Unida Unites After National Convention." *La Otra Voz* 3 (8 September 1972): 1, 4.

Gonzales, Rodolfo "Corky". "Message to Aztlán." *La Raza Magazine* 2 (1975).

———. "Yo Soy Joaquin." *El Gallo* (1967).

Gutiérrez, José Angel. "Aztlán: Chicano Revolt in the Winter Garden." *La Raza Magazine* 1 (1973): 36.

———. "José Angel Gutiérrez at the Houston Convention." *Caracol* (November 1974).

———. "La meta del movimiento Chicano es tener el control de su destino en sus propias manos." *La Raza Magazine* 2 (1974): 32–33.

———. *Regeneración* 1 (1970): 5.

Hernández, Eugene. "Partido de la Raza Unida Fresno Convention." *La Raza Magazine* (date unknown).

"In El Paso Raza Unida Party Makes Its Debut." *Nosotros* 4 (May 1974): 10.

"José Angel Gutiérrez Speaks at Valley State College." *El Popo Magazine* (date unknown).

"José Angel Speaks Out." *La Gente* (November–December 1973).

"La lomita de la libertad." *El Grito del Norte* 5 (27 June 1972).

"La Raza Unida." *El Grito del Norte* (27 June 1972).

"La Raza Unida Chairman Election." *El Chicano* 6, 17 (13 September 1972): 8

"La Raza Unida Party's National & International Conference." *El Gallo* 6 (November–December 1973 & January 1974).

"La voz de la justicia." *El Gallo*, 4 (June 1972).

López, Gilbert M. "Chicano Political Development." *La Raza Magazine* 1 (1972).

"Mujeres de la Raza Unida." *The Echo*, 5 (28 February 1974).

"Muñiz, McGovern Endorsed." *La Otra Voz* 3 (8 September 1972).

"New Facts Reported on Ricardo Falcón Killing." *El Grito del Norte* 5 (November 1972): 12.

"News of La Raza Unida Party." *El Grito del Norte* 6 (6 December 1971).

"Partido La Raza Unida." *La Raza Magazine* 1 (January 1972).

Perales, José. "National Raza Unida Conference: El Paso." *Chicanismo* 4 (Fall 1972).

"Poesía para Ricardo Falcón." *El Grito del Norte* 5 (October 1972): 6.

"Raza Unida Delegate Murdered in New Mexico." *El Grito del Norte* 5 (October 1972).

262   *United We Win*

"Raza Unida Holds National Meeting." *El Grito del Norte* 5 (October 1972).
"Raza Unida Party Attempts To Qualify Through the Courts." *La Raza Magazine* 1 (2 September 1973).
"Raza Unida Party——Northern California and José Angel Gutiérrez." *La Raza Magazine* 1 (1971).
"Reiés Comes Home." *El Grito del Norte* 4 (20 August 1971).
"Relajes, ratas, dedos y balcones." *La Raza Magazine* 1 (December 1971): 50.
"Republican Support for La Raza Unida???" *El Chicano* (7 June 1972).
"R.U. Conference Held in Denver." *El Gallo* 4 (June 1972).
Ruiz, Raúl. "Por los derechos de todos los trabajadores." *El Obrero* 1 (November 1972): 4–5.
"Se junta la Raza sobre el plan de Carter." *Para La Gente* 1 (November 1977): 13.
"The Selling of La Raza Unida Party." *La Voz Del Pueblo* 3 (April 1972).
Varela, Delfino. "Undecided Leadership and Tradition Combine to Keep La Raza in Democratic Party." *Regeneración* 8 (1970): 3.
Vásquez, Enriqueta. "Our New Nation Is Born." *El Grito del Norte* 3 (13 April 1977): 5, 7.
Ytuart, Eddie. "La Raza Unida Party in La Puente—Ernie Porras for City Council." *La Raza Magazine* 1 (1972).

Dissertations/Theses

Ambrecht, Biliana C. S. "Politicization as a Legacy of the War on Poverty: A Study of Advisory Council Members in a Mexican American Community." Ph.D. dissertation, University of California, Los Angeles, 1973.
Chandler, Charles Ray. "The Mexican American Protest Movement in Texas." Ph.D. dissertation, Tulane University, date unknown.
Cuellar, Robert A. "A Social and Political History of the Mexican American Population of Texas, 1929–1963." Master's thesis, Texas State University, Denton, 1969.
Dickens, Edwin Larry. "The Political Role of Mexican Americans in San Antonio." Ph.D. dissertation, Texas Tech University, Lubbock, 1969.
Garza, Edward D. "LULAC: League of United Latin American Citizens." Master's thesis, Southwest Texas State Teachers College, San Marcos, 1951.
González, Jovita. "Social Life in Cameron, Starr, and Zapata Counties." Master's thesis, University of Texas, Austin, 1930.
Gutiérrez, José Angel. "La Raza and Revolution: The Empirical Conditions for Revolution in Four South Texas Counties." Master's thesis, Saint Mary's University, San Antonio, 1968.
Kenneson, Susan Reyner. "Through the Looking-Glass: A History of Anglo-American Attitudes Towards the Spanish-Americans and Indians of New Mexico." Ph.D. dissertation, Yale University, 1978.
Lee, Robert T. "Rhetoric of La Raza." Ph.D. dissertation, Arizona State University, 1971.
Navarro, Armando. "El Partido de la Raza Unida in Crystal City: A Peaceful Revolution." Ph.D. dissertation, University of California, Riverside, 1974.
Pacheco, Henry Joe. "Chicano Political Behavior." Ph.D. dissertation, Claremont Graduate School, 1977.

Parker, Benny. "Power-in-Conflict: A Chicano Political Party of Social Disequilibrium and Anglo Chicano Power Relationships as Expressed Through a Situational Analysis of Public Address in Crystal City, Texas, in 1972." Ph.D. dissertation, Southern Illinois University, 1974.

Santillán, Richard. "The Politics of Cultural Nationalism: El Partido de La Raza Unida in Southern California, 1969–1978." Ph.D. dissertation, Claremont Graduate School, 1978.

Wallace, Frederick Leo. "Legitimacy and the Youth Movement of the 1960s." Ph.D. dissertation, University of Connecticut, 1976.

Interviews/Questionnaires

Anaya, Flores. Austin, TX, 29 December 1986.

Baldenegro, Salomón. Tucson, AZ, 17 September 1987.

Bernal, Joe. San Antonio, TX, 6 January 1987.

Bustamante, Daniel. San Antonio, TX, 28 December 1986.

Bustillos, Nellie. Tucson, AZ, 3 September 1987.

Canales, Alma. Raza Unida Party questionnaire, 1985.

Canales, Eddie. San Antonio, TX, 28 December 1986.

Castro, Rosie. San Antonio, TX, 6 January 1987.

Cavada, Abel. Victoria, TX, 1985, Raza Unida Party questionnaire.

Compean, Mario. Madison, WI., 12 December 1984 and 25 May 1986; Boulder, CO, 15 April 1988.

Daniel, Alberto. San Antonio, TX, 28 December 1986.

Garza, Manuel. San Antonio, TX, 31 December 1986.

Gutiérrez, José Angel. Independence, OR, January 1985; Madison, WI, 25 May 1986; Houston, TX, 24 May 1988.

Hernández, Inez. San Antonio, TX, 28 December 1986.

Martínez, Leodoro. Cotulla, TX, Summer 1985.

Martínez, María Elena. San Antonio, TX, 27 December 1986; Austin, TX, 26 May 1988; Austin, TX, 1985, Raza Unida Party questionnaire.

Martínez, Roberto Garza. Raza Unida Party questionnaire, 1985.

Mindiola, Tatcho. Salt Lake City, UT, 10 April 1987.

Miréles, Irma. San Antonio, TX, 1 January 1986.

Navarro, Armando. Madison, WI, 24 December 1986.

Peña, Albert, Jr. San Antonio, TX, 31 December 1986.

Peña, Juan José. Albuquerque, NM, 22–23 January 1988.

Rangel, Jesse. San Antonio, TX, 28 December 1986.

Sánchez, Ricardo, San Antonio, TX, 1985, Raza Unida Party questionnaire.

Vásquez y Sánchez, Ramón. San Antonio, TX, 3 January 1987.

Velásquez, William. San Antonio, TX, 22 December 1986.

Villarreal, Raúl. Kingsville, TX, Summer 1985.

Youngblood, Guadalupe. Robstown, TX, Summer 1985.

Zamora, Alfredo. Cotulla, TX, Summer 1985.

Articles

"Activists Discuss the Issues Facing Raza Unida Party." *The Militant* (11 January 1974).

"After the Revolution in Cristal." *The Texas Observer* (5 July 1974).

Alaniz, Yolanda, & Cornish, Megan. "The Chicago Struggle: A Racial or a National Movement?" *Freedom Socialist* 10 (June–August 1988).

Allsup, Carl. "Education Is Our Freedom: The American G.I. Forum and the Mexican American School Segregation in Texas, 1948-1957." *Aztlán* 8 (1979): 27–50.

Alvarez, Rodolfo. "The Psycho-Historical and Socioeconomic Development of the Chicano Community in the United States." *Social Science Quarterly* 53 (March 1973): 920–942.

"Another Selma." *The Texas Observer* (date unknown).

Baldivia, Albert. "Colorado Raza Unida Fields Slate." *The Militant* (8 September 1972).

————. "They Were the Kind We Cannot Afford to Lose." *The Militant* (21 June 1974).

Ball, Skip. "La Raza Unida vs. Henry B. Gonzales." *The Militant* (26 October 1973): 18.

Barrera, Tank. "Raza Unida Party Campaigns in Texas." *The Militant* (20 October 1972): 24.

————. "Texas RUP: Muñiz Campaign Makes Impact." *The Militant* (8 September 1972).

Barrera, Tank, & Blackstock, Nelson. "Muñiz Wins Six Percent of Texas Vote." *The Militant* (24 November 1972).

Blackstock, Nelson. "Texas Raza Unida Party Looks Toward 1974 State Elections." *The Militant* (26 October 1973): 18.

————. "Texas RUP Leader Raps McGovern." *The Militant* (3 November 1972).

Bogardus, E. S. "Mexican American Youth and Gangs." *Sociology and Social Research* 28 (September 1943): 55–66.

Brown, Lyle C., & Charlton, Thomas L., interviewers. Gutiérrez, Angel José, interviewee. "Oral History Memoir." Baylor University Program for Oral History (8 July 1971).

Calderón, José. "Reflections on La Raza Unida Party." Paper presented at the National Association for Chicano Studies, Sacramento, CA, 13 April 1985.

Camarillo, Albert. "Research Notes on Chicano Community Leaders: The G.I. Generation." *Aztlán* 2 (Fall 1971).

Camejo, Antonio. "Colorado Raza Unida Party Discusses Campaign." *The Militant* (30 June 1972).

————. "La Raza and the '72 Elections." *The Militant* (28 January 1972).

————. "La Raza Unida Candidates Discuss Berkeley Election Issues." *The Militant* (2 April 1972): 12.

————. "National Chicano Caucus Maps Independent Course." *The Militant* (5 May 1972).

————. "Over 500 at Michigan Raza Conference." *The Militant* (4 February 1972).

————. "Raza Unida Nominee Discusses Party Stands." *The Militant* (17 July 1970).

————. "Raza Unída Parties Plan First National Gathering." *The Militant* (30 June 1972).

————. "Raza Unida Parties Say No to McGovern and Nixon." *The Militant* (22 September 1972).

————. "Raza Unida Party Wins Texas Elections." The Militant *(26 May 1972)*.

————. *"Texas Raza Unida Party Maps Statewide Election Campaign." The Militant* (23 June 1972): 24.

————. "What Strategy for Raza Unida Parties?" *The Militant* (13 October 1972).

————. "What's Wrong with Senator McGovern's Program for La Raza?" *The Militant* (16 June 1972).

"Cantu's Reply to Gutiérrez." *The Militant* (1 February 1974).

Castro, Tony. "La Raza Convenes." *The Texas Observer* (22 September 1972).

Chapa, Evey, & Gutiérrez, Armando. "Chicanas in Politics: An Overview and a Case Study." In *Perspectivas en Chicano Studies I*, edited by Reynaldo Flores Macías. Los Angeles: National Association of Chicano Social Sciences, 1977.

"Chicano Candidate Wins Place on Illinois Ballot." *The Militant* (1 June 1973).

"Chicano Runs for Office in Chicago's 7th C.D." *The Militant* (23 March 1973).

"Chicanos Boycott Mayor's Bank." *The Militant* (2 October 1970).

Coles, Robert, & Huge, Harry. "Thorns on the Yellow Rose of Texas." In *America's Other Youth: Growing Up Poor*, edited by David Gottlieb. Englewood Cliffs, NJ: Prentice Hall, 1971.

"Colorado Raza Unida Spokesman! The People Are Starting to Move Collectively." *The Militant* (4 December 1970).

Cook, Joy. "La Raza Unida Party." *La Luz* (August 1972): 24–26.

Corona, Bert. "Why Labor and La Raza Should Break with the Republican and Democratic Parties." *The Militant* (7 April 1972).

Curtis, Tom. "Raza Desunida." *Texas Monthly* 5 (February 1977).

————. "Viva La Raza!" *Texas Monthly* 14 (January 1986).

de la Garza, Rodolfo, & Vaughn, David. "The Political Socialization of Chicano Elites: A Generational Approach." In *The Mexican American Experience*, edited by Rodolfo de la Garza, Frank D. Bean, Ricardo Romo & Rodolfo Alvarez. Austin: University of Texas Press, 1985.

Dick, Robert C. "La causa política de los Chicanos." *Indiana Speech Journal* (February 1976).

Dugger, Ronnie. "González of San Antonio—Part 5—The Politics of Fratricide." *The Texas Observer* (12 December 1980).

————. "San Antonio Liberalism: Piecing It Together." *The Texas Observer* (27 May 1966): 1, 3–5.

————. "The Struggle for P.A.S.O." *The Texas Observer* (14 June 1963).

"Echeverría: Friend or Foe of La Raza?" *The Militant* (8 September 1 1972).

"Election Results and Comments Thereon." *The Texas Observer* (1 December 1972).

"Energy, Land, and Natural Resources." *The Texas Observer* 67 (26 December 1975): 4–5.

Espinoza, John L. "Raza Unida Conference: Unidos Quedaremos." *La Luz* (October 1972): 10–12.

Fislow, M. "Poncho Flores Is Dead." *The Texas Observer* (26 February 1971): 1

Fogel, Walter. "Education and Income of Mexican Americans in the Southwest." Advance Report 1. Mexican American Study Project, University of California, Los Angeles, November 1965.

Folks, Lyle. "Colorado Raza Unida Makes Good Showing." *The Militant* (24 November 1972): 12.

"Gabacho Racists." *The Texas Observer* (29 September 1972).

García, Armando R. "Institutional Completeness and La Raza Unida Party." In *Chicanos and Native Americans*, edited by Rudolph O. de la Garza, Anthony Kruszewski, & Tomás A. Arciniega. Englewood Cliffs, New Jersey: Prentice-Hall, 1973.

García, Ignacio. "Crystal City: A Decade of Commitment." *Nuestro* (December 1979).

———. "Mexican American Youth Organization: Precursors of Change in Texas." Working Paper Series, 8. University of Arizona, January 1987.

———. "Is the Party Over for La Raza Unida?" *Nuestro* (December 1979).

García, Mario T. "In Search of History: Carlos Castañeda and the Mexican American Generation." *Renato Rosaldo Lecture Series Monographs*, 4, edited by Ignacio García. Tucson: Mexican American Studies & Research Center, 1988.

———. "Mexican American Labor and the Left: The Asociación Nacional Mexico Americana." In *The Chicano Struggle: Analyses of Past and Present Efforts*, edited by John García. Binghamton: National Association for Chicano Studies, 1984.

García, Richard. "The Chicano Movement and the Mexican American Community, 1972–78: An Interpretive Essay." *Socialist Review* 8 (July–October 1978): 124–127.

———. "The Mexican American Mind: A Product of the 1930s." In *History, Culture and Society: Chicano Studies in the 1980s*. Ypsilanti: National Association for Chicano Studies, 1983.

"The G.I Forum at 25." *The Texas Observer* (7 September 1973).

"Gonzales: No Compromise to Any Other Party or Any Other Candidate." *The Militant* (13 October 1972).

González, Rafael Jesús. "Pachuco: The Birth of a Creole Language." In *Perspectives in Mexican American Studies* 1: 75–87, edited by Juan R. García and Ignacio García. Tucson: Mexican American Studies & Research Center, 1988.

Guerra, Carlos. "Discrimination in South Texas." *The Texas Observer* (27 December 1974).

"Guerra Responds." *The Texas Observer* (28 December 1973).

Gutiérrez, Armando G., & Hirsch, Herbert. "Political Maturation and Political Awareness: The Case of the Crystal City Chicano." *Aztlán* 5 (1974).

Gutiérrez, David G. "CASA In the Chicano Movement: Ideology and Organizational Politics in the Chicano Community." Working Paper Series, 5. Stanford Center for Chicano Research, August 1984.

Gutiérrez, José Angel. "The Knock on the Door." *The Texas Observer* (28 December 1979).

———. "Chicanos and Mexicans Under Surveillance: 1940–1980," *Renato Rosaldo Lecture Series Monograph*, 2, edited by Ignacio García. Tucson: Mexican American Studies & Research Center, 1986: 29–58

———. "The Chicano in Mexicano-Norte Americano Foreign Relations," *Chicano Mexicano Relations, Mexican American Studies Monograph*, 4. Houston: University of Houston, 1986: 20–34.

"He Told Us So." *The Texas Observer* (18 January 1974).

Harlan, Doug. "On Electoral Reform." *The Texas Observer* (26 March 1971).

"Hidalgo County Raza Candidate Wins Ballot Fight." *The Militant* (7 August 1980).

Howard, Carl D. "Mexican-Americans 'Want To Get on Top' and They're Gaining." *National Observer* (12 April 1965).

"I Am Joaquín/Yo soy Joaquín." *The Militant* (12 January 1973).

Juárez, Alberto. "The Emergence of El Partido de la Raza Unida: California's New Chicano Party." *Aztlán* 3 (1973).

Knowlton, Clark S. "Patrón Peón Pattern Among the Spanish Americans of New Mexico." In *Social Forces* 41 (October 1962). Chapel Hill, N.C.: University of North Carolina Press.

"La Raza Turns to the Courts." *The Texas Observer* (11 April 1969).

"La Raza Unida." *The Texas Observer* (29 October 1976): 10.

Laws, Bart. "Crystal City Is a Hot and Dirty Town." *The Organizer*, published by Institute for Social Justice (date unknown).

———. "Raza Unida de Cristal." *Southern Exposure* 10 (March/April 1982): 67–72.

Lipsky, Michael. "Protest as a Political Resource." *American Political Science Review* 62 (1968): 1144–1158.

López, Juan. "Which Way La Raza Unida?" *People's World* 35 (2 September 1972).

"McGov Fails to Get Nod From MAPA." *The Militant* (10 November 1972): 16.

"A March in El Paso." *The Texas Observer* (date unknown).

Margolis, Richard. "How Popeye Socked It to the Crystal City Chicanos." *Rural America* 3 (1978).

Margolis, Ron. "Denver Raza Headquarters Raided: Candidates Score Significant Vote." *The Militant* (13 November 1970).

Maxwell, Steve. "Raza Unida Parties Plan Campaigns in Los Angeles; Colorado." *The Militant* (16 June 1972).

Miller, Michael V. "Chicano Community Control in South Texas: Problems and Prospects." *Journal of Ethnic Studies* 3 (Fall 1975): 70–89.

Miller, Michael, & Preston, James D. "Political Conflict in a Bifurcated Community: Anglo-Chicano Relations in a Small Texas Town." Paper presented at the Southwestern Sociological Association Meeting, Texas A & M University, Dallas, Texas, 25–27 March 1971.

Miller, Walter M. "Lower Class Culture as a Generating Milieu of Gang Delinquency." *Journal of Social Issues* 14 (1958): 5–19.

Mindiola, Tatcho, Jr., & Martínez, Max, eds. "Chicano-Mexicano Relations." Monograph 4. University of Houston Mexican American Studies Program, 1986.

Mindiola, Tatcho. "Marxism and the Chicano Movement: Preliminary Remarks." In *Perspectivas en Chicano Studies*, edited by Reynaldo Flores Macias. Los Angeles: National Association of Chicano Social Sciences, 1977.

Mittlebach, Frank G., & Marshall, Grace. "The Burden of Poverty." Advance Report 5. Mexican American Project, University of California, Los Angeles, July 1966.

Moore, Joan W., & Mittlebach, Frank G. "Residential Segregation in the Urban Southwest: A Comparative Study." Advance Report 4. Mexican American Study Project, UCLA, June 1966.

Muir, John. "La Raza's Community Farm Plan." *The Texas Observer* (15 October 1976).

"Muñiz Running." *The Texas Observer* (1 February 1974).

Muñoz, Carlos, Jr., & Barrera, Mario. "La Raza Unida Party and the Chicano Student Movement in California." *Social Science Journal* 19 (April 1982).

"New Gains for Raza Unida Party in South Texas." *The Militant* (19 April 1974): 19.

"New Worlds or Old Words?" *Corpus Christi Caller*, a seven-part series (22–29 September 1975).

"1974 Texas Raza Unida Campaign Opens." *The Militant* (14 April 1974).

"No Bull Bullock." *The Texas Observer* (3 March 1972).

"North California RUP Wins Election Suit." *The Militant* (8 September 1972): 14.

"Notes on La Raza." *The Texas Observer* (29 March 1974).

Pendás, Miguel. "California Raza Unida Party To Enter Governor's Race." *The Militant* (21 September 1973): 14.

———. "Carrizo Springs, Texas." *The Militant* (7 May 1974): 14.

———. "Guardian and Raza Unida." *The Militant* (16 November 1973).

———. "Guardian and Raza Unida—II." *The Militant* (23 November 1973).

———. "Obreros unidos." *The Militant* (17 May 1974): 13.

———. "Raza Unida and California Ballot." *The Militant* (30 November 1973).

———. "Raza Unida Election Campaigns." *The Militant* (26 April 1974): 14.

———. "Raza Unida Party in Southern California Race." *The Militant* (26 January 1973): 16.

———. "A Reply to Gutiérrez." *The Militant* (28 December 1973).

———. "RUP and Political Action." *The Militant* (24 May 1974).

———. "South California Campaigns Made Gains For RUP." *The Militant* (8 December 1972): 14.

"Phooey on La Raza." *The Texas Observer* (18 January 1974).

"Phooey on the *Observer*." *The Texas Observer* (18 January 1974).

"The Politics of Outsiders." *Texas Monthly* 2 (September 1974).

Proctor, Ben H. "The Modern Texas Ranger: A Law Enforcement Dilemma in the Rio Grande Valley." In *The Mexican American: An Awakening Minority*, edited by Manuel Servín, pp. 212–227. Austin: University of Texas Press, 1970.

"Pros and Cons on the Cristal Story." *The Texas Observer* (26 July 1974).

"A Quiet Revolution in Pharr." *The Texas Observer* (9 August 1974).

"Raza Militants Picket L.A. McGovern Rally." *The Militant* (22 September 1972): 24.

"Raza Unida Answers 'GOP' Smear." *The Militant* (23 November 1973): 21.

"Raza Unida Denies Republican Funding, Peace and Freedom Defends 'Tactic.'" *The Militant* (20 July 1973): 14.

"La Raza Unida Party Wins Seats in Texas Elections." *The Militant* (1 June 1973): 18.

Reece, Ray. "An Obstructed View." *The Texas Observer* (19 January 1979).

"Representative Frances Farenthold: A Melancholy Rebel." *The Texas Observer* (9 April 1971)

Ring, Harry. "Chicano Moratorium Leader Says He Was Federal Agent." *The Militant* (18 February 1972).

———. "Chicano Workers Organize in Crystal City Cannery." *The Militant* (17 March 1972).

———. "Colorado Raza Unida Candidates Speak Out." *The Militant* (3 November 1972).

————. "Corky Gonzales: Evolution of a Chicano Leader." *The Militant* (9 February 1973): 18–19.

————. "Ex-agent Discloses Entrapment Evidence." *The Militant* (10 March 1972).

————. "Raza Unida Candidate in San Antonio Gets 35 Percent of Vote." *The Militant* (1 December 1972).

————. "Raza Unida in New Mexico/A Talk with Juan José Peña." *The Militant* (15 October 1976).

————. "Raza Unida in New Mexico/Evolution of a Chicano Leader." *The Militant* (22 October 1976): 15.

————. "Raza Unida Leaders Blast McGovern Smear." *The Militant* (27 October 1972): 5.

————. "Raza Unida Organizes Throughout Texas." *The Militant* (10 November 1972): 16.

————. "Raza Unida Running for Harlingen, TX Council." *The Militant* (7 December 1973): 18.

————. "Texas Raza Unida Leaders Discuss Issues Facing the Party." *The Militant* (13 December 1974).

————. "Union Support Is Step Forward for Texas Raza Unida Party." *The Militant* (8 November 1974): 10.

————. "Where Texas Raza Unida Party Stands Today." *The Militant* (20 December 1974).

"RUP Makes Progress in Brownsville, Texas Race." *The Militant* (7 December 1973): 18.

"San Antonio, and San Juan, Texas, Follow Cyrstal City Lead." *The Militant* (28 May 1971).

San Miguel, Jr., Guadalupe. "Mexican American Organizations and the Changing Politics of School Desegregation in Texas, 1945 to 1980." *Social Science Quarterly* 63 (December 1982).

Santillán, Richard. "El Partido la Raza Unida: Chicanos in Politics." *The Black Politician.* Los Angeles: Urban Affairs Institute, 1971.

————. "Third Party Politics: Old Story, New Faces." *The Black Politician.* Los Angeles: Urban Affairs Institute, 1971.

"Should the Chicano Movement Support McGovern for President?" *The Militant* (8 September 1972): 12.

Sierra, Christine Marín. "Latinos and the 'New Immigration': Responses from the Mexican American Community." *Renato Rosaldo Lecture Series Monograph*, 3, edited by Ignacio García. Tucson: Mexican American Studies & Research Center, 1987: 33–61.

Smith, Tom G., interviewer. Ernesto Calderón, interviewee. "Oral History Memoir." Baylor University Program for Oral History (27 March 1973).

"Smith vs. Gutiérrez." *The Texas Observer* (22 September 1972).

Sosa Riddle, Adaljisa. "Chicanas and El Movimiento." *Aztlán* 5 (Spring/Fall 1974): 155–165.

Stanford University Library (Chicano Newspapers). "Chicano Prisoner of Liberation La Raza Unida." "The Border": special report written and edited by the staff of the *El Paso Herald Post* (Summer 1983).

Swadesh, Francis L. "The Alianza Movement: Catalyst for Social Change in New Mexico." In *Chicano: The Beginning of Bronze Power*, edited by Renato Rosaldo, Gustav L. Seligmann, & Robert A. Calvert, p. 27. New York: William Morrow, 1974.

"The Struggle for P.A.S.O." *The Texas Observer* (14 June 1963).

"Texas Chicano Union Wins Certification Fight." *The Militant* (7 December 1973).

"Texas Needs Farenthold." *The Texas Observer* (3 March 1972).

"Texas Raza Unida Gears Up for Fall Campaign." *The Militant* (25 October 1974).

"Texas Raza Unida Leader Elected as Judge," *The Militant* (29 November 1974): 21.

"Texas Raza Unida Plans Big '74' Campaign." *The Militant* (28 December 1973): 19.

"Texas Sleeping Giant—Really Awake This Time?" *The Texas Observer* (11 April 1969).

Tirado, Miguel David. "Mexican American Community Political Organization: The Key to Chicano Political Power." *Aztlán* 1 (Spring 1970): 53–78.

Trillin, Calvin. "U.S. Journal: Crystal City." *The New Yorker* (17 April 1971): 102.

Uhl, Judy. "Suit to Challenge California Election Code." *The Militant* (26 January 1973): 16.

Ultermeyer, Chase. "The Politics of Outsiders." *Texas Monthly* 3 (September 1974).

"Union Supports RUP." *The Militant* (10 November 1972).

"Walkout in Crystal City." *The Texas Observer* (2 January 1970).

Weeks, Douglas O. "The Texas-Mexican and the Politics of South Texas." *American Political Science Review* (date unknown): 606-627.

Weissberg, Arnold. "Raza Unida in New Mexico/A Dynamic Chicano Party." *The Militant* (17 September 1976): 23.

"Ya basta!" *The Texas Observer* (25 August 1972).

"Zavala County Co-Op: Waylaid Again." *The Texas Observer* (22 September 1978): 10–11.

Newspapers

Albuquerque Journal, 1972–80
Austin American-Statesman, 1976
Corpus Christi Caller, 1972–76
Corpus Christi Times, 1973–74
The Cotulla Record, 1984
Dallas Herald Times, 1970
Denver Post, 1970–85
El Chile (Kingsville, TX), 1975
El Paso Herald-Post, 1972
El Paso Times, 1972–83
Houston Chronicle, 1970
La Otra Voz (San Marcos, TX), 1972
La Verdad (Crystal City, TX), 1973
La Voz del Barrio (Norte, CA), 1972
Laredo Morning Times, 1984
Laredo News, 1979
Los Angeles Times, 1970–72

The New Mexican (Albuquerque), 1972
Oakland Tribune, 1972
Para La Gente (Austin, TX), 1978
Rocky Mountain News (Denver, CO), 1977
San Antonio Express, 1969–73
San Antonio News, 1969–71
San Francisco Chronicle, 1972
Waco Tribune-Herald, 1980, 1984

Government Documents

Congressional Record, April 3, 15, 16, 1969. Washington, D.C.
"Current Population Report, Population Characteristics of Spanish Speaking Population in United States." U.S. Department of Commerce, March 1970.
Harlan, Douglas S., ed. "U.S. Census of Population and Texas State, 1972."
Mexican Americans and the Administration of Justice in the Southwest. U.S. Commission on Civil Rights, U.S. Government Printing Office, March 1970.
"U.S. Census of Population, General, Social and Economic Characteristics." U.S. Department of Commerce PC (1) C45, Texas, 1970.

Unpublished Documents/Letters

"The Albuquerque, New Mexico Meeting." Minutes, 2 October 1977. Mimeographed. Chairman, Juan José Peña. CASA Collection, Stanford University.
Anchondo, Jorge. "Cotulla Tejas." Mimeographed. Date unknown.
Armendárez, Alex. Memorandum to Fred Malek, 8 October 1972.
———. Memorandum to Fred Malek, 9 October 1972.
———. "Raza Unida Convention." Memorandum to Charles Colson, 14 September 1972.
Berry, Miguel; Cavada, Armando; Sánchez, Richard; & Flores, Ernesto. "Latent Resentment Against the Political Order: An Interpretation of Chicano Voting Behavior." Manuscript, 1971. Personal collection of Ignacio García.
"Bienvenidos." Mimeographed. Flyer welcoming people to the party's first state convention in California, date unknown. CASA Collection, Stanford University.
"C.A.S.A. General Brotherhood of Workers Salutes National Chicano Forum." Mimeographed. A brochure explaining CASA, 1976. CASA Collection, Stanford University.
Casanova, Stephen. "La Raza Unida Party Press." Manuscript, 1986. Personal collection of Ignacio García.
———. "The Movement for Bilingual/Bicultural Education in Texas: School Boycotts and the Mexican American Youth Organization." Manuscript, date unknown. Personal Collection of Ignacio García.
"Confidential Internal Newsletter." Mimeographed. La Raza Unida Party, New Mexico, date unknown.
"Congreso de Aztlán." Mimeographed. Preamble, 24–26 November 1972.
"El Congreso de Aztlán Resolutions." Flyer, La Raza Unida Conference, 26–28 November 1971.
Federal Bureau of Investigation Affidavits by Crystal City Opponents of José Angel Gutiérrez. File #SA 56-172, 4/29/74, and File #SA 56-172, 2 May 1974.

Flores, Estevan. "A Call to Action, an Analysis of our Struggles and Alternatives to Carter's Immigration Program." Mimeographed. Pamphlet, date unknown. CASA Collection, Stanford University.

———. Letter to Armando Navarro, 5 August 1971. CASA Collection, Stanford University.

Gutiérrez, Angel José. "A Chicano Position on Proposals for Action by the Next President of Mexico: 1982–1988." Manuscript, date unknown. Personal collection of Juan José Peña.

———. "The Foreign Policy Initiatives of La Raza Unida Party." Manuscript, date unknown. Personal Collection of Ignacio García.

———. "Immigration Conference and Meeting." Letter to Mario Compean, Albuquerque, NM, 9 October 1972.

———. Letter to Mario Compean, 10 October 1977. CASA Collection, Stanford University.

"Join La Raza Unida Party Now." Mimeographed. Recruiting flyer carrying the preamble of the San Joaquin County Central Committee of La Raza Unida Party, date unknown.

"Justice." Mimeographed. Campaign flyer for New Mexico Raza Unida Candidates, New Mexico, date unknown. Personal Collection of Juan José Peña.

"La Raza Unida Party State of California Resolutions: Los Angeles Conference." Program and agenda, 1–2 July 1972. CASA Collection, Stanford University.

"La Raza Unida Party State of California Resolutions: San Jose Conference." Mimeographed. Program and agenda for state meeting, San Jose, CA, 8–9 April 1972. CASA Collection, Stanford University.

"La Raza Unida State Convention Resolutions." Mimeographed. Minutes of 10, 11, 12 August 1972. CASA Collection, Stanford University.

"A Manual and Political Program." Manuscript. Raza Unida de Nuevo Mexico, 1971.

Muñiz, Ramsey. Letter of appointment of local campaign managers. Mimeographed. Date unknown.

———. Thank You Letter II. Mimeographed. Date unknown.

"National Coalition for Fair Immigration Laws and Practices: Position Paper." Mimeographed. Date unknown. CASA Collection, Stanford University.

"National La Raza Unida Party Priorities." Mimeographed. Paper listing the resolutions passed at the National Convention of La Raza Unida Party, El Paso, TX, date unknown.

"National Preamble and Principles of the Raza Unida Party." Mimeographed. Second meeting of El Congreso, Albuquerque, 24–26 November 1972. CASA Collection, Stanford University.

"On the Status of La Raza Unida Party in Califas, Aztlán: A Position Paper." Mimeographed. Paper presented at the LRUP Organizing Committees Southern Region, California, 21 August 1972. Sent to all RUP organizers in California. CASA Collection, Stanford University.

"The Partido Raza Unida Caucus." Internal Report, 9 June 1979. Manuscript. Mimeographed. Personal collection of Juan José Peña.

Peña, Juan José. "Aspects of the Debate on the Chicana Question." Mimeographed. Position paper, 12 May 1981.

———. "The Socialist Workers' Party Question." Mimeographed. Discussion Bulletin #4. July 1979.

————. "Una décema del partido Raza Unida." Artículo del Noticiero para la Mesa Chicana, 1 February 1980.

"Politics of the Chicano—Recommendations, Workshops." Flyer, La Raza Unida Conference, 26–28 November 1971.

"Position on 1972 Elections." Mimeographed. Press Release, Partido de La Raza Unida, 30 October 1972.

"Proposals to National Convention of P.R.U. of the State of New Mexico." Mimeographed. Manuscript, 1980. Personal collection of Juan José Peña.

"Ramsey Muñiz, A Short Biography." Mimeographed. RUP campaign literature, 1972.

"Ramsey Muñiz's Announcement Address." Mimeographed. 1974. Ramsey Muñiz file, Latin American collection, University of Texas Archives.

"Reporte sobre la conferencia nacional sobre inmigración y política pública." Mimeographed. Minutes of 28–30 October, 1977, and 16 December 1977. CASA Collection, Stanford University.

"Resolutions, etc." Mimeographed. Flyer, La Raza Unida State Convention, 10–12 August 1973.

Rojas, Rev. Antonio M. Letter to Alfredo Zamora (then mayor of Cotulla, TX), August 1970.

Sánchez, David (prime minister of the Brown Berets). "Chicano Power Explained." Mimeographed. Date unknown. CASA Collection, Stanford University.

Schey, Pete A. "Carter's Immigration Package: A Windfall for Big Business, and Anathema For Undocumented Persons." Mimeographed. Date unknown.

Ulloa, Irma I. "Awakening of a Sleeping Giant." Mimeographed. Paper from Chicano Studies Library Project at Arizona State University, 7 May 1973. Personal collection of Mario Compean.

Vásquez, Carlos. "National Conference on Immigration and Public Policy." Mimeographed. Memo from Carlos Vásquez, CASA Political Commission, to all local committees and organizations, 7 October 1977. CASA Collection, Stanford University.

Zamora, Alfredo, Jr. "Que Viva La Raza! Que Viva La Causa! Que Viva La Revolución!" Mimeographed. Chicano songs booklet, date unknown. Personal collection of Ignacio García.

Zungi, Alma. "Chicanos for the Raza Unida Party." Manuscript, 9 May 1978. Personal Collection of Ignacio García.

NAME INDEX

Tijerina, Reies López (*continued*)
   at national RUP meeting,
     111–112;
   calls own *Congreso*, 135.
Tower, John, 130.
Treviño, George, 120.
Treviño, Mario, 48.
Truan, Carlos, 73.

U

Urriegas, José, 21.

V

Valdez, Juan, 96.
Vásquez, Arturo, 103, 116.
Vásquez, Enriqueta, 172.
Vásquez, José, 31.
Velásquez, Willie, 16, 19–21, 30;
   calls Raza Unida meetings, 19;
   represents MAYO in El Paso, 20;
   heads MAUC, 23;

leaves MAYO, 60–61;
   comments on RUP, 231.
Villarreal, "Guero", 160.
Villarreal, Raul, 161–164, 198.

W

Wallace, George, 86.

Y

Yarborough, Ralph, 48.
Ynosencia, María, 44.
Youngblood, Guadalupe, 18;
   organizes in Robstown, 62, 157;
   becomes state chairman, 186;
   moves away from state RUP, 193.

Z

Zamora, Alfredo, Jr., 62, 66, 153.
Zamora, Emilio, 127.

SUBJECT INDEX

Designed by The University of Arizona Graphic Services